Reworking the Ballet

Challenging and unsettling their predecessors, modern choreographers such as Matthew Bourne, Mark Morris and Masaki Iwana have courted controversy and notoriety by reimagining the most canonical of Classical and Romantic ballets.

In this book, Dr Vida Midgelow examines the ways in which these contemporary reworkings unveil and dismantle the basic assumptions of their texts, reconfiguring ballet to encompass changing attitudes towards gender, sexuality and cultural difference.

Reworking the Ballet: Counter-Narratives and Alternative Bodies articulates the ways in which audiences and critics can experience these reworkings, viewing them from both practical *and* theoretical perspectives, including:

- eroticism and the politics of touch
- the performativity of gender
- cross-casting and cross-dressing
- reworkings and intertextuality
- cultural exchange and hybridity.

Vida L. Midgelow is a reader in Performance Studies and Dance at the University of Northampton, specialising in European dance practices, choreographic methodologies and the radical reworking of the classics. She is also an accomplished choreographer and director of the Choreographic Lab.

Reworking the Ballet

Counter-narratives and alternative bodies

Vida L. Midgelow

Routledge
Taylor & Francis Group

LONDON AND NEW YORK

First published 2007
by Routledge
2 Park Square, Milton Park, Abingdon, Oxon OX14 4RN

Simultaneously published in the USA and Canada
by Routledge
270 Madison Ave, New York, NY 10016

*Routledge is an imprint of the Taylor & Francis Group, an informa
business*

Typeset in Baskerville by
Book Now Ltd, London
Printed and bound in Great Britain by
Antony Rowe Ltd, Chippenham, Wiltshire

British Library Cataloguing in Publication Data
A catalogue record for this book is available
from the British Library

Library of Congress Cataloging in Publication Data
Midgelow, Vida.
Reworking the ballet: counter-narratives and alternative
bodies/Vida Midgelow.
     p. cm.
Includes bibliographical references and index.
1. Ballet. 2. Choreography. I. Title.
GV1787.M553 2007
792.8–dc22   2007020596

ISBN10: 0–415–97602–2 (hbk)
ISBN10: 0–415–97603–0 (pbk)

ISBN13: 978–0–415–97602–2 (hbk)
ISBN13: 978–0–415–97603–9 (pbk)

For Naomi

Contents

Plates

Acknowledgements

Cherry Hyde has a lot to answer for! As my first ballet teacher she introduced me to dance through her commitment and passion for ballet, and continued to support me while I spread my wings and entered the world of modern dance. These early formative experiences reside within me and in my dancing – for, as reworkings make clear, we carry our histories within us. So it is with gratitude that I thank Ms Hyde and all the many teachers and dancing partners that followed. The experiences they have given me inform my writing and own choreographic work – a few instances of which are discussed here in this book. These dances, these reworkings, were fundamental, informing my understanding of this field.

It is, however, the other choreographers whose works are the main subject of this book to whom I owe most thanks. It is their dances, their creativity and vision, their willingness to tussle with the dances of the past that inspired this research. In particular I thank those dance artists who so kindly allowed me access to video materials and gave of their time to answer my questions. Also I am grateful to the photographers who have provided me with the evocative images that grace this book.

This book has evolved over many years. It developed out of my doctoral thesis (University of Surrey, 2003), and I owe a great debt of gratitude to my PhD supervisors, Professor Janet Lansdale (University of Surrey) and Professor Alexandra Carter (Middlesex University), whose patience, continuing support and critical acuity were crucial to the development of this work at various stages. Ideas have been shared at conferences, in particular those of the Society of Dance History Scholars, and I appreciate the patience of all those who listened to evolving ideas and asked such good questions – pushing my thinking forward and encouraging me to go further.

Still others assisted me – Fran Barbe took the time to share her specialist knowledge and George Savona (former Head of Cultural Studies, University of Northampton) skilfully read and commented on earlier versions. Also from the University of Northampton, my good friend, colleague and sometimes dancing partner, Jane Bacon, deserves special mention. She has been there all the way, encouraging me to finish. It was Jane and Robert Daniels who together edited video material that formed a key element of O (a set of footnotes to Swan Lake) – one of my own reworkings that is discussed in this book.

All the while I have been involved in the processes of researching and writing, my family – my parents, my sisters and their families – have been dancing alongside, holding me up. This book would not have been possible without them and their continual support. Finally, my daughter, Naomi: she reminds me every day that as women we have a duty to make the world a better, fairer place for our daughters – for they are the future.

Project funded by Arts and Humanities Research Council (research leave award) and University of Northampton.

Introduction

The choreographers of reworkings have contradicted, criticised, dislocated, fragmented, updated, celebrated, refocused and otherwise reimagined the ballet on
stage. *Reworking the Ballet: Counter-Narratives and Alternative Bodies* illuminates this
choreographic praxis, discussing the context and politics of reworkings. In particular I investigate dances that rework Classical and Romantic ballets, viewing them
as critical practices that resonate with canonical counter-discourses – as unruly
acts framed (and sometimes held) within the status quo of the canon.

Since 1980 there has been a proliferation of dances that have used and abused,
reworked and revisioned dances from the Classical and Romantic ballet canon. Mark
Morris in his work *The Hard Nut* (1991) presents a reworking of *The Nutcracker* (1892).
In *The Hard Nut* Morris creates a modern family with mutant offspring and oversized
toys to tell a tale of love and acceptance in a playful and parodic style. *Coppélia*, created by Maguy Marin and adapted for television in 1994, presents the mechanical
doll in the media age. Coppélia, in this version, is a blond-wigged, red-suited figure
that steps out of a celluloid film and rapidly replicates into multiple copies. *Aurora*
(1994), by Meryl Tankard and her Australian Dance Theatre, is a version of *The
Sleeping Beauty* (1890). Playfully making use of an eclectic range of styles, the dance is
formed as a gleeful hotchpotch, cutting across boundaries, happily mixing traditionally disparate elements. This is an uncompromisingly contemporary work that
Tankard has suggested was inspired, at least to some extent, by all the press attention
given to Lady Diana Spencer and the British royal family (Hallet 1994). British
choreographer Matthew Bourne produced a much publicised 'all male' *Swan Lake*
(1995) in which he recasts the traditionally female swans with a *corps* of men. These
male swans, with bare torsos and wearing feather-covered pantaloons, emphasise the
powerful and the untamed in contrast to the ballet's conventionally tragic and passive female swans. More recently, Raimund Hoghe toured his austere and pared-
down reworking of *Swan Lake* (2005). Through poignant contrast, this work painfully
brings to the fore the idealised concept of the body that ballet perpetuates.

While reworkings in dance have become more accepted (that is, if the commercial
success of Matthew Bourne's *Swan Lake* can be used as an indicator) they are still not
as common as they are in theatre, opera, and literature. In these forms canonical
texts are rewritten and restaged regularly (although not always counter-discursively).
Roger Copeland pointed out in 1994:

Granted, one can cite Dance Theatre of Harlem's *Créole Giselle*, or Mats Ek's madhouse *Giselle*, or Béjart's male *Firebird* or Mark Morris' nutty *Nutcracker*, but these are exceptions to the rule, much less common than say, Peter Sellars transposing the setting for a Mozart opera to Trump Tower or Harlem.

(Copeland 1994: 19)

To add to these examples, consider *Qui est là* by Peter Brook, or the multimedia *Elsinore* by Robert Lepage, or the solo *Hamlet: A Monologue* by Robert Wilson – all three, created within the space of one year (1995–6), are reworkings of Shakespeare's *Hamlet* that have played to sold-out houses (Lavender 2001). Before this, in a chapter entitled 'Production and proliferation', Susan Bennett (1996) lists no fewer than seventeen versions of *King Lear*, all made between 1980 and 1990. Crossing geographical and gender lines, these plays give rise to questions that 'challenge the authority of Shakespeare, the cumulative power of mainstream production, and the operation of that authority in the politics of culture' (Bennett 1996: 51). Given that Bennett claims these works 'challenge the authority of Shakespeare', it is interesting, and somewhat ironic, that it is Shakespeare and the prolific adaptations of his work that has given rise to much of the debate in this field – by default maintaining the Shakespearian voice as central in the politics of culture.

In literature, the rewritings of fairy tales by Angela Carter, Anne Sexton and Margaret Atwood, among others (see Zipes 1993 and Warner 1995), similarly give rise to questions about ownership and boundaries between genres. Significantly these writers refigure female characters in light of feminist perspectives. Carter, in works such as *The Company of Wolves*, in which she reworks the tale of *Little Red Riding Hood*, explores the erotic and conjures the lure of the wild. Challenging conventional misogyny, she refuses 'the wholesome or pretty picture of female gender (nurturing, caring) and deal[s] plainly with erotic dominance as a source of pleasure for men – and for women' (Warner 1995: 310).

Commonly authors in the field of reworkings have focused upon translations across generic forms – from novel to film, from drama into musical, for example. Discussions around these reworkings have often debated the fidelity between one mode and another, yet these reworkings also encompass other crossings – temporal and geographical. Patricia Rozema's (2000) film version of Jane Austen's *Mansfield Park* makes explicit the novel's British colonial context and the slavery practices on Antiguan plantations, thereby making visible contexts which are absent in the book, while Neil La Bute's film version of A. S. Byatt's novel *Possession?* (1991) shifts across cultures, enlarging the scope and, arguably, the appeal of the novel. Similarly, returning to Shakespeare, Baz Luhrmann's (1996) *William Shakespeare's Romeo + Juliet* adapts the play text for film, in the process updating it, complete with gangland warfare and frenetically paced action, to target a wider (perhaps generally younger) audience.

Dance reworkings have received attention in the popular press, yet very little academic consideration of these dances exists.[1] This discussion of the practice and theory of reworkings focuses on the ways in which narratives have been told anew and in which bodies have been refigured across the lines of race, gender and sexuality. I write from the premise that reworkings can effectively be considered as a group of dances and that they can be seen to operate in relational ways. Importantly, as is implicit throughout, I consider the identification of these dances *as* reworkings as a significant feature of the ways in which they are received, perceived and interpreted.

While the contemporary dances discussed in this book are described throughout as reworkings, I note in chapter 1 that a number of related terms could be used to describe the dances in question. I choose not to attempt to classify the different approaches to the task of reworking too tightly. Instead I focus on dances that might broadly be perceived to depart from a source text (or texts) in order to give rise to a new dance that has a significantly different resonance, while evoking a purposeful extended and intertextual relationship with that source. The works I discuss can be seen to intervene, altering the dances of the past, for, while classical revival has always meant revision, and every theatrical age remakes texts in their own image, these dances represent a much more self-conscious insurgence.

This book is limited to reworkings since 1980 (although a few earlier examples are included) and to reworkings of dances from the Classical and Romantic ballet canon (with a particular emphasis on post-1980 reworkings of *Giselle* and *Swan Lake*). This is not to suggest that the only dances to be reworked are those from this canon, or that reworkings are not found before 1980. For instance, in the mid-nineteenth century *Giselle* was remade in various guises. Dance historian Ivor Guest (1955) describes six versions of this ballet, crossing the theatre, burlesque and ballet stages. All of these six dances might be considered reworkings and would make an interesting case study, incorporating, as they do, a source text that is variously parodied, extracted from, and altered. I also do not, for instance, discuss *Créole Giselle* (1984) by Dance Theatre of Harlem. This dance significantly recontextualises the libretto and shifts the characters of the ballet in order to comment upon the black slave experience in America. However, as the work maintains the coded ballet vocabulary I choose not to include it here, for the reconceptualising and rechoreographing of the movement language is seen as an important and defining aspect of reworkings. For the same reason I also do not include the fascinating, complex and lighthearted plays of gender evident in Les Ballet Trocadero's cross-dressed performances of the ballet. The significance of a re-formed movement language is discussed in chapter 1 and exemplified further in chapter 2.

Some other recent reworkings could also have proved interesting, but are similarly not included. For instance, *Rome and Jewels* (2001), by Rennie Harris, takes *Romeo and Juliet* by Shakespeare and *West Side Story* and reformulates them into a hip-hop and rap style. As an example of a reworking which crosses cultures, asserting a black American street culture into the heart of what is, predominantly, a white Western high art canon, this work is worthy of note. But as it focuses on adapting Shakespeare, rather than focusing or commenting on ballet, I choose not to discuss it here. *O* (1994) and *OO* (2006) by Michael Clark incorporate extended references to Ballet Russes ballets (in particular Stravinsky's *Apollo*), using music and movement images to the choreographer's own ends. These dances are fascinating examples of reworkings but are not within the remit of this book, as they refer to Modern ballets rather than Romantic or Classical styles.

While, before my post-1980 frame of reference, I do, however, include brief discussions of two examples of reworkings from the mid- to late 1970s – *I, Giselle* (1981) by two British choreographers, Fergus Early and Jacky Lansley, and *Sunrise* (1979) by Early. Both dances are based on *Giselle* (see chapter 1), and I include them as they can usefully be seen to reflect counter-discursive perspectives and as precursors to the current phenomenon of reworkings.

The boundaries I set for this book nevertheless do reflect a common thrust. While reworkings of Modern ballets, such as those by Clark, can be found, more commonly choreographers have tended to revisit the most well-known and most canonical ballets of the nineteenth century. Arguably, as is implied in chapter 1, the reason for this is because canonical dances represent a body of works that perpetuate particular ideologies that need to be questioned. Conversely, they also represent values, themes and ideas that might be seen by some to traverse historical and cultural bounds and thereby be worthy of revisiting. Also pertinent is the very popularity and visibility (not to mention commercial success) of dances such as *Swan Lake*, *Giselle* and *The Nutcracker*. Reworkings in many ways rely on, or at least use, an audience's prior knowledge of the dance which they reference. By using a well-known ballet, references can be mobilised with at least some confidence that an audience will recognise the allusions.

Swan Lake represents the pinnacle of the classical canon and, possibly because of this status, has been restaged and reworked somewhat more than most ballets. Of reworkings which purposefully and explicitly change the character, movement and meanings of *Swan Lake*, I have gathered a list of some thirteen dances, dating from 1976 to 2005.[2] As almost half of these dances are small-scale or little-known works and only a few were premiered before 1995, I am quite sure that there are others in existence that have evaded my searches. Nevertheless these examples already encompass a wide range of choreographic approaches to the task of reworking – reimagining and exploiting the ballet in different and innovative ways. Many of these reworkings of *Swan Lake* appear through the journey of this book, becoming a recurring theme and enabling comparisons, as well as differences, across different dances to emerge.

The ballet *Swan Lake*[3] is arguably one of the most well-known classical ballets, which has captured the popular imagination and has come to stand as the epitome of all things balletic. Christy Adair similarly writes:

> *Swan Lake* has become synonymous with ballet. The major companies' productions of this ballet are performed to packed audiences and little-known ballet companies attract audiences when *Swan Lake* is in their programmes. For many people, the virginal Odette and the whorish Odile are the essence of ballet.
>
> (Adair 1992: 105)

Swan Lake, then, offers an enticing case study both because of the ballet's canonical and iconic status and on account of the wealth and complexity of the different reworkings that have been staged. The reworkings of *Swan Lake* discussed here reconfigure the dances of the past in the light of the cultural, critical and artistic climate formed by the insights of poststructuralism, feminism, postcolonialism and queer theory. Representing an egalitarian stew of approaches, reworkings abandon the modernist quest for historical authenticity and open classic texts to an infinite range of possibilities. Thereby the dance texts discussed in this book generally take up a polemic stance towards their source text as they operate to open up the canon, at times entering the canon from discordant directions and at other times revealing gaps and omissions. These gaps become the very foundation of reworkings, making what is usually hidden manifest. Through this book I investigate the extent to which these dances demythologise the dances of the canon and participate in canonical counter-discourses.

Part I is made up of two chapters, '*Reworking the ballet: (en)countering the canon*' and '*Canonical crossings: narratives and forms revisioned*'. These chapters present an overview of the context and practice of reworkings and provide the starting point for a theoretical understanding of this choreographic practice. Chapter 1 establishes the language and critical framework used and developed in the discussion that follows. Working towards a definition of reworkings, I outline salient features and contexts. Of particular interest are the construction and deconstruction of the canon, the processes of myth, the strategies of intertextuality and the potential of the hybrid or bidirectional text.

Chapter 2, 'Canonical crossings', provides an overview of the various counter-canonical strategies employed by choreographers. The contemporary reworkings of the ballet canon discussed here encompass works from America, Australia, Britain and Sweden. The dances considered give a sense of the breadth of the field, and the examples have been selected in order to illuminate particular choreographic strategies and themes. The choreographers of these works reconstruct notions of identity, and in this chapter I begin to draw out the specific ways in which reworkings have altered the ballet and refigured the body in unruly ways. However, it is also consistently apparent that the canon is not surpassed but continues to reverberate within these dances.

Following this overview of contexts and practices I turn in '*Refiguring the body and the politics of identity*' (Part II) to consider the work of specific choreographers who have variously used the act of reworking to (re)construct notions of identity. The dances discussed here are radical reconfigurations of *Swan Lake* and *Giselle*, and are performed solo or are duets/small groups. Through this section dances are analysed individually and particular attention is paid to the specifics of each work.

Chapter 3 uses feminist perspectives to discuss the reclaiming of the phallus and the erotic by Susan Foster and myself. In this chapter gender is shown to be especially fictive owing to the explicit reappropriation and reinscription of the female body. In chapter 4, I consider the work of Javier de Frutos and Raimund Hoghe, discussing the ways in which their dances query and queer the canon such that they open up representations of masculinity and the body *per se*, to reveal the power and pleasure of (homo)sexuality without recourse to dominant orthodoxies. Chapter 5 turns to focus upon intercultural reworkings, which complicate discussions of gender and sexuality, in the work of two contrasting dancers – Masaki Iwana and Shakti. These two artists give rise to further debate around the potential of hybridity while also bringing attention to the risks of commodification and globalisation.

Through these chapters I invoke various theorists of difference, including Bhabha, Braidotti, Butler, Deleuze and Guattari, Grosz, Irigaray and Spivak, examining how far it is possible for contemporary dance makers to de/reconstitute and locate the ballet for current contexts, and importantly consider the extent to which they reflect *and* problematise ontologies of the body. These dances can be seen to refigure the body, making it clear that the body needs to be considered beyond the binary nexus of male/female, homo/hetero, subject/object and self/other. Identity (in the singular) has given way to identities (in the plural), and binaries between gay and straight, female and male, and black and white have been undermined. Thereby the dances evoke performative, plural and fluid bodies, as opposed to a closed or universal body. This increasing fluidity impacts on both the range and the meaning given to representations. For, as Judith Butler (1990) notes, perhaps the very proliferation and deregulation of representations are part of the process towards the production of a chaotic multiplicity that may undermine the restrictions of the terms of political identity.

The concluding chapter draws these various strands together to assert that reworkings celebrate the simultaneous habitation of multiple and overlapping formulations. What comes to the fore is that each reworking, in its own distinctive way, attempts to refigure the body. For, through diversity and difference, reworkings (re)inscribe the body and evoke the pleasure and power of the (re-)eroticised body.

Through this book I present the new and relatively unknown (the radical reworking), reflecting on the relationships established between this and the seemingly well known (the classic ballet). The analysis of these dances thereby traces the symbiotic relationship established between the present contemporary performance (the reworking) and the historical source text (the nineteenth-century ballet which is revisited by the reworking). I investigate the extent to which the re-reading of the ballet evident in reworkings represents not simply an unrelenting critique but may demonstrate both a distance and a yearning. Through these dances, it is proposed, it may be possible to come to know the dances of the past but to know them differently. This is important for, as Adrienne Rich tells us, 'we need to know the writing of the past, and know it differently than we have ever known it; not to pass on a tradition but to break its hold over us' (1980: 35).

Part I

Approaching reworkings of the ballet in theory and practice

Chapter 1

Reworking the ballet
(En)countering the canon

No text is ever completely imagined in any one production. It can continue to be dreamed in different ways, with different people, at different times. This can be regarded as one of the central truisms of theatre. And yet, what remains enigmatic is not the multiple lives of a text, but the unknown lives that are concealed *within* it.

(Bharucha 2000: 85)

Reworking the ballet

What cultural and artistic period reworks *The Nutcracker* as a 1960s comic book, characterises Aurora in *The Sleeping Beauty* as a drug addict, and replays *Swan Lake* as a homoerotic love story?[1] Choreographers have increasingly presented cherished ballets from the past in maverick and radical ways, challenging the edifice of received meanings. In this chapter I outline choreographic reworkings of canonical ballets, considering how they might be accounted for within the context of the current milieu, and establish the critical frame within which reworkings exist and can be discussed, for I am interested to know how we experience reworkings and how we come to 'understand,' or 'make sense of', reworkings when they are discussed *as* reworkings.

I start, in 'Defining the terms of the discourse', by providing an overview of terminology. I outline particular classification systems proposed within the fields of dance, theatre, film and literary studies for use in the analysis of differing versions of a source text. The section that follows, 'Reviewing five *Giselles*', compares reworkings of *Giselle*. These dances exemplify typical practices associated with reworking, and the brief analysis offered here begins to illuminate the choreographic strategies and recurring themes within these dances. The following section, 'Counter-discourses and the canon', outlines the tenacious web within which these dances operate. This web is woven with threads that emanate from, among others, poststructuralist, postcolonialist, feminist and queer discourse – forming counter-canonical positions. These bodies of knowledge, as they intersect with postmodernism, have provided the critical climate of the current era. Strands of these discourses are unravelled in the two following sections in order to give rise to a critical language and analytical method with which reworkings, analysed in detail in subsequent chapters, can be discussed. Particularly influential threads evident in the acts of reworking discussed in this book are the challenges to the discursive production of power and knowledge, especially as exemplified by re-formations of the artistic canon. This, together with challenges to notions of authorial authority, authenticity and truth, and the corresponding awareness of the historical and social construction of identities, forms the critical basis from which these works can be considered. The final section, 'Towards a definition of reworkings', begins to delineate the common features of reworkings.

Reworkings can usefully be considered as hybrid, 'palimpsestuous' texts that evoke a particularly bidirectional gaze, as they exist within a double frame, simultaneously evoking and questioning their sources. While, as shall become evident, it is difficult to suggest 'newness' in reworkings, for they are always at some level 're-presentations', I nevertheless note the ways in which many of the dance works discussed throughout this book embody alternative or subversive agendas such that many (although not all) of them play a part in counter-canonical discourse. The choreographers discussed produce transformed visions of the ballet and its narratives to create new texts that can help us to recognise our assumptions and shift our perceptions about both the past *and* the present.

Defining the terms of the discourse

The term 'reworking' is not a standardised or commonly understood term, and the dances I here term 'reworkings' do not demonstrate a single set of easily definable features. There are almost as many approaches and terms as there are dances and writers. The following proliferation of terms – revivals, remakes, reconstructions, re-creations, restorations, reworkings and revisions – among others, represents a contradictory mix of approaches. While definitions of these terms are somewhat illusive, it is nevertheless useful to attempt to delineate approaches and define features in order that effective analysis may be undertaken. What is similar in the dances that are here called reworkings, and what is reflected in this set of terms, is the prefix 're'. These terms all describe dances that have a pre-existing dance text, or pre-text(s), as a source that they 're'-visit in a variety of ways. They all describe dances that have a source text that is variously altered, revised or turned over – a source text that is at the very least a significant reference point for the new work.

The relationship between the source text(s) (or sometimes it might be more appropriate to describe it as a target text(s)) and the newly constructed text is an important one which distinguishes one mode of 're'-visiting from another. The emphasis here is upon dances that substantially alter the ballet in order create a new work that has a significantly different resonance. Reworking, as I use the term, needs to be differentiated from other essentially more restorative trends, for revivals and reconstructions in ballet have tended towards a securing of tradition, while reworkings, in contrast, are engaged in a dialogue with tradition, often challenging established premises.

In truth, reworkings cannot be totally dissociated from processes of restoration and reconstruction; rather, they operate at opposite ends of a continuum, as both restorations and reworkings are on a scale of 'authenticity and interpretivity' (Thomas 2003: 144) – with reconstructions emphasising the aura of 'authenticity' and reworkings stressing 'interpretivity'. However, as Helen Thomas argues, even though reconstructors tend to highlight notions of 'repeatability' in their search for the 'original', the processes of reconstruction and the ephemeral nature of dance means that 'interpretivity' plays a part.

Indeed, taking this one step further, Mark Franko argues against the embedded notions of replication in reconstructions, stating that reconstruction's 'master conceit is to evoke what no longer is, with the means that are present' (1993: 135). Franko suggests that constructing through deconstruction lets loose new forms of reconstruction. 'It consists', he writes, 'of inscribing the plurality of visions[,] restoring, conceptualising and/or inventing the act' (ibid.: 152). The result of this process, he maintains, is to reinvent, rather than reconstruct, the work – in what might be considered a manner analogous to the process of reworking. However, reworkings, as distinct from reconstructions, explicitly and demonstratively break the chain of 'repeatability'. Reworkings, using a viewer's knowledge and arguably, in some instances, the canonical and commercial success of a source, also enter into a conscious and overt dialogue of change and difference. For, unlike reconstructions, they make no pretence to authenticity – indeed they deliberately mark themselves as other than the authentic in order to emphasise their difference. Bypassing the obsessive yet unattainable search for an authentic version, reworkings deconstruct the past, engaging with it only to enter into an interpretive discourse – often wilfully reinterpreting or misinterpreting their sources.

Various authors have attempted to clarify these different trends and have sought to establish frames of reference for discussing the relationships between a source text and the newly produced text. Interestingly, most of the authors cited in the following overview discuss theatre, literature or film rather than dance. They also tend to discuss shifts across art forms rather than reworkings within an art form, but across styles/genres – it is the latter of these approaches that is my focus. Either way there has been little attention paid to this enterprise in dance. However, a few dance scholars have entered this thorny territory, and Smith (1992) suggests that the terms *reconstruction, recreation, resetting* and *revival* could be described in the following ways.

> *Reconstruction* suggests intensive labor, research, piecework, maybe educated guesswork about some details, and generally implies a date of performance distant from that when the work was first produced. *Recreation* implies that the spirit of a dance is captured [even] though the details may be totally wrong, and the term is often used, for example, when discussing a modern performance of medieval entertainment in which descriptions from the period are

scarce. If a dance with costumes and sets from one production is being set on another cast within a relatively short interval of time, the term *resetting* is often used. The term *revival* is often used when a dance is produced, usually under the direction of the choreographer, after not being performed for several years.

(Smith 1992: 248–9)

Ann Hutchinson Guest follows a similar vein of thought when she suggests that *reconstruction* implies 'constructing a work anew from all available sources of information aiming for the result to be as close as possible to the original' (2000: 65). In this category she offers the work of Millicent Hodson and Kenneth Archer as an example.[2] *Revival*, she suggests, is a term that describes the bringing to life of choreographic work from notation. Of a *reworked* dance she has little more to say than that, if the choreography is reworked, it should be indicated clearly whether it is by the original choreographer or by some other person (ibid.: 65–6).

These dance writers essentially focus on recuperative approaches. Theatre analysts have emphasised works that are more distant from their source texts. Amy Green, in *The Revisionist Stage* (1994), cites Robert Brustein's formulation, which categorises two approaches to the conceptual rewritings of classic plays. These are *simile* productions, in which plays are recontextualised wholesale into different historical contexts, and productions which are conceptualised on the basis of *poetic metaphor*. Such productions are 'suggestive of the play rather than specific, reverberant rather than concrete' (Brustein, in Green 1994: 13). Geoffrey Wagner (1975) and Darko Suvin (1988) similarly identify and categorise productions as they become progressively distant from the source text. Wagner, discussing adaptations from novels to films, uses the terms *transposition*, *commentary* and *analogy*. Of these, *transposition* has the minimum of apparent interference, whereas the *commentary* re-emphasises or restructures the work in some way. These changes might include modifying characters, dealing with inner stories, or altering the context or surrounding imagery. The final term, *analogy*, represents a parallel argument to Brustein's *poetic metaphor* in that this approach may only hint at the source text.

The set of terms established by Suvin provides perhaps the most concrete model of categorisation, but, in attempting to be definitive, it is problematic. Suvin formulates what he calls 'interpretative pragmatics' (1988: 395) in order to discuss directorial interpretations. He argues that any signifying situation in printed or performed dramas induces a 'Possible World' in the reader or spectator (ibid.). Therefore, he goes on, each world will unavoidably have some limits and central features. While acknowledging that diverse readings of these possible worlds are probable, he argues that 'they will have to have what Wittgenstein called a family likeness, that is some parameters in common: negatively, limits; positively, features' (ibid.: 376). He labels these central features *invariants*. Suvin develops a system of identifying these invariants and attempts to distinguish between different stagings of plays based on their preservation, or not, of significant *invariants*. He calls these *variants*, *adaptations* and *rewrites*.

A *variant* observes the central structural features of the text being interpreted. In this formulation *any* staging is a *variant*. An *adaptation* uses only some of the central invariants, but these 'are sufficient to establish its "family likeness" to other members of that family' (Suvin 1988: 410). His final term, *rewrite*, indicates a work that 'is no longer, strictly speaking, an interpretation but a use of some elements from the anterior structure as a semi-finished product'; in such works only a few invariants may be evident (although at least one must be evident), although they may be 'used for a radically differing purpose' (ibid.).

Dance reworkings, as I use the term, are found across what Suvin categorises as *adaptations* and *rewrites*. For the term reworking, in that it is an active term, implies a process, a rethinking, a reconceptualising, and a revising of the source text in order to bring about some new resonance. For one of the purposes of reworkings is to alter the convention, and, while not all revised texts are progressive, the basic premise evident in these dances is that the source needs to be gone over or re-examined. The creators of reworkings can be seen to map out an alternative aesthetic terrain, which, to varying extents, diverges from the perspectives evident in the dances that they rework.

However, Suvin's formulation is not easily adapted for dance for, while possible worlds are inevitably evoked in the viewer in dance texts and play texts, he relies heavily on the written play text as a fixed anterior source to establish his *invariants* or central features. Without this anterior source, as is mainly the case for dance, the *invariants* are harder to establish, for in live performance there are an infinitely greater number of features to consider. The closest that it may be possible to approach the identification of *invariants* in dance is the discernment of form and the relationships between typical components in a particular work.[3]

More recently, continuing this plurality of terms and definitions, Julie Sanders (2006) discusses the differences between *adaptations* (which may be *amplificatory* or *proximations*) and *appropriations* (which may be *embedded* or *sustained*). Emphasising the intertextual nature of both adaptations and appropriations, Sanders notes that 'adaptation … constitutes a more sustained engagement with a single text or source', whereas 'appropriation carries out the same sustained engagement as adaptation but frequently adopts a posture of critique, even assault' (2006: 4). This differentiation is interesting in that it brings attention to differing methodologies, yet it is also slippery, as the defining line between these two approaches is inevitably imprecise.

Linda Hutcheon (2006) also notes the ways in which adaptations are intertextual, and helpfully differentiates adaptations from other related terms such as plagiarisms, sequels and prequels, for, she writes, 'plagiarisms are not acknowledged appropriations and sequels and prequels are not really adaptations either . . .. There is a difference between never wanting a story to end … and wanting to retell the same story over and over in different ways' (2006: 9). It is this strong desire to 're'-visit old texts from new directions that is the driving force behind dance reworkings. Yet I suspect that, rather than wanting to 'retell the *same* story', many choreographers seek to use source texts to tell new stories. Hutcheon (ibid.: 8) usefully attempts to summarise the features of adaptations in the following way:

- an acknowledged transposition of a recognisable other work or works;
- a creative act of appropriation/salvaging;
- an extended intertextual engagement with the adapted work.

This broad-sweep approach is helpful in that it is encompassing and avoids the prolific generation of terminologies that other writers, by establishing models of classification, have tended to create. In the main I find the range of terms, definitions and classifications evident in this field overly schematic, resulting in unhelpful and simplistic pigeonholing while still not exhausting of the range of possibilities. Suvin's model, for example, could usefully distinguish between, say, Mats Ek's reworking of *Swan Lake* and Susan Foster's as two reworkings that represent what Suvin would term an *adaptation* and a *rewrite*. However, it does little to identify the differences between *Giselle* by Ek and *Aurora* by Meryl Tankard. Nor does his model help distinguish between Javier de Frutos's use of *Swan Lake* and my own references to the ballet in *O (a set of footnotes to Swan Lake)*. And although the definitions offered by Hutcheon and Sanders remain more open and give rise to important frameworks for analysis, they do little to illuminate the ideologies and methodologies of dance reworkings, for, while Hutcheon mentions dance (if only in passing), dance is not the focus for either writer.

Through proliferation, however, these models and classifications do point to the disparate aims and intentions, methods and results of reworkings which make this such a fascinating area. Nevertheless the question that remains for an analysis of dance reworkings is not: How can a reworking be recognised or classified as a version (however it is adapted) of source?, but rather: How can different types of reworkings be understood and analysed in relational terms? For my purposes I do not find it necessary to classify different approaches tightly as specific types. Rather, I use the term reworkings to cover a range of dances which depart from their source text(s) in order to give rise to a new dance. To understand these differences, a much more detailed analysis needs to be undertaken of individual works so that one can identify the differing relationships to the source texts and choreographic strategies used. So what is important here is not the identification of terminology or the categorisation of different versions but an analysis of the features of these dances, and the conceptual, aesthetic and political terrain established in and by them.

Reviewing five *Giselles*

While *Giselle* has been presented in many forms by choreographers, interpreting the conventional ballet to suit different ends – I am thinking, for example, of Alicia Alonso's film version in Cuba in the early 1960s, Mary Skeaping's 1970s version for London's Festival Ballet and *Créole Giselle* (1984) by Arthur Mitchell and Frederic Franklin for the dance Theatre of Harlem – each of these works remains within the ballet genre. The five reworkings of *Giselle* discussed here depart more significantly, however, such that this overview reveals different choreographic approaches to reworkings and begins to illuminate the concepts embedded in, and applied to, these dances.

In chronological order the dances that I review here are *Sunrise* (1979) by Fergus Early; *I, Giselle* (1980) by Fergus Early and Jacky Lansley; *Giselle* (1982) by Mats Ek, my own work *The Original Sylph* (1997) and Michael Keegan Dolan's *Giselle* (2003). These reworkings, which range from large-scale theatre works to small-scale dances with small casts in non-traditional spaces, exemplify differing relationships towards the conventional *Giselles* which they rework.[4] For example, at what might be considered opposite ends of a continuum are *Sunrise* by Early and *Giselle* by Ek. *Sunrise* is a solo dance work which refers only in passing to the ballet, while using the character of Giselle and illuminating a previously absent narrative. *Giselle* by Ek has a large cast and is a dance that parallels the ballet closely, while also significantly altering the context, characterisation and dance vocabulary.

Although some of these five *Giselles* are more explicit than others in their radical politics and revisionary purpose, all reflect and participate in artistic and cultural agendas. *I, Giselle* embodies the agendas of the 1970s feminist movement, representing a critique of *Giselle* and the ballet genre while at the same time maintaining a respect for the ballet. Lansley and Early state in their programme notes that they wished to 'reclaim some of [ballet's] positive elements and skills, particularly its theatrical quality and use these in new contexts' (cited in Huxley 1988: 167). This dance, akin to other reworkings, does not treat the ballet flippantly; rather, while deconstructing *Giselle*, Early and Lansley find aspects of the ballet of value and of interest. *I, Giselle* takes the established narrative and examines its politics, ideology and sexual roles. The piece was performed by five artistes dancing the roles of Albrecht, Hilarion, Berthe and Myrtha (this last danced by the same person and presented as two aspects of a single powerful woman) and two Giselles (in act I by an actress and in act II by a dancer).

Consonant with the growing trend in new and postmodern dance in the 1970s, *I, Giselle*, while maintaining the central narrative, is an eclectic work which crosses styles and refuses boundaries. The music score by Steve Montague uses and distorts a recorded version of the conventional music by Adolphe Adam alongside atmospheric sound, and the live performance contains speech and songs. Set on a plain cloth-draped stage, the dance incorporates slide projections of the various famous ballerinas who have danced Giselle and, in act II, slides of ever multiplying Wilis. The movement crosses genres and includes mime, gesture, ballet, and movements influenced by release-based dance forms.

In discussing her experiences of the ballet, Lansley has commented that she felt that traditional versions have held Giselle in the position of the eternal victim, and that the power of the Wilis as a group of women often went unacknowledged (Early and Lansley, personal interview, 1999). This conceptualisation of the Wilis as an independent group of women who live in and enjoy a female realm is evident in *I, Giselle*. Similarly, Giselle is represented as a strong, assertive character in charge of her own fate. Rather than falling into madness and death, this Giselle makes a clear choice to join the powerful Wilis. When she enters this realm it is not a tragedy but a celebration of sisterhood; she does not have to be coerced by Myrtha. Giselle joins in a dance full of energy and circular patterns – reflecting feminist celebrations of womanhood and community (ibid.).

Of Albrecht, Huxley writes that, in '*I, Giselle* Albrecht is trapped by the Romantic role accorded him, in a version where Giselle discovers his subterfuge in Act One, and he is punished for his deception rather than his noble love' (Huxley 1988: 168). This reinterpretation disrupts the values embedded in *Giselle* and in the Romantic style. Early, who danced the role of Albrecht, has 'a distinctive performance style, a somewhat diffident presentation which belies the expected macho role of the male dancer' (ibid.: 165). Within this reworking the gendered vocabulary of ballet is extended as Early performs the steps of the ballet but with a different dynamic and body attitude. This anti-virtuosic language and 'softer', alternative physicality may challenge conventional expectations of the male dancing body.

Early took a similar approach to the vocabulary of ballet in *Sunrise* – a one-act, one-man 'ballet', with music from *Giselle* by Adam. In this dance Early enters the stage from an escape route in the roof of the theatre. Emerging down a ladder, wearing a white wedding dress and veil, while playing Adam's music on a recorder, Early walks slowly down the space on his toes. In the centre of the space he kneels down and removes the wedding dress to reveal underneath a pair of white Y-fronts. Early then goes on to perform sequences of mime that allude to the gestures in the ballet *Giselle* – hinting at the ballet's story. Performing in his Y-fronts, he moves along the green mats laid out on the floor and displays a relaxed balletic virtuosity. Jacky Lansley, in her review of the dance, said that she found it 'extremely satisfying to see the energy and skill of a ballet dancer', and that 'many of the movements which have evolved for the proscenium arch are, close up, larger than life and amazing' (Lansley 1979–80: 13).

Sunrise takes place after act II of the *Giselle* libretto. In this way the dance takes place 'in the gaps', filling out and shifting the understanding of Giselle's experience. My own reworking of *Giselle*, ironically entitled *The Original Sylph* (1997), like *Sunrise* by Early, takes place in the gaps of the ballet. Rather than rechoreographing the ballet while retaining the structural form, as Ek does, Early and I make references to *Giselle*, exploring intersecting themes without reworking the narrative or specific parts of the ballet. *The Original Sylph* is a small-scale solo dance that begins with the overture to *Giselle* by Adam. I lie under a mound of earth over which white flowers are spread. As the music reaches its climax I burst from under the mound of earth, gasping for air. The images of the grave, death and resurrection recur throughout the dance. These images clearly refer to act II of the ballet but are also used as a metaphor for the process of reworking, of the resuscitation of the past. Drawing on poststructuralist accounts of history (see below), this dance works through the past that is 'dead', which can only be found in history, and resurrects it in a different form. This new form comments on past forms and acknowledges its debt to the past, but is also a dance clearly of the late twentieth century.

Leaving the grave, I struggle in pointe shoes and totter towards the audience. When I reach the front of the stage I stop, look up and gaze back at those gazing

Plate 1   The Original Sylph (1997) by Vida Midgelow

Photograph: author's own

upon me. Looking down at my feet encased in pink ribboned shoes, I squat and begin to untie the ribbons. Whether this is a rejection of the shoes or an inability to conform to their requirements is ambiguous. Either way I assert myself/Giselle as flesh not fantasy, real not ethereal. In an ironic and playful reference I begin to gesture with my arms and hands. The gestures are drawn from the ballet but they are pared down and abstracted in such a way that they become like an encoded semaphore. Alongside these gestures I speak of love.

> I love you madly.
> A woman who loves a very cultivated man knows she cannot say to him 'I love you madly.'
> Because she knows that he knows (and that he knows that she knows) that these words have already been written by Barbara Cartland.
> Still, there is a solution to this problem. She can say, 'As Barbara Cartland would have put it, "I love you madly".' At this point, having avoided false innocence, having clearly said that it is no longer possible to speak innocently, she will nevertheless have said what she wanted to say: that she loves him, but that she loves in an age of lost innocence.
>
> (After Eco 1984: 67–8)

The reference to Umberto Eco's work on the postmodern condition contextualises this reworking. Operating intertextually, in the manner described by Riffaterre (1990) and de Marinis (1993) (discussed later in this chapter), the dance cites a number of sources. The conventional *Giselle* is the most overt and obligatory reference. It is *Giselle* that resonates throughout the work via set, music, costume, movement vocabulary and characterisation. Other references embodied in the dance are those of writers: Eco, as paraphrased above, Salman Rushdie and Susan Foster. These self-conscious intertexts form the basis of the spoken text and create a self-commentary within the dance. Cutting across the character of Giselle, while being voiced by her, these references help signify a woman who is multifaceted, aware of her own past, her own history, and able to refer to others. In this way *The Original Sylph* represents a disruptive account recalling Foucault's assertion that the task of genealogy is 'to expose a body totally imprinted by history and the process of history's deconstruction of the body' (Foucault 1977b: 148).

The incorporation of spoken text, following other postmodern dances, presents a sylph who refuses to be safely silent, refuses to evoke an ephemeral world within which she need not be taken too seriously (Foster 1996b: 219). Using physicality and voice, the sylph evokes a sense of 'knowingness'. She embodies the role of sylph, albeit a different kind of sylph, and also comments upon and critiques her role, going some way towards countering the ballerina's thwarted impulse to speak. In asserting an alternative vision of this canonical work which foregrounds the female as creator and interpreter as well as subject, the dance seeks to reclaim and affirm female agency within dance history. Tracing the construction of her identity, Giselle in this reworking suggests the possibility that she might shun her mythical status and dance out of her grave.

Both Early and I present *Giselle* in a very pared-down form using only a few direct elements of the source ballet within the new text's own structure. In contrast, the most well-known reworkings, presented by choreographers such as Matthew Bourne, Mark Morris and Mats Ek, follow the narratives and use the traditional music to maintain a close structural link to their sources. Ek updates *Giselle*, placing it into a twentieth-century context. His approach removes the supernatural elements of the dance and locates the tale in a Freudian-inspired, symbolically painted stage (designed by Marie-Louise Ekman). In the first act the painted 'landscape' loosely resembles a woman's body, with boldly coloured hills shaped like breasts out of which trees sprout and under which green grasses grow, which are reminiscent of pubic hair. This concept is developed on the painted backdrop in the second act when female body parts (fingers and breasts) are represented as dismembered and fragmented objects.

Ek, speaking in 1983 of his reworking of *Giselle*, comments that:

> Over ten years ago I saw it [*Giselle*] for the first time – with Markarova. She was the one who really grabbed me. Already then, I thought the traditional story of *Giselle* contains many hidden possibilities which are not recognized. There are various trails leading inside, but they are not utilized. They lie fallow or else are powdered over.
>
> (Cited in Tegeder 1983: 19)

Bringing into focus subtexts from the ballet, his work highlights class differentiation and the tensions between individuality and conformity. Following the traditional narrative, Giselle, a country girl, falls in love in act I with Albrecht, who in this version is not a fairy-tale aristocrat but a sophisticated, rather spoilt young 'townie'. Giselle is not an innocent virgin but a passionate, if rather peculiar, woman. Giselle's love for Albrecht is a sexual love, and themes of sexuality and fertility are to the fore. These themes are particularly evident in the backdrop and the giant eggs with which the women dance.

From his first entrance Albrecht is clearly of a different class from Giselle, for, while Giselle's movement is grounded as she shifts, slides and twitches across the floor, his is a more upright alignment and his movement emphasises flow. And, if these differentiated movement styles do not mark his difference from Giselle enough, his white tailcoat, distinct from Giselle's 'peasant' brown, certainly does. However, Giselle, unbridled by social constraints, loves him. She refuses to acknowledge that they cannot be together simply because they have been brought up in different classes. Because of her infatuation with Albrecht, Giselle is positioned apart from her fellow country folk. She is a woman who attempts to transgress the bounds of societal norms and subsequently is accepted neither in her own social group nor in that of Albrecht. Indeed, rather than dying of a broken heart, in this version she is punished for her open sexuality and for attempting to transgress her social background. At the end of act I her own people trap her – pinning her down like a dangerous animal with their two-pronged forks and banishing her to what appears to be a lunatic asylum, the context for the second act.

In act II the traditional Wilis are replaced by a host of female hospital patients and Myrtha by a strict matron. Whether these women are supposed to be truly mentally ill or, like Giselle, are women society would rather ignore is not clear. For whatever reason, they are restricted and controlled. Confused and intense, they rock, shuffle and lie on the floor, their bodies held in tense contortions. It has been suggested that they were conceived as nymphomaniacs (Poesio 1994: 695), and they certainly demonstrate an obsession with sex and pregnancy. They are also fearful of men, and their at times violent response to Albrecht seems to be driven by this fear. Hilarion, a more three-dimensional character in this version, is allowed to leave the hospital, but Albrecht, the focus of the women's attentions, is stripped naked and left exposed and vulnerable.

Ek's representation of the workings of psychology and social strictures upon female sexuality is particularly evident in this *Giselle*. Problematically, however, the way in which the imagery on the painted backdrop, Giselle's sexual desires and the red doll/cushion (which Giselle cradles and pushes inside her top) combine suggests in Ek's *Giselle* that 'sexuality, fertility and the maternal instinct are one' (Ulzen 1990–91: 45). Further the representation of women as psychologically unstable, and as unable to control their sexual desires, may also reinforce negative images of women.

'Worse still', critic Karen van Ulzen points out, is 'the overly simplistic portrayal of country life as equated with earthy, natural sexuality and its comparison

Plate 2   Giselle (2003) by Michael Keegan Dolan

Photographer: T. Charles Erickson

with the sanitised, modern medical world' (1990–91: 45). While these issues are present in conventional versions, but perhaps hidden by the Romantic form, Ek's modern work emphasises these points and does little to 'correct' them. Indeed in this version Giselle, while more assertive, is chastised for her wilful sexual transgression rather than her folly of being too innocent in love, as in the ballet, and the potential strength and power of the Wilis and Myrtha has been lessoned by Ek. However, while containing contentious elements, Ek's reworking brings new perspectives and depths of understanding to our dancing heritage. Full of original ideas, this dance will make you think again.

The most recent reworking of *Giselle* discussed here is by Michael Keegan Dolan and his Fabulous Beast Dance Theatre. This *Giselle* also operates within a narrative structure, yet here the plot and form is significantly altered. This Dublin-born choreographer has created a work that strongly asserts its difference from the ballet – radically reconceiving and recharacterising Giselle, placing her in Ballyfeeny, an imagined modern-day Irish village – and which is soaked in violence and reilluminates the sexual aspects of the traditional narrative. Keegan Dolan states that what interests him are 'the themes of betrayal, selfhood and forgiveness. Ballyfeeny could be anywhere but what I've created is very hard-hitting. It goes deep into subjects such as bisexuality and other taboos' (cited in Brennan 2003). His work attempts to use the existing darkness in Giselle, portraying her as a mute woman, abused by her family and most of the other village inhabitants.

The first half is filled with an eclectic mix of styles, including a camp, kitsch hoedown, folk songs, spoken narration, simulated sex scenes and powerful physical theatre. Giselle, surrounded by an abusive all-male family, becomes sexually involved with Albrecht, who in this reworking is a line-dancing teacher, new to the village. Through the work it becomes clear that, while involved with Giselle, Albrecht, a closet bisexual, is also having sexual liaisons with the Butcher's son – by whom he is buggered in a dark alley. Here Albrecht's deceit is one imposed by a dysfunctional uninformed community, yet Giselle is still left betrayed.

Giselle's death of an asthma attack – brought on by being forced to watch her lover have sex with the Butcher's son – brings us to the second part of the work. As in the ballet, pure movement takes over. The stage darkens and white ghost-like figures appear through trapdoors. These figures climb, hang and swing on looping ropes. The movement is darkly magical yet violently intense. The figures are joined by Giselle, who dances a stunningly beautiful duet with Albrecht, which ends with the last few bars of Adolphe Adam's original ballet score.

This reworking uses the ballet narrative as a background text – it consistently exists in the shadows but is rarely brought into the foreground. The narrative has been refocused and extended in such a manner that attention is less on 'spot what has been done to the ballet' and more on Keegan Dolan's commentary upon sexuality, patriarchy and repression. These themes and the heightened sense of violence amplify that which exists in the ballet, but refocus them to comment upon the 'developed history of violent and sexual repression in this country [Ireland]' (Keegan Dolan, cited in Brennan 2003).

The five dances implicitly embody the socio-cultural and critical climates reflected and created by poststructuralism, postmodernism, feminism and queer theory. These theories bring to the surface debates about the nature of human existence and relationships: they are fundamental because they are political and result in a questioning of power and discrimination, to demonstrate how power and knowledge are constructed and thereby help to deconstruct the edifice of received norms. It is to these concepts, among others, as they relate to reworkings that I now turn.

Counter-discourses and the canon

While the history of ballet is one of reinvention and restaging, the parallel and interactive operations of the canon and history have served to imbue Classical and Romantic ballets, the dances that are most commonly revisited in reworkings, with the gloss of transcendence and ahistoricism. This gloss tends to hide the process of constant change that is a continuing aspect of ballet companies' repertoires. Contemporary discourses have dispelled this gloss and opened up canonical texts to reveal their artistic, cultural and political specificity. Reworkings both reflect and add to this discourse – requiring the existence of the canon and conversely contributing to its deconstruction, reformulation and expansion. For reworkings enter the canon metaphorically, and sometimes in actuality, from alternative, and at times discordant, directions.

The term 'canon' traces back to the Greek 'kanon', denoting notions of rule, ruler, model or standard. The establishment of a canon has been part of church practice. One of the most pertinent meanings of 'canon' is as an authoritative list of books accepted as Holy Scripture (hence the description of canonical works as 'sacred'). Thereby the canon may be understood as a consolidated narrative of origin that forms the legitimating backbone of a cultural and political identity. Other definitions of 'canon' that are particularly useful are as the authentic works of a writer and as a criterion or standard of judgement. Marcia J. Citron, in *Gender and the Musical Canon*, writes that 'canons are exemplary, act as models, instruct, represent high quality, endure, and embody at least some degree of moral or ethical force' (1993: 15). Canons therefore exert formidable power, setting the standards of what is considered to be worthy, to be of quality and good. Associated with the authority of the canon is a set of transhistorical aesthetic values evidenced by the unquestionably 'great' creators which establish models to be studied (and aspired to) by those wishing to gain entry to the practice (Pollock 1999: 3). Works are judged as to whether they 'match up', and works which fail to meet the criterion are then excluded and, as a result, partially ignored.

As a potent symbol of the identity of a culture, the canon is not value free but value laden. As Citron states, 'the canon is seen as a replication of social relations and a potent symbol on their behalf' (1993: 1). Those who have control over it are in commanding positions, for the canon tends to reflect and perpetuate the ideologies of particular points of view. Almost invariably, especially until more recently, it has been the points of view of privileged, white, heterosexual, middle-class Western males that have formed the criteria of canonicity.

The canon appears to present a unified vision of quality, for although the works included within canons do shift, the process takes place over long periods of time. Thereby the works included within the canon become, over time, entrenched as canonical. This 'entrenching' is further enhanced by the perception that a work should be able to 'stand the test of time' in order to be considered truly canonical. Works within the canon take on a normative significance, and the dance canon has tended to perpetuate a particular type and approach to the making of dances – and by extension to present only certain representations of race, gender, sexuality and class.

Through the operation of the canon the rows of identically dressed women that form the *corps de ballet*, the extended linear positions of the ballet vocabulary, and fairy-tale narratives that are the basis of many ballet librettos come to be hold the status of what Roland Barthes calls myth. He writes that myth 'consists of overturning culture into nature or, at least, the social, the cultural, the ideological, the historical into the "natural"' (1977: 165). Barthes argues that myth is a collective representation that is socially produced but inverted in order to appear 'a matter of course' (ibid.). Myth, like the canon, acts to deny social and political development and refuses to be named, producing the effect of an eternal, historical, apolitical artefact.

Barthes reads beyond the apparent neutrality of texts in order to uncover their covert meanings and considers the way texts become myth.[5] His perspective can help to reveal the way in which canonical ballets have come to seem, through mythification, universal and transcendent, rather than specific and contextualised. Thereby temporal, geographical and artistic particulars of dancers, makers, steps, patterns and narratives are discounted such that these elements are formed all together under the mythical sign that is 'the ballet'. This process can be seen to homogenise differences between one ballet and another such that a ballet as a specific creative act becomes lost in dense layers of signification and comes to seem to be just as it 'always has been' and, perhaps more problematically, as 'it should be'. Ballets thereby transpire to appear static and unchanging, as differences between specific ballets and specific performances are eroded by the workings of myth. The result of these processes is that, although current productions of Classical and Romantic ballets are themselves of course consummate palimpsests – bearing the traces of successive transformations – these transformative marks are hidden within a unified aesthetic.

It is this mythic, generalised and standardised source that is referred to in reworkings. So, although some reworkings may reference a particular version, in general the references, and the audience's perception of the references, are to a mythic version. Reworkings both reveal and utilise the mythic status of the ballet, for, to a certain extent, they rely on the generalisation of ballet, as they use the audience's shared knowledge of convention and choreographic codes. They do not differentiate between one version of their source and another but 'use' a generic marker recognisable as the source. At the same time, however, the process of reworking also brings to the fore the individual and specific in contrast to myth. Radical or alternative reworkings offer readings of ballets in which the reality behind the myth and the fantasy are made known. They can question and illuminate the mythic, opening up myth, unmasking it, to reveal the particular and hidden, thereby reversing the processes myth.

The potential of the demythologising features of reworkings enables the assumed authority and embedded socio-cultural values of the 'classic' or 'canonical' text to be unveiled and dismantled. This process can usefully be seen to be part of counter-discourses that have established bodies of scholarship concerned with countering the literary and theatrical canons. These studies have revealed how the canon is based on dominant economic and social systems and have highlighted the resultant race, gender, sexuality and class bias. In order to challenge its hegemony, the canon has been expanded, with the aim of creating a more balanced canon that more adequately reflects the work of women and non-Westerners who, through history, have been disenfranchised. This approach seeks to rediscover the 'lost' works of women and non-Western artists. The inclusion of these works, traditionally considered as 'other', seeks to add diversity and difference which, because of the normative power of the canon, tends to be papered over. However, while an important project, this approach encourages the separation and continuing marginalisation of the 'other'. 'The real history of art', suggests Griselda Pollock, 'remains fundamentally unaffected because its mythological and psychic centre is fundamentally or exclusively to do not with art and its histories but with the Western masculine subject. ... The Story of Art is an illustrated Story of Man' (1999: 24).

From this perspective the addition of 'other' voices to the canon, or the establishment of a counter but parallel canon, while in many ways necessary and positive, runs the risk of resembling an 'add and stir' approach in which the flavour may be changed but the overall product does not. The danger is that the addition of a more diverse range of works to the canon does not challenge the concept of canonicity itself. In fact such a methodology can be seen to support those existing structures by buying into them, which, when the concept of canonicity is shown to reside in a patriarchal approach, is problematic. The values that implicitly form the canon need from this perspective to be brought to the foreground and questioned.

More recent approaches seek to reveal that the canon is a discursive formation. Through deconstruction the canon becomes visible as 'an enunciation of Western masculinity' (Pollock 1999: 26). The deconstruction of the canon has led to radical new knowledge that undercuts its seemingly 'ungendered' and 'universal' domains and insists that sex and race is everywhere. Re-reading canonical texts as a charged signifier, and re-reading for what is not said as much as for what is, allows meaning to be produced in the space between. This permits the canon to be seen and understood anew; thus canonical objects can be reconsidered and challenged.

Reworkings, as a form of counter-discourse, provide opportunities for refiguring canonical texts. They bring heritage to the fore while asserting their difference from canonical forms, suggesting a deep ambivalence, and in so doing they persist in slipping into and around the canon – into the heart of dominant Western culture. These reconsiderations of the canon are closely tied to the challenges that have been raised to traditional concepts of history. It is to these concerns, and the place of reworkings in them, that I now turn.

Reconsidering the past: reworkings as postmodern historiography

In reworkings, historical contexts are reinstalled as significant, while they are also problematised. Reading against the grain of canonical dances, reworkings adapt, embrace and question our dancing heritage, drawing attention to history and processes of historiography (my own *The Original Sylph* does so explicitly, as described previously). The historical referent in reworkings is recognised as 'textualised', as the past only comes to us in the form of indirect representations, through collections of textual traces. Reworkings are thereby unavoidably discursive, as the textual traces of history are opened to interpretation. The choreographers of these dances enter the canon and reveal the discursive production of history in a manner akin to that of post-'ist' historiographers.

In poststructuralist and postmodernist accounts there is a distrust of the gloss of neutrality and an acknowledgment of the pretence of objective recounting evident in traditional history writing. Instead postmodernist history becomes histories and questions. It asks, Whose history gets told? And, For what purpose and in whose name? 'Postmodernism is about histories not told, retold, untold. History as it never was. Histories forgotten, hidden, invisible, considered unimportant, changed, eradicated' (Marshall 1992: 4). Thereby, rather than coming towards the end of history or a rejection of history, as suggested by some commentators,[6] history is proliferating. We now have multiple histories that are inclusive of herstories and your stories, for postmodern histories attempt to tell the stories of the winners and the losers, those at the centre and at the periphery. History has become overtly narrativised as the facts of the past become known as constructed accounts. So, rather than forming a grand narrative, postmodernism constructs a montage of narratives that are provisional and problematic. Hence history becomes recognised as 'hybrid tracings' rather than as historical fact because history has been shown to be a shifting discourse within which changes of gaze and new interpretations may appear. This challenge to the totalising impulse of the continuity of history, and of history writing, creates a position in which history is seen as unstable, relational and provisional.

Reflecting what Lyotard has called 'the postmodern condition', reworkings bring the fluid and transient nature of history to the fore. Lyotard notes that grand narratives of legitimisation are no longer credible, for metadiscourse purports to narrate a story about the whole of human history. In contrast postmodern narratives become plural, local and immanent. Following Lyotard's concept, reworkings might usefully be considered *petits recits* (little stories), in contrast to *un grand recit* (one grand overarching story or narrative) (Lyotard 1984). While reworkings range from approaches that suggest a complete narrative (for example, Ek's version of *Giselle*) to those which are fragmentary in form (for example, my own work *The Original Sylph*), the very proliferation of reworkings of a single source serve to reveal and contest the conception of the source as a unity, as a single history. The spaces between and conflicts across different versions preclude any assumption that only one narrative exists.

Through such revelations it is evident that any claim to a single objective 'truth' is not plausible. Through postmodernism, 'truth' is interrogated as to its power and politics, and it becomes inconsistent to speak of objective knowledge or absolutes, for they are only formulated on the prevailing and generally dominant ideologies of knowledge. Rather than searching for a truth within postmodernism, the historian, author and choreographer construct persuasive and meaningful hypotheses. The challenge to the concept of 'truth' offers freer rein to the possibilities of fancy and imagination. Rather than events being presented as fixed monoliths, they can be put forward in new lights and are open to constant modification. Alternative possibilities can be exposed which make us aware of alternative options for the future.

The interest in revisiting history is also evident in postmodern dance practices, and reworkings, consonant with these practices, reinstall history as an issue. Previously for modern dancers the appropriation of existing representations was considered taboo, as Roger Copeland makes clear in 'Mark Morris, postmodernism, and history recycled' (1997). In this essay Copeland argues that modern choreographers placed their emphasis on originality and prided themselves on having 'broken with history and tradition'. For example, Martha Graham, as a modern dancer, 'practised a scorched earth policy with regard to the past: her mission was to "begin again"' (Copeland 1997: 20). In contrast, for postmodern choreographers,

> there's no starting over, no returning to innocence, no going home again. More important, the 'frame of mind' in which many postmodern choreographers create has itself been historicised in that they possess a divided or double consciousness, being acutely aware of their relationship to both the past and present.

And further:

> Rather than deceiving themselves into believing that at this late date in the twentieth century it is possible to be wholly original ... many postmodern choreographers use a heightened consciousness of dance history as their point of departure.
>
> (Ibid.)

Reworkings reflect this general thrust in postmodern dance practice and embody a tendency towards recycling and the retro. However, we might consider – as Mark Franko (1993) does in relation to reconstructions in dance – whether this tendency connotes a radical critique of the past, a nostalgic return, or a rather more sinister cynical commodification. These arguments resonate with Hal Foster's 1985 positioning of the postmodern *per se* which he discusses in terms of resistant and reactionary approaches.

> A postmodernism of resistance, then, arises as a counter-practice not only to the official culture of modernism but also to the 'false normativity' of a reactionary postmodernism. In opposition (but not only in opposition), a resistant postmodernism is concerned with a critical deconstruction of tradition, not an

instrumental pastiche of pop- or pseudo historical forms, with a critique of origins, not a return to them. In short, it seeks to question rather than exploit cultural codes, to explore rather than conceal social and political affiliations.

(Foster 1985: x)

Foster's insightful discussion usefully points towards two intersecting yet contrasting directions of postmodernism. In practice, however, these two directions are less clearly defined, less clearly marked. A reworking may embody both the liberating potential of counter-practices while also exploiting the cultural status of the ballet. Thereby the historical form (the ballet) is fulfilled *and* lost, uncritically celebrated *and* questioned, for reworkings operate in between the continuum of resistive and reactionary postmodernisms. While varying in degree, these dances, like the ballets they rework, are a strange mixture of highly elitist and popularist, generating ambiguous political sites. For example, reworkings such as those by Matthew Bourne (see chapter 2) tend to be accessible to a non-specialist audience as his works follow clear narratives, echo the recognisable styles of musical theatre, and also, in pragmatic terms, have been extensively toured and publicised. They risk, however, being rendered so safe and so commodified that they lose their liberating, and certainly radical, potential.

In contrast, others, such as the deconstructive reworkings by Foster and Hoghe (see chapters 3 and 4), tend towards a more reified audience. For while they both embody an overtly critical stance towards the ballet, they risk becoming insiders' games that render dance traditions and institutions not as more open and public but as more hermetic and narcissistic. They are in danger of articulating their critique for initiates only. Such is the doubleness of reworkings. At once inside and outside the institution, both more and less accessible, they are duplicitous in their retaining of the status of canonical art while propounding critiques of those very hegemonic constructs.

However duplicitous in form and/or politics, reworkings are part of the postmodern reconsideration of history, overtly and self-consciously revisiting the dances of the past to create dances that comment on both the present and the past. Decolonising and deconstructing the canonical order, these dances can serve to reveal traditional ballet as a form of cultural imperialism and to destabilise the way in which canons disguise their own histories in order to present an illusion of a natural aesthetic order. In the light of poststructuralist accounts, choreographers can be seen to insert themselves creatively into past texts, which have been shown to be unstable texts. This insertion by choreographers of reworkings does not help 'make sense' of past texts (although this is a feature of some reworkings) but engages with the past in conscious play. While reworkings are not all, by any means, radical or deconstructive in purposeful or explicit ways, by interpreting old texts from new directions these dances open up the canon and demythologise the texts within it. Thereby, reworkings, by their very nature, represent a potential strategy for creating discursive counter-texts.

Reworkings as intertextual practices

Theories of intertextuality have made it clear that all texts are part of a 'general discursive structure (genre, discursive formation, ideology)' (Frow 1990: 46) and are shaped by other textual structures. Recognising the intertextual nature of all texts relies on the ability of the reader/viewer to reconstruct the codes which are realised, or contested, within them (ibid.). Janet Adshead-Lansdale writes that the theory of intertextuality maintains

> the idea of a text as a series of traces, which endlessly multiply and for which there can be no consensus of interpretation. In this area the reader's [the reader here is understood to be the viewer, choreographer, critic, etc.] activity becomes one of unravelling threads, rather than deciphering fixed meanings, choosing which colour in the tapestry to follow, where and when to start, change direction and conclude.
>
> (Adshead-Lansdale 1999: 8)

If intertextual analysis is understood to be a deliberate positioning of a creative product within a network of other texts, then reworkings can usefully be positioned as a particular type of intertextual practice. Reworkings involve liberal references to, and quotations from, their source text(s), and the choreographers of reworkings can be seen self-consciously to embed, cite, and allude to other pretexts in their dances. This relates to common devices within intertextuality which, as de Marinis states, involve the 'complex and variegated play of borrowing, citation, implicit or explicit references, dialogues from afar, and substitutions, which substantiate the relationships between the texts of a given culture (and even between texts of different cultures)' (de Marinis 1993: 4). However, while many choreographers may cite or quote other dance texts in an intertextual practice, this doesn't necessarily result in the more crucially acknowledged, embedded and sustained engagement that is a characteristic feature of reworkings.

Reworkings form a relationship between texts such that a conversation arises (either explicitly in the work or implicitly via the reader's connections). These intertextual sites in reworkings, like all intertexts, may seem more or less visible to particular viewers depending upon their ability to see, and their knowledge of, the allusion being made. Indeed, reworkings encompass layered acts of reading by the choreographer and the viewer. They are often founded upon the choreographer's ability to make an open reading of a source, working within the gaps and from different perspectives to be able to imagine it otherwise. The viewer of a reworking is then required to make connections between texts in order to enjoy the intertextual play. These dances encourage the simultaneous consideration of the reworking and the source alongside the numerous other texts at play. As Adshead-Lansdale suggests, the reader becomes an 'aggressive participant' in the construction of meaning as, in works of this kind, the 'knowledgeable reader is expected and invited to pick up the appropriate references when required to do so by the text' (Adshead-Lansdale 1999: 19).

Reworkings as performative acts are the practical realisation of creative interpretation and, as Michael Worton notes, 'performative interpretation must bring
about its own criteria and persuade the unknown reader of their worth' (Worton,
in Adshead-Lansdale 1999: xi). Further, as performative acts of interpretation,
'they move between numerous discourses in order to liberate us and the works
they consider from the tyranny of singular concepts of telling, showing, explaining'
(ibid.).

However, while shifting between discourses and operating in the manner of
intertextual texts, reworkings also have a vested interest in maintaining an identifiable, if mythic, source text to which they repeatedly, however literally or
obscurely, refer. The relationship in reworkings to this source gives rise to questions about the connections between such dances, source criticism and intertextual practices. John Frow comments:

> Intertextual analysis is distinguished from source criticism by this stress on
> interpretation rather than on the establishment of particular facts, and by its
> rejection of a unilinear causality (the concept of 'influence') in favour of an
> account of the work performed upon intertextual material and its functional
> integration in the later text.
>
> (Frow 1990: 46)

And Barthes writes that the

> intertextual in which every text is held, it itself being the text-between of
> another text, is not to be confused with some origin of the text: to try to find
> the 'sources', the 'influences' of a work, is to fall in with the myth of filiation;
> the citations which go to make up a text are anonymous, untraceable, and yet
> *already read*: they are quotations without inverted commas.
>
> (Barthes 1977: 160)

Intertextual approaches, as distinguished from those of source criticism, avoid the
search for a 'source' or 'origin' and emphasise instead playfulness and ambiguity.
While reworkings, to be identified as reworkings at all, must contain clear and
'known' sources, these sources are not treated by the choreographers of such dances
in terms of 'influence' but rather in a dialectic exchange. While knowledge of the
ballet that is being reworked will undoubtedly provide the viewer with an added
pleasure, the identification of the 'source' text is different from the search for a
source of meaning. Frow argues that the 'identification of an intertext is an act of
interpretation. The intertext is not a real and causative source but a theoretical construct formed by and serving the purposes of a reading' (1990: 46). However,
reworkings rely on what Michael Riffaterre has described as the 'obligatory intertext', that is, the text(s) which the reader must know in order 'to understand a work
of literature in terms of its overall significance' (Riffaterre 1990: 56). The pre-
textual intertext at the source of reworkings is particular and causative. Failure to

note this intertext would be to miss an overt and distinguishing feature of these dances. But this is not to say that the audience member who does not recognise the ballet intertext will be unable to make a reading of the reworkings – rather that the latter consciously mobilise their pre-text(s). However, rather than their 'known' source existing in the manner of an originary text, such dances open up and unfix their pre-texts such that they become in the new work one (albeit key) intertext among many. While, like all texts, reworkings are open to multiple readings, the knowledge of the source invokes another level of enjoyment and can assist in the reader's capacity to generate 'appropriate' meanings. It is this relationship between the new and the surprising alongside the known and the comfortable that is at the heart of our pleasure in reworkings.

Through a politicisation of theories of intertextuality, it is possible to note how reworkings might foreground the politics of representation. For example, Linda Hutcheon, in a discussion of parody as a form of intertext, writes that parody 'contests our humanist assumptions about artistic originality and uniqueness and our capitalist notions of ownership and property' (1989: 93). Further, she notes that postmodern ironic parody engages 'the history of art and the memory of the viewer in a re-evaluation of aesthetic forms and contents through a reconsideration of their usually unacknowledged politics of representation' (ibid.: 100). This denaturalising (to use Hutcheon's term) of past representations is parallel to Barthes's notion of demythologising that which appears 'natural'. This is not to suggest that *all* reworkings have a political agenda, or that those with political agendas are necessarily overt, for, as Helen Gilbert and Joanne Tompkins (1996) note, while counter-discourse is inherently intertextual, not all intertextual texts necessitate a rewriting project. Rather, I propose that the act of reworking itself inherently denaturalises representation, bringing to the fore continuity and, importantly, difference. Thereby these dances can make us think again about the dances of the past, and the ideologies embedded within them.

The inherent ambiguity of intertextual strategy makes this approach doubly dangerous for the politically motivated artist. For, as Hutcheon stresses, 'one of the lessons of the doubleness of postmodernism is that you cannot step outside that which you contest, you are always implicated in the value you choose to challenge' (1988: 223). In other words, that which is quoted or referenced as an obligatory intertext in reworkings carries its own embedded values which cannot be escaped. The use of, and choice to use, a particular intertext is not 'free' but carries with it a set of implications, perspectives and assumptions. This perspective runs throughout the analyses undertaken in this book. While remaining implicated within the canon, these dances reveal strategies that have the potential to subvert the discourse of power – a potential inherent in reworkings.

Towards a definition of reworkings

I now turn to discuss the delineating features of reworkings, and outline the mode of analysis that will follow. Reworkings, it has so far been suggested, can denaturalise, or demythologise, the mythic dances of the ballet canon. Creating against the grain and deconstructing the canon, reworkings can reveal the limited representations of gender, sexuality and ethnicity in a process analogous to the strategies of canonical counter-discourse. Further, emulating postmodern historiography, reworkings are like *petit recits*, in that they represent the local and the specific rather than the global and the ahistorical. As particular kinds of intertextual practice, reworkings operate through extended and acknowledged references to an obligatory intertext (the source) while simultaneously unfixing or recoding that very intertext.

While canonical dances, owing to changing contexts of production and, importantly, reception, are in constant metamorphosis, reworkings suggest a much more conscious interpolation. Reworkings are particularly discursive and evoke multiple gazes. These dances must, at the very least, mobilise a bidirectional gaze – to itself and backwards to the source.[7] This bidirectionality, this double vision, may be both inter-temporal and/or intercultural, for our experience of these works operates in overlapping layers of familiarity and memory, as we experience both the familiar and the new at the same time.

As a delineating feature of reworkings it can be seen that a text that does not signal a clear enough relationship to a source text may not be able to be recognised as a reworking at all. If the signifier of the source, or to use Riffarterre's phrase the obligatory intertext, is absent or too obscured, it becomes just another intertextual work, not a reworking. Conversely a dance that does not clearly signal its difference from the source so as to be recognised as being sufficiently 'new' may only reiterate or imitate the source text, and therefore would not be considered a reworking either.

Through the following chapters I explore the extent to which the bidirectional gaze evoked by reworkings might be able to operate in a fluid, rather than a fixed, form. I review the shifting nature of reworkings and argue that they may be seen hybrids that inhabit the 'inbetween'. As hybrids, to apply the concept of postcolonialist writer Homi Bhabha (1991), these dances embody not a singular alterity but a myriad of shifting markers. The hybrid nature of reworkings is at times explicit, through strategies such as parody, but always implicit, via the signifiers of the obligatory intertext. Reworkings express a multifaceted identity, an identity which takes into account tradition while refusing to be locked under the sign 'authenticity'. Rather than reversing or replacing the established order (the canonical ballet), these dances provide an implicit critique of the illusion of fixed and stable forms.

The viewer of these works has the opportunity to move beyond binaries – beyond one and its other – for these dances do not seek to displace (as if that were possible or desirable), but stand as 'differences' (or Derridian *différance*).[8] It may be that these dances can avoid the hierarchical relationship between binaries in which the 'other' (the reworking) is always placed in opposition to, and is perceived to be less than, the dominant norm (the canonical ballet). For, by opening up the possibilities of their source texts, reworkings do not ignore the past; they interact with it such that the previously 'pure' is replaced with plurality.

In reworkings, the source text(s) is(are) simultaneously and paradoxically insignificant and highly important. Even the most radical of reworkings thereby enters into a discourse with the canon, evoking a double-edged relationship. As contemporary works (full of socio-cultural imperatives that cannot be avoided) that simultaneously evoke source texts (with all their own histories), these dances exist within a double frame. This means, at least to a certain extent, that they exist within the status quo of the canon. At one level reworkings might be seen to challenge the canonical texts upon which they are based, but in other ways they also reinforce canonical works through the implicit value given to the canon by revisiting the works within it. So while the content and form of any particular reworking may in and of itself be transgressive, or include transgressive elements, via the return to the canon the importance of canonical texts may be seen to be restated. Reworkings operate polemically. As Barthes states when reading myth:

> we constantly drift between the object and its demystification, powerless to render its wholeness. For if we penetrate the object, we liberate it but we destroy it; and if we acknowledge its full weight, we respect it but we restore it to a state which is still mystified.
>
> (Barthes 1993: 159)

If the makers of reworkings find something of interest in the source – something worthy of exploration, celebration or exposition – then the 'reworker' mirrors Barthes's problematic. The challenge of reworking is thereby how to penetrate the source text, how to liberate it, without either destroying it or restoring it. This view is also voiced by Helen Tiffin when she points out that the risk of counter-discursive strategies in postcolonial contexts is that they may be neo-assimilative in their use of colonialist models of production (Tiffin 1995: 96). In a similar manner to postcolonial texts and contexts, reworkings always risk being contaminated by that which is hegemonic. There is no going back or being free of the contaminant. This neo-assimilative and conservative impulse in reworkings is particularly evident when dance reworkings are perceived as buying into the commercial success of their canonical sources. The cache of the source may be used to attract programmers, media attention and audiences. The existing stature of the source text as canonical may be perceived to 'rub off' on the reworking – providing the reworking with more recognition than it would otherwise achieve. This view implicates reworkings in the commercialisation of the canon. As Foster (2001) and Manning (2001) note, Bourne's *Swan Lake* is implicated in just this way. Bourne remains uncritical of the way his dance exists within and is commodified by global capitalism, limiting its potential challenge to dominant masculinities and the heterosexual matrix (see chapter 2). The context of commodification is also highlighted as a particular problem in Shakti's reworking of *Swan Lake* in chapter 5. This dance risks commodification by the global economy of sex. Reworkings operate on a tightrope between that which re-enshrines the canon and that which alters and exposes the canon, creating a dynamic counter-discourse, and, as shall become evident, while varying in degree, reworkings tend to operate in both of these ways at the same time.

While reworkings maintain a complex and at times tense relationship to their influential forebears, this relationship is not consonant with, indeed may contest, what has been called 'the anxiety of influence'. Literary critic Harold Bloom (1997) (originally published 1973) developed the critical concept of influence, arguing that for artists to achieve significant originality they need to bear the burden of influence of existing canonical works/artists. For Bloom, standards are only maintained when artists (Bloom uses the more specific term 'poets') enter into an interpersonal (if imaginary) antagonistic struggle with past artists. He writes that 'tradition is not only a handing-down or process of benign transmission; it is also a conflict between past genius and present aspiration, in which the prize is literary survival or canonical inclusion' (Bloom 1995: 9). While in some senses Bloom's concept is consistent with theories of intertextuality, as he acknowledges the way in which all literary works come into being and are resonant with precursor works, his focus upon the 'genius' (which is already a highly gendered concept) of particular authors and inheritance belies the much more open and inclusive concept of intertextuality used here. Bloom's response to calls to liberalise the canon is to suggest that quality is being replaced by ideology, labelling all 'other' voices a 'school of resentment'. What he fails to recognise is his own ideological position in the maintenance of the status quo. In his model the standards and values set by past artists are perpetuated and so the power and authority of particular groups are maintained. Bloom's position actively creates a hierarchical genealogy of father–son succession and replicates patriarchal mythologies of exclusively masculine (and white, heterosexual) creativity.

Reworkings can challenge this patriarchal model. Bearing the influence and contesting the authority of the influential source texts, reworkings question the epistemology of the canon. The model of analysis applied in this book attempts to be non-hierarchical and focuses upon the reworkings (the daughters) rather than the source (their oppressing fathers). While I acknowledge that the daughter could not have come into being without the father, the analysis that follows works from the assumption that, while the daughter is younger, it does not mean that she is by necessity less than or secondary to her father.[9] Rather I avoid any hints of 'fidelity criticism' or judgements based on a proximity to, or the authority of, the source text. Instead I emphasise the oscillating, dialogic relationship established between texts and undertake close readings of reworkings *as* reworkings. Through the following chapters what comes to the fore are the ideologies and methodologies evident across a range of reworkings, establishing the field. While I regularly refer to the source ballets, it is generally to note how a particular reworking is different from, or related to, that source, and not as a marker of quality. Tracing the stories of bodies that are often (but not always) dancing from the margins, I follow and unravel the many intertexts that I find, of which the ballet as the source text is the 'obligatory' reference (Riffaterre 1990).

Conclusion

While the character and purpose of reworkings are varied, the choreographers of reworkings clearly find something of value or interest in the dances which they choose to rework – something to celebrate, challenge, illuminate or subvert. The rationale for reworkings is neither therefore wholly subversive nor wholly celebratory. What they offer is not simply an unrelenting critique, or an uncritical homage, but rather complex and multifaceted (re)visions that implicitly (and at times explicitly) bring to the surface a variety of social and aesthetic issues. These dances say as much about the interests of contemporary performance and current cultural concerns as they do about the ballets of the past.

Reworkings then are hybrid palimpsestuous texts that evoke, at the very least, a bidirectional gaze. This gaze is fluid and shifting rather than fixed. However, reworkings are, perhaps unavoidably, implicated within the status quo of the canon such that they risk reinforcing that which they actively reinterpret and question.

Particularly relevant to an understanding of reworkings are the operations of myth that have rendered classic texts as normative. Theories of identity as they interface with poststructuralist methodologies have demythologised canonical texts to reveal they are not timeless and universal but are fundamentally entangled in the political, social and aesthetic developments of their time. Poststructuralist criticism has shifted the focus from fixed sets of received meanings to themes of motion and flux. Texts, characterised by disunity rather than unity, give rise to a multiplicity of meanings when read and re-read by the reader/viewer. These fluid texts formulated by and within discourse are inseparable from power structures, which in turn govern what it is possible to say and the criterion for 'truth'. In order to reveal the implied 'truths' in a text, poststructuralists set the text to work against itself and refuse to be fixed by single meanings, deconstructing them to reveal the power behind established knowledge.

This unfixing of texts and discourses has led to the subsequent defrocking of the canon, as an example of a particularly powerful discourse, within reworkings. The acknowledgement of the canon as a discourse, and the sense that texts are more unstable and interactive than once perceived, permeates reworkings, as choreographers embrace the freedom to reinterpret freely and activate the political dimension of the ballets at their source for our own era. However, as particular kinds of intertextual practice, reworkings self-consciously incorporate their sources as an obligatory intertext; therefore the canon embodied within reworkings consistently reasserts itself. This places these dances in a precarious position.

While terms to describe reworkings proliferate, perhaps the promising way to understand and to identify the features of such dances is through the close examination of individual works. In the following chapter I turn from this conceptual overview to a consideration of practice. This examination reveals recurring choreographic strategies, as well as differences, and provides details of the specific impulses and ideologies that are at play in these instances of reworkings. While the dances discussed may be more or less explicit in the political or ethical aspects of their acts of reinterpretation, the political dimension is nevertheless often inescapable as, by their very nature, reworkings are engaged in the destabilisation of authority and hegemony. Thereby the discussion of these contemporary dances deliberately puts the questions of representation and the embodiment of identities (in particular race, gender and sexuality) in the foreground. For, as Derrida writes, 'because it has always already begun, representation therefore has no end' (1978: 250). Thereby I emphasise the ways in which choreographers re-present the body and re-present identities in different and diverse ways, often in contrast to their source texts. Such revisionist accounts and other points of view dominate the rest of this book, as the ways in which choreographers have read against the grain of accepted history, and dismantled received meanings, emerge.

Chapter 2

Canonical crossings

Narratives and forms revisioned

I make use of the fundamental story and the original music but I am not interested in keeping to the classic tradition. Cultural heritage is the point of departure. I see it as a big bowl which I can break down, recreate and fill with my own meaning.

(Mats Ek, cited in Hutera 1999a: 44)

[My] intention is to break the mould, to bring ballet into the next century and to stop it becoming old fashioned.

(Matthew Bourne, cited in Bannerman 2000: 247)

[*Swan Lake* is] a strong cultural icon. The thing about *BirdBrain* is that it's not a contemporary interpretation of the narrative, it's all those elements of *Swan Lake* pulled apart and deconstructed and reconstituted to form something else.

(Garry Stewart, cited in Hardwick 2005)

There's a willingness to take risks ... I've had the idea to reinterpret *Sleeping Beauty* for ages – I don't know why – perhaps it's all the press that's stirred in my mind questions of love and the world [the] royals must submit themselves to.

(Meryl Tankard, cited in Hallet 1994)

Strategies of dissonance – moments of sameness

The fascinations and desires revealed in the quotations above point towards the range of rationales and methodologies evident in reworkings. Illuminating diverse choreographic strategies, this chapter focuses upon the ways in which choreographers have unhinged old dance texts to replay them upon the contemporary stage in revisionary ways. Drawing on, and elucidating, specific examples, I review the content, form and reception of six reworkings, produced in four different countries, of four nineteenth-century ballets. In tracing some of the common strategies and recurring themes evident in recent examples of reworkings, this chapter starts with dances that retain key structural invariants of their source ballets (for example, dances by Ek and Bourne) and shifts to those that use the ballet within an eclectic context and for radically different purposes (for example, Tankard and Stewart). (See chapter 1 for a discussion of invariants in reworkings.)

I consider the grip of canonical discourse, reflecting upon the extent to which the canon as traditionally constructed continues to impact upon the reading of these dances. What reverberates throughout this chapter is that, however radical or subversive a particular reworking may be, the tenacious web of canonicity always attempts to reassert itself. As Susan Bennett, in her discussion of adaptations of Shakespeare, notes, this 'remains the argument against the revival/rewriting of … [a] classical text: that containment is an inevitable effect' (Bennett 1996: 145). While containment may or may not be an inevitable effect, reworkings do offer a proliferation of reconceptualisations of bodies and identities, and a recurring theme in the reworkings discussed in this chapter is the divergence from conventional representations of identity. Whether counter-canonical or not, these reworkings have clearly rewritten and recast the ballets at their source across the lines of gender, race, class and sexuality. My writing invokes these political dimensions, for these dance reworkings have the potential to engender a rethinking of seemingly fixed identity categories and aesthetics. Thereby I bring attention to the ways in which reworkings engage in aesthetic and social dimensions to speak back to, as they simultaneously intersect with, their sources.

In the first section, entitled 'Inverting bodies: reformulating the dance vocabulary', the emphasis is on the body and the dance language itself, for in the works discussed here the vocabulary of ballet has been discarded and inverted, appropriated to different ends and placed within an eclectic range of styles. This rechoreographing of the movement vocabulary is one of the most important aspects of dance reworkings, for movement practices embody public statements of race, gender and sexuality. 'Retelling tales: new contexts, new narratives' discusses *Highland Fling* by Matthew Bourne, a reworking which retains the basic choreographic structure of its source while setting the dance in the modern day. This dance exemplifies one of the ways in which narratives are being revisited and updated in reworkings. Continuing this theme of retelling tales, I consider the ways in which reworkings have been cross-cast and cross-dressed along gender lines – further proliferating identities. I end, in 'Strategies of dispersal', with two choreographers who have fragmented the ballets at their source, cutting and slicing into the canon to form dances that emphasise textuality and provisionality. Here reworkings are positioned as part of the larger interest, driven by poststructuralism to reclaim narrative forms while also questioning those very forms.

Inverting bodies: reformulating the dance vocabulary

Shaped by years of training and performance in distinctive vocabularies and styles, dancing bodies are encoded with particular ideologies. The analysis of the

Plate 3   Highland Fling (1994) by Matthew Bourne
Photographer: Bill Cooper

dancing body presented here insists on an awareness of the manner in which our lives and our bodies are (literally) shaped by complex sets of historical, cultural and personal systems. These bodies as mediums of culture are not, however, simply acted upon by culture but are engaged in an interactive process with it. As articulated by Rosi Braidotti from her materialist corporeal perspective,

> the body is seen as the inter-face, a threshold, a field of intersection of material and symbolic forces; it is a surface where multiple codes of power and knowledge are inscribed; it is a construction that transforms and capitalises on energies of a heterogeneous and discontinuous nature. The body is not an essence and therefore not an anatomical destiny: it is one's primary location in the world, one's primary situation in reality.
>
> (Braidotti 1991: 219)

Echoing this perspective and locating the body as a primary concern, the following discussion is marked by these materialities, alongside an acknowledgement of the kinaesthetic reverberations of the body in performance. What comes to the fore is the transgressive potential of the dancing body and the complexity of dynamics of power.

The 'recoding' of the dancing body through the reformulation of the dance vocabulary is a highly significant aspect of reworkings. For the process of choreographing anew assists in making evident the ways in which the dancing body is a mobile and mobilising force. While all dancing bodies have this potential, the reframing and reformulating of dance vocabularies that takes place within reworkings brings this potential to the fore. In the dances discussed here the performing body – sometimes through mere difference – becomes a site of discourse, a site through which it is possible to see and experience the world otherwise. These 'reworked' dancing bodies enter into a dialogue with their predecessors and with history to create dynamic bidirectional duets, full of interconnections, echoes and contrasts.

The body in reworkings of Classical and Romantic ballets enters a particularly volatile space. For in ballet the dancing body has been strongly coded by convention, and that body had tended to be marked by gendered and racial boundaries of exclusion. As Susan Foster notes, 'the Romantic ballet celebrated the principle of distinct vocabularies for male and female dancers – the dainty and complex footwork, the *développés* of the leg and extended balances for women and the high leaps, jumps with beats, and multiple pirouettes for men' (Foster 1996a: 4). The gendered vocabulary of ballet has become so emphatic, and dancers' bodies have been so pressed upon through training, that it has led Foster to question the extent to which it is possible to present an egalitarian future for male and female bodies. In answer to her own question she remarks:

> The answer rests on the series of gendered bodies developed historically within the ballet tradition over the past two hundred years. Whether visible in reworked versions of the classical masterpieces – *Giselle, Swan Lake, Coppélia,* etc. – or merely in the vocabulary and style of the dancing, the weight of these past bodies presses too hard upon contemporary ballet to allow a nongendered reception of its meaning, or even to allow for the dismissal of gendered content as a superfluous formal feature analogous in impact only to that of an irrelevant cliché.
>
> (Ibid.: 3)

Departing from, and possibly inverting, this body coded in ballet traditions is thereby a salient task. Redefining the dancing body, via rechoreographing the source and rethinking the dance vocabulary, is one of the critical, if not crucial, features of a reworking if that reworking aims to be resistant of the canonical order. This reformulating of the dance language is a feature of all the dances that I here describe as reworkings.

Through the following analysis of Mats Ek's work I explore the ways in which reworking in dance implies not just an alteration in the details of choreographic patterns but a reformulation of the very codes of the dancing body. Analysing the ways in which reworkings can be seen to encompass a wide variety of bodily incarnations, I reveal strategies that allow for difference and multiplicity, as opposed to uniformity and sameness, in contrast to their sources. This is not to suggest that ballet's embodiments are homogeneous, as close inspection and attention to the specifics of performance dynamics reveal a diversity of representations and a range of performance styles (see Banes 1998). However, it is to say that reworkings, as bidirectional texts that variously bring their hybridity to the fore (see chapter 1), have the potential to make explicit their heterogeneity and to escape the mythologies of the ballet that have cast it within a myopic frame.

Mats Ek's version of *Swan Lake* (1987) exemplifies such a strategy. It is not that Ek in fact breaks totally from the vocabulary of ballet, but that he attempts to forge a cohesive choreographic language of his own which emanates from, without explicitly embodying, the classical movement language of the source. The vocabulary Ek uses can be located in expressive modern ballet of the European school. While it is evident that his reworking of *Swan Lake* carries the same signature movements that appear in all of his choreographies, because of the bidirectional nature of these dances his movement signature appears more pronounced. This bidirectional nature means that the viewer is encouraged to make connections to the source such that, in this case, movements which in another dance may seem idiosyncratically Ek's own, or clearly expressively modern in style, here may be seen to reflect the codes of ballet – and at times specifically to reference the ballet *Swan Lake*. Conversely, however, the bidirectional gaze also means that audiences can simultaneously note, and take pleasure in, the way in which Ek's choreography is differentiated from its source. This doubleness, this ambiguity, is central to the counter-canonical promise of reworkings while also being potentially problematic.

Born in 1945, the second son of the choreographer Birgit Cullberg, Ek studied dance, alongside drama, with Donya Feuer from 1962 to 1965. In 1966 he began working at the Royal Dramatic Theatre and the Puppet Theatre in Stockholm as a producer. Having been initially engaged as a dancer by the Cullberg Ballet (Sweden), he became the company's artistic director in 1982, forging the dramatic expressive style for which the company is renowned. Ek resigned his directorship in 1993 to work freelance. His earlier choreographies had explicit socio-political messages. *Soweto* (1977) is a clear example of this approach in its direct confrontation of apartheid. Later works are less explicit in their political agenda as community and family relationships become the focus, as *Old Children* (1989) and *Light Beings* (1991) demonstrate. Ek has also had an ongoing thematic interest in legendary tales, narrative form and creating characters. Ek's reworkings of the classics, *Giselle* (1982) (see chapter 1), *Swan Lake* (1987) and *The Sleeping Beauty* (1996), draw together these different aspects of his work. Through his reworkings, Ek creates alternative narratives, re-examining the legendary tales and characters. Transforming and recontextualising the traditional scenarios, he makes them relevant to current audiences.

Perhaps what is most distinctive about Ek's work is his movement language. His works are characterised by the fluid and curving movement of the torso and the recurring usage of deep knee bends, creating an earthy angularity as movements are drawn out of the dancer's centre then pulled back in. Even leg extensions and leaping actions are performed with a sense of returning inwards and downwards. The movement vocabulary developed by Ek is weighted and grounded. Alongside

Plate 4   Swan Lake (1987) by Mats Ek

Photographer: Lesley Leslie-Spinks

this is a more idiosyncratic vocabulary as dancers twitch and shuffle: legs shoot out, backs arch fully over and arms are flung. Through this movement language Ek refigures the image of the Prince and the swans to portray genders that sit in opposition to the former, more idealised representations at their source, shifting expectations through movement, narrative and models of identification.

Through the discussion that follows there is interplay between modes of spectatorship, narrative drive and choreographic/performance dynamics in order to

Plate 5   Swan Lake (1987) by Mats Ek

Photographer: Lesley Leslie-Spinks

elucidate the staging of gender that Ek unfolds as he transforms *Swan Lake* into Freudian myth. This psychological approach is typical of Ek (and evident also in his reworking of *Giselle* – see chapter 1).

Ek's *Swan Lake* shares clear parallels with its Petipa and Ivanov source but pares down the number of characters and shifts the emphasis between them. Ek has retained the original music score (with cuts and alterations to its order) and the dance, comprised of two acts, is one hour and forty minutes in duration. Central to the dance is the relationship of Siegfried, the prince, with his mother and his dreams and experiences of other women. The narrative begins with Siegfried's birthday celebrations, during which his mother presents him with a young woman – a pale version of herself. He rejects this 'gift', and following the celebrations dreams of a white swan woman, Odette. She is seemingly possessed, along with the other swans, by what appears to be an old man – yet just before Siegfried awakes this controlling figure (conventionally Rothbart) is revealed to be his mother. In act II the Prince travels around the world and meets Odile – the Black Swan. Yet in the end it is Odette whom he marries – although menacingly it is the Rothbart figure holding the veil and Odile suggestively reappears.

The Odette/Odile roles, danced by Ana Laguna (who also danced the title role in Ek's *Giselle* – see chapter 1), are the antithesis of the traditional roles while also echoing them. Ek's Odette is bald and barefoot, and her movement is grounded. Rather than performing soft lyrical movements, as a traditional Odette, she takes long strides, flexes her feet and cocks her legs. She also incorporates movements that are more linear and extended, such as positions akin to *arabesques* and *attitudes*, but these are not performed in the melting, swooning manner of her predecessors. Ek's Odette is bolder, more direct and more independent in her movements.

However, Odette is, as in the Petipa and Ivanov version, still presented in opposition to her counterpart Odile. Odile enters shrieking at Rothbart, at whom she stabs her fingers and kicks her feet. Odile is a more volatile character than Odette, and while she performs many of the same movement motifs as Odette, her movements, as in the ballet, are more assertive and provocative. While Ek's Odile doesn't perform any one step displaying such overt flamboyant virtuosity as thirty-two *fouettés en tournant en pointe*, as has become conventional in ballet versions, she does display virtuosity and is flamboyant. She performs childlike, aggressive and sexual actions. She playfully teases Rothbart, comically scratching her shoulder, and, in mimicry, menacingly wrings her hands. She also mimics herself, dragging her feet in a parody of her own childish behaviour. A sexual being, Odile protrudes her buttocks towards the Prince and Rothbart, circles her hips, and then whips away in a rapid turn. At another point she runs her hands down over her hips and then repeatedly thrusts her pelvis forward as if holding an imaginary partner. The collection of images embedded in Odile's movements suggests a complex character which, while represented by a different movement vocabulary, runs parallel to the traditional Odile.

Ek's swans, in what is known in the traditional ballet as the white act, enter not as mythical, distinctly feminine creatures floating through a mist, but as a set of independent, earthy creatures that cross the stage with weighty gallops and stamping feet. They first enter by sliding onto the stage in a half split and come to stand in a parallel *plié* with the body bent over. The swans' movements accentuate the angular and the awkward: they lift their knees high, carrying them out to the side, and their buttocks are allowed to protrude towards the audience. They walk flat-footed and thrust their heads forward repeatedly; elbows, knees and shoulders are used in isolation, and they stand feet together, hands pressed onto the front of their thighs, and wobble from their hips through their whole bodies.

These swans, which are bold yet sensitive, break gender and racial bound, mixing black and white, male and female performers. These are strong individuals as opposed to a homogenised *corps*. While they move in a group as a *corps*, performing actions in both unison and canon, there is a decidedly more rebellious quality to these swans. Whereas Petipa and Ivanov's swans stand in perfect lines, mirror each other exactly and perform their movements with decorum, Ek's swans shift through space, have individual quirks and are indiscreet.

The 'dance of the cygnets', for example, offers not four swans in line, dancing small, sharp footwork in perfect unison, but four characters with large padded hands dancing gauche, awkward movements. The four dancers walk with their knees up high, with bottoms out and with flexed feet. At the end of their dance they laugh, screech, point, and 'hump' the set as they blow 'gas' out of their bottoms. Fiona Burnside describes the swans thus:

They were definitely a much more birdlike type of swan than those in any other production I have seen even though the bird they most resembled was a goose. There was a determined uglification in this production with a general issue of bald-heads and pigeon-toed stances.

(Burnside 1996: 26)

The swans' movements are, suggests Burnside, 'very anti-balletic' (ibid.). The general impression, Peter Bohlin writes, has 'the flavour of a duck pond' (1988: 32). The description of Ek's swans by Bohlin and Burnside as ducks and geese (as opposed to swans), respectively, effectively demonstrates the extent to which Ek has refigured them. Yet it is Siegfried, the prince, the focus of Ek's reworking, whose role is the most extensively reconceived, and it is to him I turn.

At the very start of this work Ek stages an extended solo for Siegfried, establishing his character through his danced actions rather than through his interaction with others and before any extended narrative has had chance to develop. He is dressed in black, with his back to the audience and his body curled up in a foetal position, and his solo is suggestive of his introverted, even neurotic, disposition; the movements are awkward, spasmodic and tentative. His hands twitch and shake, he squats to the floor, and bows underneath his own arm in an inward curve. Interspersed between these idiosyncratic actions are occasional leaps – *grands jetés en avant* and *à la seconde*. Yet these expansive movements constantly give way to enclosed forms and scuttling walks. His signature movement is a lunging step forward on demi-pointe, his arms stretched out in front of him. His back is repeatedly towards the audience: he walks with his body bent over and knees lifted, arms swinging violently at his side, slipping along linear pathways as if to minimise his presence.

While the Prince is central to this *Swan Lake*, the narrative tends to take him over, as he almost stumbles from one experience to the next, failing to control his destiny or to follow a specific course of action. Ek centres this lack of control around Siegfried's relationship with his mother, which his choreography loads with Oedipal significance. The Queen – dressed in a scarlet dress and gloves and with vibrantly painted lips – dominates the stage and is overtly sexual. Resembling a walking phallus, she, like all the characters except the Prince, is made to appear oddly bald – wearing a flesh-coloured scalp covering. Their duet begins with Siegfried circling the Queen with his body hunched over. She places her hands over his eyes – a reference to the myth of Oedipus. Running her hands in a seductive motion across his chest, she teasingly taunts him – the touch sexual rather than maternal. He avoids the contact, taking her hand and bowing under her arm. As they curve and rotate around each other, his relationship with his mother transforms him. His movements become bold as he traverses the space in leaps and gallops, dancing in unison with his mother. He adores her, but the sexual tension between them, something she appears to relish, confuses him and he returns repeatedly to circle around her, lowering his torso and dipping in towards her body.

Symbolically speaking the Queen – a 'monstrous female' – castrates him. Following constructs of masculinity, as derived from Sigmund Freud, a boy's rejection of the mother is central in order to secure identity for himself as a man. The Oedipal project requires a turn away from the mother and identification with the father. This process, according to Freud, is set in motion by the boy's sexual desire for his mother, a desire thwarted by the presence of the father. The boy's fear of the father forces him to identify with the father and thereby become heterosexually gendered and capable of sexual union with a mother-like substitute. Siegfried's relationship with his mother emasculates him – for in failing to reject her he is unable to become fully gendered. Following Freud, his relationship with his mother, combined with the absence of a father figure, deems it impossible for Siegfried to become fully masculine and establish successful relationships with other women (although to a certain extent the Queen's lover serves the role of the thwarting father figure, and, correspondingly, Siegfried is childishly jealous of him, repeatedly attempting to usurp him for his mother's attention.)

Siegfried's failure is evident in his determined reaction against the mother-like substitute, presented to him by his mother in the form of a birthday gift. This gift, a pale pink version of his mother, enters the stage covered in a pink veil. The prince immediately crouches over – folding into himself – and has to be carried forward by the courtiers to meet her. The Queen and the birthday gift dance in unison – confirming their sameness, while the Prince lies on the floor – his body curled inwards and rigid. While he does eventually attempt to perform in the manner expected of him, taking the gift in a ballroom hold, his actions towards her are not sustained or successful.

Similarly, Siegfried's complex relationship with his mother carries through to his relationship with Odette, who is the subject of his dreams. In contrast to tradition, which asserts a confident, heroic, lover, it is Odette's actions, rather than his, which liberate and support him as they develop their relationship. Initially he attempts to catch her and lift her but she throws him to the floor and kicks him away. Slowly he does become more confident, and his actions grow childlike, carefree and unrestrained. Even in his dreams, however, he doesn't sustain this confidence and returns to his introverted movements, circling the stage, his hands nervously waving back and forth. Given the Freudian nature of this reworking it is significant that this white act is evoked as an escapist dream in which Siegfried displays his repressed sexual fantasies, and even more so that, towards the end of his dream, it is his mother who is revealed to be still controlling his sexual destiny.

Developing the Oedipal complex, Jacques Lacan asserts the Oedipal moment as the constitutive moment of language, locating the phallus (as opposed to the individual penis) as the centre of the symbolic order – as the doorway to marked gender distinctions. Thereby, through Lacan, masculinity is established outwards from the Oedipal knot into the social order as a whole. Siegfried's struggle to enter the social order, to become fully positioned as male, is located in his inability, or more positively unwillingness, to desire to take up the Law of the Father – the phallus. For to enter the symbolic 'as a social and speaking subject entail[s] the disavowal of its [the pre-symbolic] modes of corporality, especially those representing what is considered unacceptable, unclean or anti-social' (Grosz 2001: 143). Siegfried's continuing 'impure' incestuous attachment (his lack of appropriate desire), alongside his lack of affirmative action, risks marking him as a lesser man. Yet it is also this gender ambiguity that gives rise to the most potential refiguring of masculinity.

While at the very end of the dance the narrative thrust attempts to reclaim a phallic masculine space through Siegfried's marriage to Odette, this is again undercut by the last images of Rothbart (his mother) and Odile. Siegfried remains vulnerable, emasculated, such that he is portrayed as a confused young man in both narrative and performance terms. He is an emotionally wrought figure, and these emotions often threaten to overwhelm him, for he is unable to express them articulately. Thereby his body signifies not a source of male (phallic) power, but a site in which his emotional traumas are embodied. Rather than celebrating his physical virtuosity, Siegfried embodies complex physicalities. His body is marked by inner conflicts, becoming a canvas upon which his repressed trauma is written. His dancing body manifests internal disruptions – twitches, shakes, nods, flickers and glitches. Speaking his discontent, his body is abject and hystericised – for through his body his maleness is presented as incomplete and damaged.

Exposing complexities of character in an inversion of Petipa and Ivanov's far more conventional, idealised figure, Siegfried is significantly refigured. However, Ek doesn't offer a safe or singularly positive alternative masculinity – rather what is left is an abject male body that is vulnerable and elusive, entailing complex interplays between narrative, movement and viewing perspectives. For while the narrative centres on Siegfried's experiences – locating him as the protagonist, his phallic power is thwarted by his mother. Further his movement cuts between states to embody ambiguities of gender and signs of abjection. These ambiguities usefully open up masculinities, establishing a counter-image that reveals the myth of normative masculinity, giving space for a less hegemonic script. These subversions are, however, also limited by the commitment to narrative, full-scale theatricality and virtuosity. For however peculiarised these elements might be, they encourage the viewer to revert to the safe viewing positions of convention.

Further, while the movement Ek choreographs inverts the aerial language of ballet, it also echoes the structural forms of conventional *Swan Lakes*, patterning movement into marked phrases and repeats, and at times using movements which correspond to movements of the same nature in the ballet version. The cohesive feel of the movement also creates a sense of a rather closed text as opposed to offering a more open, overtly intertextual text. Operating within the bounds of a unified syntax, the dance appears to present an alternative 'truth' which creates the impression of permanence rather than opening the work to the potential of multiple visions. This is not to take away from the richness of Ek's style or the unfailing theatricality of his approach but brings again to the fore the tense relationship between reworkings and their sources.

Choreographers such as Matthew Bourne and Mark Morris (discussed below) similarly rechoreograph the ballet within their own distinctive styles while retaining many of the structural patterns and codes of the original. Examples of more divergent approaches to the reformulation of the movement and the body can be seen in Raimund Hoghe's pared-down response to *Swan Lake* (see chapter 4), Garry Stewart's fragmented *BirdBrain* (see below), or Masaki Iwana's butoh *Giselle* (see chapter 5). These dances not only radically alter the dance vocabulary, but also reshape structural forms, significantly refiguring the body on stage and participating in shifting ontologies of dance.

Retelling tales: new contexts, new narratives

Alongside the reformulation of the movement language, reworkings have also recontextualised the narratives embodied in their sources. It is noteworthy that dances with narrative structures and content have most commonly tended to be the focus of reworkings. The reasons for this are multifarious but can be seen to fall into two key areas: the revised interest in narrative and meaning-making driven by poststructuralism, and the difficulties and complexities entailed in the reworking of non-literal, or more formal work.

To address the latter of these two areas first, Sarah Rubidge, in a debate entitled 'Does authenticity matter?', points to the reworkings of Ek and Bourne and suggests: 'In non-literal, or formal, dance works such a cavalier attitude would be more difficult to countenance if only because the materials of non-literal dance works, as with some music, are themselves the subject matter of the work, rather than the medium through which the subject matter is communicated' (Rubidge 1996: 230). This supposes that the reworking of the medium (the dance material itself), without the reassurance of an extrinsic subject matter that can be retained, may be less acceptable on account of the drives of 'authenticity' – when the dance's 'authenticity' is based on the replication or preservation of the internal identity of a work and that identity is found in the dance medium opposed to an external narrative (ibid.).

While I find the placing of a clear boundary between 'medium'/'subject matter' and 'formalist'/'representational' works to be problematic, whether or not the reworking of a 'formalist' work is 'more difficult to countenance', it is certainly true that dances with subject matter 'external' to the dance material itself are the most common focus or target of reworkings. Reworkings of more formalist or abstract pieces, such as those by Balanchine, do exist (for example, *Vivaldi Suite* by Les Ballets Trockadero de Monte Carlo and *O* by Michael Clark), and these work on the basis of the recognition of a specific dance vocabulary and (parodic) play with a highly defined style. This type of reworking is less common, perhaps due to the more limited scope in the play between subversion and recognition.

As mentioned above, the focus on narrative in reworkings echoes a renewed interest in narrative generally that is part of the poststructuralist fascination with conventions and meaning-making, and the deconstruction and demystification of those narratives and meanings. This thrust is evident across the arts and in postmodern dance from the 1980s onwards. Sally Banes (1994) discusses this shift from the 'pure' postmodern dance works of the 1960s and 1970s, which repudiated expression and narrative, to a concern with narrative in the 1980s and 1990s.

She writes, 'the generation of choreographers that emerged in the eighties has outstripped the earlier postmoderns in its insatiable appetite for narratives of all kinds: autobiography, biography, fiction, political document, interview, the use of sign language and other emblematic gesture systems' (Banes 1994: 281).[1]

Given that the ballet, in its Romantic and Classical forms, is arguably the epitome of the narrative form in dance, it is perhaps not surprising that choreographers have turned their attention to the ballet. The form is not accepted wholesale, however, but in reworkings the ballets' narratives have been contextualised anew, refocused and fragmented, resulting in established meanings being turned inside out.

One of the ways in which narrative has been typically reworked is the relocation of traditional libretti into new time periods, most often into more contemporary contexts. To name but a few dance examples: Mark Morris relocated *The Nutcracker* (1892) to a 1970s American comic book context (see below); *Coppélia* (1870) has been taken out of her rural village and resituated, by Maguy Marin, in a modern inner-city housing block; *Giselle* (1841), when reworked by Mats Ek, becomes a Freudian analysis of sexuality and class (as discussed in chapter 1) and is also relocated into modern-day, if rather surreal, Ireland by Michael Keegan Dolan (see chapter 1); and Matthew Bourne shifts *La Sylphide* (1832) to 1980s Scotland. One potential value of these dances is that, by recontextualising traditional narratives, they give the originals a new relevance to current audiences. The last of these examples is discussed at more length here.

Bourne has created a series of reworkings, including versions of *The Nutcracker* (1992), which retained a sense of historicity and a commitment to fantasy; *Swan Lake* (1995) (see below), which replayed (while significantly challenging) the aristocratic narrative of its source; and *La Sylphide*, renamed *Highland Fling – A Romantic Wee Ballet* (1994, restaged 2005), which shifts the context, character and movement vocabulary while working closely within the traditional storyline and ballet structure. In this short analysis I am concerned with two questions. Firstly, what affect does this updating have on our understanding of the traditional *La Sylphide* and the new reworking? Secondly, how does *Highland Fling* represent its characters and contemporary Scotland?

Bourne's company, New Adventures (formerly Adventures in Motion Pictures), was founded in 1987 with David Massingham and Emma Gladstone. Bourne, now sole artistic director of the company, has a reputation for creating light-hearted theatrical works and has created a number of dances which rework ballets. His best-known work, *Swan Lake*, is discussed below, but previous to this are works such as *Spitfire* (1988) that use references to ballet in general. As critic Jennifer Grant notes, in *Spitfire* 'Matthew Bourne has created a piece encompassing the male image in two areas, underwear and the ballet world' (1988: 31). She continues, 'they soon get into their stride as Bourne's creativity flaunts a knowledge of the classical ballet vocabulary' (ibid.). In these dances, suggests Burnside, Bourne 'pokes fun at the sentimentality of his originals, he solicits the complicity of the audience as his contemporaries rather than provoking a head on collision' (1994: 40).

In 1994 *Highland Fling* toured the UK and had a three-week season at the Donmar Warehouse in London. In 2005, drawing on Bourne's subsequent successes, it was performed again with a somewhat larger cast and higher profile tour schedule. Allen Robertson writes that *Highland Fling* is 'a sincere re-evaluation of a nineteenth-century masterwork newly minted for late twentieth-century eyes' (1995: 7). Brought up to date through the new 1980s setting, the work becomes, arguably, more accessible and appealing to a broad contemporary audience. Rather than representing Scotland as a remote, unknown, even exotic world (to the 1832 Paris audience), Bourne presents a contemporary Scotland, familiar to his UK audience, of clubs, drink and drugs. Throughout the first act Bourne makes reference to a number of dance styles, from modern to disco, and to steps taken from folk dances – including the Highland fling. The work opens with James leaning in a drunken stupor against a graffiti-covered urinal. James and his friends are, we discover, enjoying a night out at the 'Highland Horse Social Club Disco'. This prologue added by Bourne is a far cry from the mist-covered, quiet opening of the Romantic version. This dance, full of lively, hip-grinding club dancing and ending in a fistfight, locates the viewer in the modern day and dispels the possibility of a 'happy ever after' tale.

Scene 2 is set in a Glasgow council flat, complete with plaid-covered walls and sparse furniture, and begins with James and his friends lounging and sleeping in front of a television after their night of drinking. From the television the music 'Once in the Highlands' blares. After James's friends leave, the scene picks up the ballet narrative. The sylph visits James, caressing him while he slumbers in a chair. At this point the references to the ballet are clear, and James and the sylph dance a duet that mirrors the ballet version. The correspondence between the two duets is such that Burnside writes, 'here Bourne and Bournonville meet' (1994: 40). The opening image of the duet is a clear and obvious reference to what occurs in the ballet. However, while in conventional versions the sylph poses at the side of James's chair, looks and gestures towards him and dances light steps around him, only once touching him with a gentle kiss on the cheek, Bourne's sylph is far more tactile in approach. Pulling at his hands and head, she playfully notes his drink- and drug-induced daze. Rolling her whole weight onto him, she slides and sits upon his back. Later, as he stumbles about the room, she sits upon the top of the doorframe; as he reaches up to her she appears to lift him up and then passionately kisses him on the lips. While both the Romantic sylph and Bourne's sylph might be seen to represent an other-worldly, living dead, Bourne's sylph is more garish in her appearance. This sylph is more like a waif from a Goth club than a woodland spirit. She has black paint surrounding her eyes, and the rest of her face and body is painted white, which looks as if it is peeling. This deathly and direct sylph is, however, no less elusive; echoing the earlier sylph, she is 'both dangerous and enchanting' (Aschengreen 1974: 11).

While the sylph remains a supernatural figure, Madge is recharacterised as a drug-pushing 'friend' with an interest in tarot cards. She retains the manipulative characteristics evident in the ballet, and her interest in tarot cards links her, if rather tangentially, to foreknowledge and insights of another world. However, casting Madge as a drug-pushing friend removes the witches from the work. While Banes and Carroll describe them as 'monstrous inversions of humanity' (1997: 99), in fairy tales witches can be seen as strong wise women (Rowe 1993). Taking out this third key group (the other two are the sylphs and the ordinary folk) from the dance perhaps creates a more modern and believable tale (as James's visions are explicitly represented as drug related) but it also limits the range of female characters on stage. Bourne problematically follows gender stereotypes through this dance. At the point in the ballet narrative where Effie would normally enter with her mother and girlfriends, for example, *Highland Fling* offers a domestic scene in which Effie and her friends iron clothing and rearrange and tidy the flat. While the sylph later, in a parody of domesticity, stands at the ironing board mimicking the action of ironing in a 'zombie' fashion, Effie and her girlfriends maintain their traditional roles.

The second act is set on a piece of wasteland that overlooks the city, complete with a derelict car. In this mundane setting James is compelled to dance by the fascinating sylphs that are here both male and female. Like their nineteenth-century counterparts, these sylphs lightly cross the stage. Shifting through the space, dancing in unison and canon, they resonate with an unearthly spirit. As James tries to capture his elusive fantasy, this spirit world turns to nightmare. Retaining a disturbingly misogynist aspect of the ballet, James asserts his desire to contain the sylph. Taking a pair of gardening shears he cuts off her wings. Blood-smeared, the sylph, with her arm linked to James, walks a grotesque and sinister wedding march. This horrific modern ending highlights James's violent act. Whereas in the ballet James's violence is softened by the gentleness of a scarf,[2] here his unforgivable selfishness is marked as aggressive and abhorrent.

The recontextualising of the narrative contemporises the ballet. The emphasis throughout *Highland Fling* is upon the everyday interactions between friends and peers in the form of a danced drama. The stress on friendship removes the concepts of family and formality evident in the ballet and makes this present-day version seem less about duty and responsibility and more to do with peer groups and individual desires. The work makes explicit themes of drug-induced visions, domestic life and violence, which are present but tend to be only implicit within ballet versions. The reiteration of the ballet in a modern context suggests that the ballet's themes and narrative have something to offer modern-day audiences beyond nostalgia for the Romantic ballet form. Problematically, however, the reinstatement of the importance of the ballet's themes may also reinforce the notion that *La Sylphide* is ahistorical and universal. The work also risks maintaining modern-day stereotypes of Scotland as surely as it was previously exoticised. These criticisms of Bourne's dance provide evidence of ways in which a reworking may simultaneously reflect more contemporary sensibilities and reveal the possible limitations of conventional versions, while still not always creating more positive portrayals of location or gender.

Gender bending: cross-casting and cross-dressing

Using parodic and hyperbolic strategies, Matthew Bourne and Mark Morris have both reworked the ballet through cross-casting and cross-dressing.[3] Their strategies parallel John Berger's suggestion that we should take any painting of a traditional female nude and in our imaginations turn the woman into a man and notice the 'violence which the transformation does. Not to the image, but to the assumptions of a likely viewer' (1972: 64). This process of transformation is echoed in cross-casting and cross-dressing, similarly challenging the viewer's assumptions. Thereby both of these dance-makers subvert dominant codes of gender – specifically masculinity – for here gender is exposed and estranged.

Feathered pantaloons and homoeroticism

Casting men as the swans, conventionally an all-female territory, Bourne's *Swan Lake* is arguably one of the most well known of all recent reworkings. Receiving attention and accolades within popular and academic contexts, the dance was premiered on 9 November 1995 at Sadler's Wells Theatre, London. It then went on to a long run in London's West End, successfully transferring to Broadway, New York, and touring extensively. This work, similarly to Ek's version, retains Tchaikovsky's music, shares a commitment to full-scale theatricality and parallels the conventional libretto. Indeed in the programme notes musical director David Lloyd-Jones makes much of the status and quality of Tchaikovsky's score. He celebrates his restoration of the music to claim that this is 'the fullest and most authentic version presented in recent times' (Lloyd-Jones 1995: 7). I find this somewhat of a paradox. In the light of the inherent challenge to authenticity by reworkings, this reinstatement of the music sits at odds with the dance. However, this approach is not uncommon as other reworkings, such as those by Mark Morris (*The Hard Nut*) and Mats Ek (*Giselle* and *Swan Lake*), also privilege the full musical scores.

Bourne choreographs the dance anew to create a different movement form, this time reflecting release-based practices and social dance forms, Susan Foster, in her illuminating essay 'Closets full of dances', suggests that the movement material is reminiscent of Humphrey technique. She writes that

> these swans do not perform ballet, nor do they execute the well-known choreography of Act II ... The swan's vocabulary contorts classical ballet stipulations for bodily geometry. Hips raise with legs; torsos duck and undulate; legs rotate inward and frequently extend at 45-degree angles to side front or side back. Where the ballet vocabulary constantly presses up and away from gravity, in order to inhabit the aerial, the swans give into gravity, then surge up out of its depths on curving pathways reminiscent of the modern dance choreographer Doris Humphrey's fall and rebound.
>
> (Foster 2001: 191)

Plate 6   *Swan Lake* (1995) by Matthew Bourne

Photographer: Bill Cooper

While changing the vocabulary, Bourne, as in *Highland Fling*, still echoes the choreographic form of ballet. He retains the relationship between characters and musical sections, for example, the leading swan dances to the Swan Queen adagio and the 'Dance of the cygnets' is still a light and amusing quartet. He also retains the pattern of the music and dance phrasing, using dynamics, repeats and variations typical of the ballet. He similarly maintains a hierarchical stage arrangement, with clearly marked differences for central characters (front and centre) and the rest of the troupe, who form an, albeit rather untamed, *corps de ballet*.

The Odette and Odile roles are performed by Royal Ballet dancer Adam Cooper, who performs not in drag but as a sensual and compelling male Swan and as the Stranger, with whom the Prince falls in love. This reworking can be seen as a gay love story. While Bourne and others have repeatedly played down the homosexual implication of this cross-casting (more of this later), the swapping of gender roles is a substantial alteration of the canonical ballet, and it brings to the fore the previously restricted images of gender and sexuality presented on the ballet stage.

The dance begins with the music of the prologue. A large bed is centre stage, in which the sleeping boy prince is tossing and turning. In what we suppose are his dreams, a male Swan rises, phallus like, over his bed. (The Prince is to become enthralled by the idealised figure of the Swan, which offers an escape from his failures as a prince and as a young man.) In the morning the court servants dress the boy and, as the waltz begins, the Queen leads her son and entourage on a round of royal appointments, from launching ships to awarding medals. During this period the Prince grows up and acquires a fluffy-haired blonde girlfriend. The group all goes to view a ballet. This is a papillonesque ballet-within-a-ballet. Parodying the ballet form this is a metatheatrical device that playfully makes light of what are perhaps an audience's expectations of a reworking. During this 'performance' the Queen, disgusted by the girlfriend's behaviour, leaves. Later the Prince pleads for his mother's understanding but receives no support from her. He goes out with his girlfriend and proceeds to get drunk and to fight in a sleazy bar. The Private Secretary attempts to pay off his girlfriend, which she refuses. However, the Prince only sees her being offered the money, and, dejected, for he assumes the worst, he goes to the municipal park to drown himself.

The entrance of the Swan, in contrast to convention, reveals a confident and knowing creature. There is none of the fright and panic of Odette, nor is there any explanation of the man-swan's existence (besides the earlier images of the Swan in the young Prince's dreams). The Prince and the Swan dance together. This Swan and the rest of the male swans maintain the 'otherness' of their predecessors, yet claim territories the conventional Odette has never been allowed to take.

In act III the action returns to the royal court for a ball, parallel to the ballet. Various female dancers – the foreign princesses – dance for the Prince. The party is disrupted by the arrival of the Stranger (a role that echoes, but is not the same as, that of Odile – Black Swan). The Stranger is a mysterious figure, clad in black leather, with whom all the women, including the Queen, are enchanted. The Stranger taunts the Prince who, in his turmoil, seizes a gun. When a shot rings out it is the Private Secretary who has fired and (mistakenly?) shot the Prince's girlfriend. In act IV, the Prince returns to his bedroom; he is confused and distraught. The swans appear, sliding out from under the bed and pouring in through the window. The Swan comforts the Prince but then the flock viciously attacks them both. This is a vengeful and harsh group action that leaves the Prince dead.

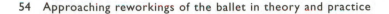

Plate 7   Swan Lake (1995) by Matthew Bourne
Photographer: Bill Cooper

The representation of the Prince, similar to Ek's Prince, is the antithesis of the male heroic figure. While the narrative is told from his perspective and is focused around his experiences, his presence on stage is often hesitant and overshadowed by his mother, the Swan and the Stranger. As if swept along by the unfolding events, the Prince fails to understand the behaviour of those around him and is unable to control or understand his own emotions. From the start, when we see him as a young boy, he is portrayed as troubled – suffering from nightmares, distressed by the swan appearing in his dreams. On waking he reaches out to his mother as she walks away from his bedside.

Once the Prince has grown up, 'Bourne clearly shows that there is no social space in which [he] is fully competent' (Hargreaves 2000: 239). He clings to his mother in a duet of withheld embrace, desperate for her recognition. Dipping to her waist he repeatedly goes to her, grasping for attention. Failing to receive the response he craves, he pitifully crawls towards her on his hands and knees, only to be chastised once again as she insists he stand upright, pulling back his shoulders and straightening his back. Her action is clearly resonant of the phrases 'pull yourself together', 'be a man' and 'chin up'. These admonitions directed at a young man seek to deny emotional display, reinforcing expectations of hegemonic masculine behaviour.

While the Prince constantly fails to be 'man enough' – becoming emasculated through his Oedipal relationship with his mother and his homosexual desires – the reverse is true of the Swan. While echoing the convention of white and black incarnations of the swan, Bourne does not mimic the ballerina's costume or movement. He consciously avoids any association of drag in his portrayal of the usually female swans (which are already, if you consider it, in drag, playing overly femininised white birds).

The Swan takes centre stage. His torso bare, displaying his muscular frame under white body paint, and dressed in white feathered pantaloons, he dances large sweeping actions, full of ebb and flow, dynamic swings and curving leaps to engulf the space. Like the idealised masculine figure of a Grecian sculpture, this Swan manages to encapsulate an athletic virility – associated with maleness – and to present his body for erotic contemplation – which usually evokes the spectre of femininity. Yet, while taking pleasure in the Swan's body, critics' responses repeatedly note and reinforce his presence and agility. For example, 'He is ravishing in his solo, legs cutting through the air for quick changes of direction or arching over huge circles as he finds his balance' (Sacks 1996: 1161). Gilbert agrees: 'Adam Cooper's Swan ... well to judge by the way he danced on Wednesday he's scarcely less than a god' (Gilbert 1996: 1162), while Mackrell finds that 'Adam Cooper in the Odette/Odile role dominates the stage as a savagely beautiful force of nature, his arms braced like an eagle's wings' (Mackrell 1996: 1164). And Christiansen states: 'This is not the timid, vulnerable creature familiar from Ivanov, but a potent figure, not so much predatory as commanding and knowing' (Christiansen 1996: 31).

The confident physicality of the Swan is established in contrast to that of the Prince and the conventional image of Odette. Martin Hargeaves has interestingly argued that it is this very contrast with the ballerina that secures the Swan's maleness: 'if Bourne's swan is *not* Odette, who is femininity par excellence, then he is masculine, if only through default of being not-feminine' (2000: 236, emphasis in original). Continuing this line of thought, Hargreaves (2000) suggests that, in order to remain masculine, the Swan relies on the continued absent presence of the ballerina, maintaining his distinct gendered identity through difference. The risk then is that the difference between Odile and the Swan breaks down, that her presence enters our consciousness, and thereby our reading of him, hence of the Swan, is emasculated.

For reworkings, this risk is very real, for our reading of difference in reworkings exists simultaneously with our reading of sameness such that the ghostly presence of the ballerina inevitably lingers. Failing to wipe away the tainting presence of the ballerina, the male swan, in a parallel fashion to his female forebears, evokes a transcendental figure. As Emilyn Claid (1998) argues, the swans, as represented by Bourne, parallel the mythic signification of the male androgynous body, and therefore transcend sexual desire and evoke spiritual beauty. Following Barthes's discourse of myth, in a similar manner to my own use of myth in chapter 1, Claid suggests that on account of the likely event of an audience's prior knowledge and seduction by the classical swan, these male swan bodies become, in Barthes's third order, 'the ideal empty form which the myth of androgyny fills with its concept' (Claid 1998: 30). The swans thereby become symbols of transcendence, beyond earthly pleasure. This is a compelling argument and interestingly illuminates the tension in reworkings generally between deconstruction and the mythic properties of the source texts, which continually assert themselves. In this case the mythical transcendence of classical swans works to hide the maleness of these newly refigured swans. Claid remarks: 'The identity of the male body becomes ambiguity, a secret, seductive as a shadow, all of which displaces and disguises conventional "truth" about man while his maleness remains unquestioned' (ibid.: 31).

While the Swan risks emasculation through association with Odette, his maleness becoming ambiguous, the Stranger (the Black Swan) is presented by Bourne as a hyperbolic figure. Trussed from head to toe in black leather, this swan embodies a more male than male masquerade of gender. At his entry in act III he struts across the floor, and all eyes turn to him. His presence is excessive: taking the Queen's hand, he licks her arm, and pulling out his cane, he whips his leg and holds it to the face of one of the many women who throughout the ball will throw themselves at him. In dancing with a series of these women he leads with his hips, performs sharp changes of direction, and flicks his legs. He caresses his partners' necks and breasts, diping backwards and leaning his body over theirs in lustful 'macho' delight.

This is phallic-driven masculinity played out at its most obvious and most narcissistic. Emphasising his sexual performance, thrusting his penis at all comers, the stranger perpetuates dominant male sexual behaviour. Yet its very hyperbolic nature has the promise to unsettle masculinity, for, like a drag performance, its heighten properties expose the usually masked performativity of masculinity. As thoroughly argued by Judith Butler (1988), gender is performative, which means, quite simply, it is 'real' only to the extent that it is performed.

Hypermasculinity has also been appropriated by underground gay male subcultures, and Bourne's Stranger resonates with images common in gay male pornography. His 'macho style', emphasising physical strength, black leather and muscled body can be read as gay. And, as Richard Dyer has suggested, the adoption of dominant cultural constructions of masculinity in a gay context can be destabilising.

> By taking the signs of masculinity and eroticising them in a blatantly homo-sexual context, much mischief is done to the security with which 'men' are defined in society, and by which their power is secured. If that bearded, mus-cular beer drinker turns out to be a pansy, how ever are they going to know the 'real' men any more?
>
> (Dyer, in Weeks 1985: 191)

Operating at the boundaries of masculinity, Bourne adds another twist. The Stranger consistently taunts and teases the Prince, who, enthralled, hangs on his every movement, his every gesture. When they dance together it is a mere reflec-tion of the *pas de deux* that is usually a central feature of the ball scene. Here the Stranger plays tricks on the Prince and pushes him about the space, manipulating him while provoking clearly expressed desires. Their duet is both (homo)sexually passionate and, from the Stranger's behaviour, homophobically incessant. Either way there is an ambiguity as regards the sexuality of the Prince, the Swan and the Stranger. This ambiguity provokes instabilities in the discourses of masculinity and sexuality.

Thereby the strategy of cross-casting the swans significantly shifts the reading of the ballet and has the potential to challenge heterosexist frameworks. Whether the dance fulfils this potential, however, is debatable. As Susan Foster convincingly argues, the representation of homosexuality in this dance is exciting (as it has vis-ibly placed homosexuality within the mainstream context) but also problematic. Foster describes the end scene in which the Prince is cradled by the Swan, having been gay bashed by 'his own kind', and notes that this scene brings to the fore 'how the closet in Bourne's *Swan Lake* operates'. For Foster, both 'the causal relationship between homosexuality and inadequate mothering that the dance depicts and the attack on Swan by his fellow swans issue from a framework of het-eronormative assumptions about gay life' (Foster 2001: 198).

Acknowledging Foster's perception of disavowed homosexuality, Martin Hargreaves writes that 'homosexuality never fully disappears but, like a ghost, is always in the process of simultaneous manifestation and dematerialisation'. The death of the Prince and the Swan, he argues, 'shows not only the punishment brought on any attempt to love, but also the degree to which this prohibition is internalised within any cultural context that deals with male homosexuality'. For Hargreaves, this reworking gives evidence of self-regulation in terms of homosexu-ality while also revealing the murderous workings of this regulation. He argues that Bourne's *Swan Lake* hovers 'between conservative and transgressive, homophobic and homophilic, it is a complex series of hauntings and visitations at the site of melancholic masculinity' (Hargreaves 2000: 235). Rather than performing a radical critique, Bourne enacts and exposes the interdependency of homosexuality on the normative codes that *Swan Lake* represents. His closeted representation of homo-sexuality serves to mark and ensure the construction of heterosexuality. This is reinforced by the residing presence of femininity in spite of, or perhaps because of, Bourne's efforts to rid *Swan Lake* of the ballerina.

Hyperbole and eccentricity

The Hard Nut (1991) by Mark Morris is based on the ballet *The Nutcracker* (1892) and the story by E. T. A. Hoffmann, and in this work Morris, like Bourne, interrogates gender and (homo)sexuality. But Morris foregrounds gender via parody, as characters are cross-dressed in the manner of drag and ballet as a form is critiqued.

Conventional versions of the ballet are set in an upper-class nineteenth-century context and tell the tale of a girl who is given a nutcracker by her godfather, Drosselmeier, for Christmas. She falls asleep and dreams that the nutcracker changes into a handsome prince who takes her on a journey through a snowstorm and a kingdom of sweets. Morris sets his version in the 1960s/1970s. At the Christmas party given by Dr and Mrs Stahlbaum the guests are a 'pop nightmare: bouffant hairdos, push-' em-up bras, hip-huggers, skirts with slits' (Acocella 1993: 184). While the first act follows generally the same narrative as the ballet, the second act focuses upon the story of the Hard Nut, in which a queen rat attacks and spoils the face of Pirlipat (the baby princess). The rat explains that the princess will only regain her beauty after a young man cracks the hard nut with his teeth. Drosselmeier sets off around the world to find the hard nut. On his return it is Drosselmeier's own nephew who cracks the nut and kills the rat. Pirlipat rejects the young nephew as he begins to turn ugly – just like a nutcracker. At this point Dr and Mrs Stahlbaum's daughter, Marie, interrupts the story (which is being told to her by Drosselmeier) and offers her love to the young nephew. And, as described in the programme notes, 'everyone in the world joins Marie and the young Drosselmeier in celebrating their love. The two go away together forever' (Morris 1995).

The Mark Morris Dance Group was formed in 1980 and has since toured widely. The dances Morris has produced for the company demonstrates a concern for gender issues. For example, as early as 1982 he created *Jr.High* and *New Love Song Waltzes*. *Jr.High* dealt with a teenager's feelings as he realised he was homosexual, and in *New Love Song Waltzes* Morris portrayed sexual desire as freely shifting within and across genders. Morris has also been particularly open and vocal about his own homosexuality. He has often referred to this in press interviews, noting that he 'got tired of pretending to be a straight guy in love with a ballerina' (cited in Tobias 1984: 30). Morris also demonstrates a willingness to incorporate a range of different physicalities into his dances. Morris himself has a sizeable build, which has a fleshy quality and from which protrudes a generous belly. His own physicality is therefore not typical of ballet or modern dance notions of a dancer, and the members of his company too vary in shape and size, from the extremely diminutive to the large and fleshy. Acocella also notes that his dancers are older than average American dancers and represent a 'vivid ethnic assortment' (1993: 75).

It is Morris's continuing interest in dealing with gender issues, combined with his ability to reference a wide range of dance styles, that is at the heart of his strategic plays with gender in *The Hard Nut*. Gay Morris convincingly argues that this overtly parodic work creates 'a proliferation of gender identities' (1996: 150). 'The waltz of the snowflakes' in *The Hard Nut* incorporates movements from the ballet canon in such a way as to create conflicting gender cues. The waltz, in traditional versions, is danced by the female *corps de ballet*, whereas in Morris's version it is danced by both male and female performers, who are all dressed in tutu-like skirts and satin halter-neck cropped tops, have ice-cream swirl headdresses, and a mixture of bare feet and pointe shoes. The movements in the waltz are derived from ballet, including steps and positions such as *bourrées*, *arabesques* and *grands jetés*, but there is little attempt to re-create the quality of ballet. This 'Waltz of the snowflakes' is a delightful caper; the dancers enter in groups with coltish pleasure, creating criss-cross patterns and spraying fistfuls of powdery snow with their very leaps. The leaps, and corresponding puffs of snow, are timed to occur with the accents in the music, creating a veritable overflow of orgasmic bursts. This is 'The waltz of the snowflakes' *à la* Busby Berkeley, with a good dash of irony thrown in.

The incorporated ballet movements, which are usually performed for spectacular effect, are in Morris's work made to look awkward and difficult. The dancers clearly do not have perfect ballet technique and they look heavy footed as they land from *grands jetés* which are not fully extended. They throw their bodies rather than place them, and the lines through shoulders, hips and knees are allowed (or forced) to go awry. Also many of the dancers on pointe, especially the male dancers, do not have the expected technique. As Ann Nugent points out, the dancers' feet in pointe shoes resemble 'gnarled bananas' (1995: 18). Morris seems to push the dancers past their physical limits deliberately and to place ballet movements in situations in which they cannot possibly achieve their usual effect. The dancers are not allowed to hide their efforts but are made to struggle. Describing such a moment, Acocella notes how, towards the end of *The Hard Nut*, Morris has his dancers perform the spectacular *pirouette à la second*.

> [P]irouette a la second is normally done solo; if two people tried to do it together, they would tend to go out of unison and thus rob the step of its look of focused perfection. Morris, however, has not just one or two people but ten people – none of them professional ballet dancers, many of them struggling to keep the leg from bending and drooping – perform pirouettes a la second in unison, with no allowance for ending early. The effect, and the goal, is not the look of perfection but of good-humoured effort.
>
> (Acocella 1993: 80)

The effect also provides a commentary upon the vocabulary of ballet itself. The parodic reprise of the vocabulary seemingly states, 'look, it is not so special after all'. The use of the usually rarefied steps of ballet, as performed by his modern dancers, suggests a more casual, relaxed approach to ballet technique, one which undermines the elitist and hierarchical perceptions of the form.

A number of critics have played down the ironic and parodic aspect of Morris's work, valuing instead his musicality, phrasing, and use of narrative and emotion. These critics, notes Ramsay Burt, place Morris within 'an ahistorical tradition of "great" choreographers' (1995: 184). The critic Arlene Croce is quoted as an example. She states that Morris 'doesn't try to be more than a good choreographer and a completely sincere theatre artist' (cited ibid.). Burt argues that, because Morris makes use of traditional dance vocabularies and skills, he may be unable to stop his work from being viewed from the dominant androcentric, heterosexual position (ibid.: 187).

This may well be the case, but it would be impossible for any sensitive viewer to miss the ironic tone of *The Hard Nut*, especially as it pertains to gender. As Nugent notes, 'gender play was an essential element, and men were so regularly disguised as women that it was not always possible to know who was what. Morris's point was that it didn't matter' (1995: 18). In both 'The waltz of the snowflakes', described above, and 'The waltz of the flowers', a mixture of men and women perform in what is traditionally a female dance. They dress and cross-dress, and perform ballet movements from both the male and female canon alongside movements from a modern idiom. Through such methods Morris 'proliferates gender to the point of erasing it altogether, since', as Gay Morris points out, 'the spectator can no longer make gender attributions' (1996: 154). This inability to ascribe gender, in a society that is based on the making of distinctions between male and female, has the potential to be an effective strategy.

Another and perhaps the most commented upon and overt way in which *The Nutcracker* has been refigured by Morris is through cross-dressing in the form of drag. Cross-dressing is a time-honoured tradition in dance and theatre. In dramas, ballets, pantomimes and music halls, from the Greeks through to Shakespeare and beyond, performers have been cross-dressed. What is at stake in this analysis is the extent to which the instances of cross-dressing in Morris's work operate to question the cultural and social assumptions of gender, and thus challenge heterosexist discourse, or whether they simply work to reinforce the status quo.

Cross-dressing or, more specifically, performing in drag,[4] as Morris's characters do, can potentially highlight the negotiability of gender but, problematically, it can also present a misogynist view of women and stereotypical images of men. Drag, analysed by Butler, 'plays upon the distinction between the anatomy of the performer and the gender that is being performed' (1990: 137). Three dimensions constitute drag: anatomical sex, gender identity and gender performance. The potential of drag is thereby found in the dissonance between these dimensions. As Butler writes:

> If the anatomy of the performer is already distinct from the gender of the performer, and both of these are distinct from the gender of the performance,

then the performance suggests a dissonance not only between sex and performance, but sex and gender, and gender and performance.

(Butler 1990: 137)

The Stahlbaum family incorporates three drag roles: Fritz, the youngest in the family, is an ill-behaved boy played by Marianne Moore, the female Housekeeper is performed by Kraig Patterson, and the Mother, Mrs Stahlbaum, is also played by a man. Acocella contends, however, that most of Morris's characters are not drag because 'most drag acts, by dint of their energetic but always imperfect imitation of one sex by the other, reaffirm the separation between the sexes' (Acocella 1993: 94). Further, she argues that 'the point of a drag act is that you can still tell the difference: gender is permanent, immovable' (ibid.). Morris, Acocella tells us, is not trying to conceal the difference or imitate gender but is offering us both in one body. Within Butler's theoretical frame, drag is not an attempt to copy or imitate an original gender but, through parody, imitates an imitation. Indeed it is the potential of dissonance between the act, sex and gender that makes drag performance interesting. Acocella suggests that, while *The Hard Nut* does contain what she describes as travesty roles, these roles 'like most modern travesty roles … are based on an acceptance of difference between male and female, and they are played for comic effect' (ibid.: 101). This casts aside the drag roles in a tone that suggests these are limited to comedy and strangely discounts Morris's repeated interrogation of gender through his work.

Gay Morris (1996) convincingly discusses the different approaches that these drag characters encompass. Fritz runs, slides and bashes around the Stahlbaum's living room. He teases and snarls at his sister, shadow boxes with the guests, and undertakes mock military charges around the furniture and through the guests. Morris states we 'see a "girl" who looks like a "boy" but still looks like a "girl" moving like a "boy"', and we are struck by a series of jolts that constantly refocus our attention on the instability and performative aspects of gender' (Morris 1996: 151). These 'jolts' come from the tension between our knowledge that we are watching a female dancer perform typical boy-like behaviour and the treatment that he/she receives from the guests. For example, Fritz is generally allowed to run amok, and when he is disciplined it is with a physical reprimand. In many ways Marianne Moore presents us with a character who is more boy than boy, a virtuoso rendition of boy-like actions. What this calls to our attention is the performative nature of gender; it is the actions of Fritz that allow us to recognise the character as a 'boy' rather than assume any prior gender identity. As Morris argues, 'that is to say, the performativity of gender on the surface of the body causes identity rather than performativity being the result of a natural or interior core of gender identity' (ibid.: 151).

Mrs Stahlbaum can be seen to foreground the discontinuity between the anatomy of the performer and the performance of gender even more overtly than Fritz. Peter Wing Healey plays Mrs Stahlbaum. She/he has a large build and wide fleshy shoulders that are revealed by a sumptuous off-the-shoulder dress in green velvet and satin. When we first see Mrs Stahlbaum she flits across the stage, her arms held out from the elbows as she gestures with her wrists and circles her shoulders. Throughout the opening party scene she performs in mime with a few movements and gestures which are clearly balletic in style. For example, she performs small beaten steps, gallops, and *relevés* with *port de bras* into fifth position. Overall she is presented as a larger than life 'fluttery' mother. In some respects she is the stereotypical drag queen or pantomime dame. Mrs Stahlbaum is like a female impersonator who attempts to celebrate the feminine ideal (in this case the ideal mother) and generates humour from the 'womanish' mannerisms employed. Yet the incongruous nature of physical anatomy, gender and gender act belie any attempt to 'pass' as a woman – rather we enjoy the self-conscious and purposeful enactment. Through drag Mrs Stahlbaum presents a revision of the mother figure in *The Nutcracker* (1892), disrupting the traditional mother image through hyperbole not only of gender but also of class. Mrs Stahlbaum, as played by Healey, is not the gracious upper-class figure presented in conventional versions, but a suburban housewife worrying about specks of dust while trying to discipline her children and fussing around her guests.

The Housekeeper 'is a drag queen who has "become" a woman and savours every moment of it', states Morris (1996: 151). She performs the actions of femininity with pleasure and delight – as perhaps only a person who does not take such actions for granted could. She pushes the drinks trolley with a sway of her hips, delightedly opens Drosselmeier's box of nuts, smells her perfumed wrist, having circled it on a perfume sample in a magazine, and tests Marie's temperature – placing the back of her hand on both her own and Marie's forehead in a dramatic gesture. Whether Mark Morris intends us to view the Housekeeper as a transsexual or drag queen is uncertain, but she is highly feminine in looks and behaviour. She wears a maid's uniform that is shaped into a slim waist and is cut short on the thighs. She dances on pointe and her signature movement is the *pas de bourrée couru*. In this reiteration of the gender codes of ballet, especially such a highly recognisable canonical action as *pas de bourrée*, the Housekeeper both reinforces and confuses normally female performative actions. The Housekeeper, as distinct from the mother, attempts to 'pass' as female. This 'passing', as in the Harlem drag balls, requires the gender-crossing to become invisible. Yet the 'idea is not to dissolve into femininity but to keep the contradictions between masculine and feminine at play, to emphasize the performativity of Western culture's construction of femininity and masculinity' (Claid 2006: 166).

The extent to which any drag performance can destabilise gender assumptions has been queried by a number of feminist commentators. Alice Solomon argues that, 'precisely because "man" is the presumed universal, and "woman" the gussied-up other, drag changes meaning depending on who's wearing it … And since femininity is always drag, no matter who paints on the nails and mascara, it's easy to caricature' (Solomon 1993: 145) – hence the ambiguous status of drag. Sceptics such as Solomon, and more radically Jill Dolan, have argued that drag relies on grotesque caricature and presents misogynist views of women. It is argued that, in mirroring women's socially constructed roles, the drag performer conspires to construct a male-identified subject. In a discussion of the way gender impersonation destroys or maintains gender roles, Dolan says that

> women are non-existent in drag performance, but woman-as-myth, as a cultural, ideological object, is constructed in an agreed upon exchange between the male performer and the usually male spectator.
>
> (Dolan 1985: 8)

Butler acknowledges that drag can be part of the heterosexist domain and cites Dustin Hoffman in *Tootsie* and Jack Lemmon in *Some Like it Hot* as examples (Butler 1993: 126). In these films of high net entertainment the potential homosexual consequences of the drag roles are deflected within the narrative of the film. This type of drag can possibly be seen to function, Butler suggests, as a 'ritualistic release for a heterosexual economy that must constantly police its own boundaries against the invasion of queerness' (ibid.: 126). However, she also problematises the misogynist analysis of drag as it is presented by radical feminists. This analysis, she argues, figures male to female transsexuality, cross-dressing and drag as male homosexual activities (which they are not always) and further roots homosexuality in misogyny. The rooting of homosexuality in misogyny attempts to frame homosexuality as being 'about women', for, the argument goes, 'he is only gay because he hasn't found the right woman.' Ironically in this frame the radical feminists' argument against drag reinforces the heterosexual matrix, placing heterosexual love as the truth of drag and homosexuality (ibid.: 127–8). However, this argument still leaves drag in an ambivalent position. 'Sometimes', writes Butler, drag 'remains caught in an irresolvable tension, and sometimes a fatally unsubversive appropriation takes place' (ibid.: 128).

Laura Jacobs, in her critical review of *The Hard Nut*, suggests that Morris's drag characters are in just such an ambiguous and possibly even fatally appropriated position. Jacobs points out that, 'in *The Hard Nut*, anything maternal is played for laughs' (1993: 3–5). Morris removes the focus from the main female characters (the Sugar Plum Fairy doesn't appear and Marie is passive throughout the majority of the second act) and presents the other main female characters in drag (the mother/queen and the housekeeper/nurse). Jacobs argues, in line with feminist critics of drag performance, that in removing the female roles, or by giving those roles to men, Morris removes any of the potential matriarchal readings available in conventional versions. In doing so he shifts the focus of the work to the masculine and presents the women as objects of ridicule. The cartoon staging of *The Hard Nut* also plays an important part in the way the drag characters are perceived. The comic and one-dimensional image of the set design carries into the characterisations, which are stereotypical and emphasise the humorous. As with the pantomime dame, laughter is used to release and allay any fears of gender displacement. As a result the gender roles presented are, for Jacobs, unconvincing, and in the end 'it is the women who look most worn' (ibid.: 4).

Yet some significant shifts in focus and status do take place. While not always counter-discursive, cross-dressed, particularly drag, performance is enticing on account of its play between the theatrical and performative conventions of both genders at once in the one body. Blurring and stretching boundaries, Morris inserts his own (homosexual) body into *The Hard Nut*. He creates for himself a drag of a hyperbolic heterosexual male. Dressed in bell-bottoms and sporting a large Afro hairstyle and moustache, Morris's character is extrovert, sexually predatory and grotesque. Acting out, and playing up, the role of a drunken guest, he bumps and grinds his way through act I. His drag highlights the enactment of (hetero/homo)sexual identities in a parallel mode to 'dragging' across genders, for experiencing his homosexual body playing out a heterosexual masculine script in this way illuminates incoherence between gender and sexuality, and specifically between masculinity and heterosexuality.

The heterosexual matrix and beyond

The Hard Nut by Morris and *Swan Lake* by Bourne both rework the ballet from male homosexual perspectives. Their dances intervene in the canon in ways that have the *potential* to be deviant. This potential is particularly significant given that Classical and Romantic ballets place heterosexuality centre stage. Both the narratives and form of ballet reinforce what Sally Banes has described as the 'marriage plot' (1998: 5). The marriage institution is central to heterosexist frames of life-giving sexuality and is a powerful part of the continuing hegemony of heterosexual systems. The heterosexual matrix positions homosexuality as taboo, as sterile and as deviant, in contrast to fertile heterosexual practices. As Sue-Ellen Case (1991) points out, from a heterosexist perspective, homosexual sex is other-than-natural, as what is natural is associated with giving life, or practising life-giving sexuality, affirming the heterosexual matrix. Further, Butler defines the heterosexual matrix as:

> a hegemonic discursive/epistemic model of gender intelligibility that assumes that for bodies to cohere and make sense there must be a stable sex expressed through a stable gender (masculine expresses male, feminine expresses female) that is oppositionally and hierarchically defined through the compulsory practice of heterosexuality.
>
> (1990: 151, n.6)

Conventional plots and choreographic structures in ballet have reinforced the heterosexual matrix, for the origins and context of ballet in the Renaissance court as part of events such as weddings have become embodied within the ballet itself. The analysis undertaken by Banes considers the marriage plot within the double frame of re-reading the narrative and form of ballet, considering the way it is part of a bourgeois social imperative. While she points out that reading narrative alongside a choreographic analysis reveals views other than those of dominant patriarchy, overall the nineteenth-century ballet offers 'the most splendid celebration in the Western dance canon of the wedding theme' (Banes 1998: 42). For example, Banes argues that act II of *The Nutcracker* (1892) suggests a metaphorical wedding feast for Clara (ibid.: 60). It is a wedding feast within which Clara is a docile observer, passively watching the dancing of others, crowned by the grand *pas de deux* of the Sugar Plum Fairy and her consort.

The *pas de deux* form is a central feature of Petipa's ballets and is often used as the symbolic summation, or climax, of romantic love. The regularity of its form invites the viewer to compare duets across ballets and also across from the ballet to its variation in reworkings. Both Morris and Bourne create parallels to the male–female *pas de deux*, incorporating male–male *pas de deux*, into their dances. In *The Hard Nut* Morris creates a dance for the Nutcracker and the Uncle, while Bourne uses a duet between the Prince and the Swan as the crux of his white scene.

Bourne's duet is a touching dance in which the relationship between the Prince and the Swan develops; yet, as in his approach to this reworking generally, he tries to avoid overt homoeroticism. The duet, formed around unison, mirroring and moments of contact, starts hesitantly. The Prince follows the Swan, performing in unison with him. Failing at first fully to echo the Swan's movements – performing a hesitant imitation of them – he slowly grows in confidence. Full of movements akin to *arabesques* and *attitudes*, the pair shift across the stage space. Their bodies' tip, fall and swing off balance in fluid motions. When they come together their touch is gentle, as the Swan uses his head to nuzzle the Prince, and the Prince embraces the Swan. Supporting each other's weight, they lean and lift each other, creating moments of whole-body contact in a mode influenced by contact improvisation.

The Prince doesn't attempt to control or display the Swan – rather the interaction tends towards the symmetrical, copying as opposed to complementing. Further the Swan remains somewhat feral throughout, at moments turning suddenly on the Prince in an interesting reversal of power, for here the femininised Prince gazes at the masculinised Swan. Yet, as Hargreaves notes, this reversal of power is not complete, as the Prince doesn't look out to the audience and the Swan does not display to the prince; their inward attention and self-absorption contrast convention. Yet our relationship to the heterosexual *pas de deux* means that a Romantic reading lingers, and the narrative thrust of the Prince wanting to be the Swan becomes conflated with wanting to have the Swan.

Similarly, our experience of conventional *pas de deux* colours the narrative thrust in Morris's duet between the Nutcracker and the Uncle. Echoing the codes of Classical ballet *pas de deux* more closely then Bourne, the Uncle guides and supports the Nutcracker. Standing with his arms crossed over the Nutcracker's chest, the Uncle leads the duet, directing the gaze of the audience. Holding the Nutcracker as he leaps in *grands jetés* and springs in *sissones*, his hands are placed at his waist in a fashion akin to balletic male–female partnering. At other times they mirror each other's movements or dance in unison, traversing the stage with leaps and landing in sweeping lunges. All the while the young Marie lies prone on the floor – ignored until the two men, having finished their dance, lift her onto a sofa.

These duets challenge how men relate to other men, as the dividing line between homosocial and homosexual desire is blurred. Men touching and gazing upon other men creates ambiguities around what is acceptable/unacceptable male behaviour, pushing the norms of male–male interaction. Yet through the references back to the highly coded form of Classical ballet these duets also risk reinforcing the patterns of heterosexism. This is perhaps why, as both Acocella and Gay Morris point out, Mark Morris uses the duet form only rarely and, when he does, it can usually be found within an ensemble context.

Morris replaces the final grand *pas de deux* of the Nutcracker with a dance for the whole company, who lift and support the central couple – Marie and the transformed Nutcracker. Throughout the adagio section of the dance they do not so much dance together as be danced by the rest of the troupe. In opposite corners Marie and the Nutcracker are lifted into horizontal star-shaped positions; they are turned in the air as other dancers circle around them. Continuing the symmetry, the groups curve through space, enter and exit, turn and pose. Then, in the final coda section of the *pas de deux*, the central pair disappear altogether. The highly virtuosic steps and lifts normally associated with the coda are therefore performed not by the central couple but by twelve couples. Ironically echoing and eschewing tradition, on the last notes of the music they take up two of the most typical postures within the duet vocabulary: the fish dive and the shoulder sit.

Gay Morris suggests that dethroning the duet and locating stability within the group, rather than the couple, is one of Morris's greatest challenges to heterosexual regulation (1996: 155). However, while this may be the case, it is also true that *The Hard Nut* maintains the general thrust of the 'marriage plot'. That we do not actually see a marriage does not take away from the overall direction of the work – the pairing of Marie and the Nutcracker.

While Bourne's narrative deals with homosexuality somewhat more explicitly than Morris's, placing the (homoerotic) relationship between two males (Prince and Swan) at the centre of the dance, the other-than-natural possibilities of this *Swan Lake* are also thwarted, this time by both the signifying images in the dance and the publicity surrounding it. I have already noted the ways in which the male swans may be remythologised as androgynous creatures and suggested a plausible interpretation by Foster, who senses a homophobic thrust within the dance (2001: 198). These heteronormative features in the dance are also echoed in the publicity surrounding the production. The homosexual aspects of the work have been strangely closeted, ignored or covered over by critics and Bourne himself. For example, Debra Crane comments, 'to brand this a "gay *Swan Lake*" is to do Bourne an injustice.' She continues, however: 'there is no denying the gay sensibility of the surface love story.' She then immediately offers a more transcendent reading, stating that 'his *Swan Lake* is ultimately about the death of idealism, and the death of dreams' (Crane 1996: 1161). Clement Crisp, more directly, writes that 'theirs [Swan and Prince] is not, thanks to Bourne's controlled imagery and Cooper's rare artistry, a homosexual relationship' (1996: 1162).[5] These reviews are riddled with homophobic tendencies that Bourne does little to dispel.

The performative reiteration evident in these reworkings offers the potential for the dislocation of white Western masculinism but does not ensure it. Rather, it might well reincorporate norms, for, as Amelia Jones notes: 'Any performative act is always recuperable to its nonparodic baseline effects' (1998: 104). Further, as Butler remarks, in conventional performance settings (such as the proscenium arch stages used by Bourne and Morris) it is too easy to say 'this is just an act', and thereby derealise the act. Because of this distinction, one can maintain one's sense of reality in the face of any temporary challenge to our existing ontological assumptions about gender relations. As reworkings are explicit in their 'act-ness' this may be especially true here. The challenge then is how to denaturalise effectively that which can too easily be reassimilated.

While historically relocating the ballet, reformulating the movement vocabulary, and crossing genders, the maintance of close links to the structural form of the ballet may, as Ramsay Burt points out, be too easy to view from the dominant position, which may neutralise any transgressive representations present. For, as Burt notes when using and giving new life to traditional vocabularies, skills and forms, there is a 'danger of domestification' (1995: 187). This view emulates the now famous dictum by Audre Lorde. She states: '*the master's tools will never dismantle the master's house. They may allow us temporarily to beat him at his own game, but they will never enable us to bring about genuine change*' (Lorde 1984: 112, emphasis in original).

Reworkings that have sought to 'dismantle the master's house' more thoroughly have tended to use more overtly intertextual approaches. Intertextual structures can liberate reworkings from conventionally 'closed' narratives through multiplicity. The reworkings discussed in the following section explode narrative conventions and any sense of unified movement languages through the use of fragmentation, eclecticism and juxtaposition.

Strategies of dispersal: intertextuality and the carnivalesque

While, as discussed in chapter 1, all reworkings operate through palimpsestuous intertextual modes, some are more overt in these strategies than others. The reworkings discussed here open up their source texts and revel in the pleasure of deconstruction. The following dances by two Australian choreographers rip apart the movement language, narrative and traditional choreographic structures through intertextual methodologies, layering and inserting multiple intertexts to form overt references.

BirdBrain (2001), by Garry Stewart, and *Aurora* (1994), by Meryl Tankard, were both made for the Australian Dance Theatre while under the artistic directorship of these two distinctive choreographers. Garry Stewart has said that his approach to *Swan Lake* in *BirdBrain* was 'not a contemporary interpretation of the narrative', rather that 'it's all those elements of *Swan Lake* pulled apart and deconstructed and reconstituted to form something else' (cited in Hardwick 2005). The 'something else' he creates is a riotous high-energy mix of ballet, 1980s-style Eurocrash, hip-hop, yoga, acrobatics and break-dance. In a related, yet distinct fashion, Tankard creates an eclectic and carnivalesque version of *Sleeping Beauty* – reworking the ballet in order to bring about new resonances through tap, circus, clowning and strong design.

Both Stewart and Tankard reflect the poststructuralist drive to dismantle, as they self-consciously deconstruct classical ballet conventions. This approach has echoes in earlier postmodern dance, as noted by Sally Banes: 'in the age of post-structuralism, narrative in general has captured the intellectual and artistic imag-ination, where it has been analysed, dismantled, and deconstructed' (1994: 280).[6] As part of this poststructuralist drive these dances encompass questions about dance history, genre and style, giving voice to a range of socio-political concerns.

By questioning and constructing their sources anew, these two reworkings are particularly deconstructive in approach. For, as Jacques Derrida has made clear in a deconstructive method, the reader, or choreographer, seeks to produce the text, not simply to reproduce by providing a double commentary of a pre-existing non-textual reality. This Derridian perspective makes clear there is nothing behind the source text to 'reconstruct' – no non-textual reality, no controlling authorial voice.

But processes of deconstruction are not arbitrary, for, as Barbara Johnson has clarified: 'Deconstruction is not synonymous with "destruction", however. It is in fact much closer to the original meaning of the word "analysis" itself, which ety-mologically means "to undo" – a virtual synonym for "to de-construct" ' (Johnson 1980: 5). Derrida's own description asserts that a deconstructive reading 'must always aim at a certain relationship, unperceived by the writer, between what he commands and what he does not command of the patterns of language that he uses' (Derrida 1976: 158).

Similarly, deconstructive reworkings do not destroy that which they rework, nor do choreographers proceed unwittingly in relation to that which they rework. Rather reworkings are usefully understood as critical analysis in practice. These dances evidence complex relationships with their sources, and the themes, myths and histories referred to by choreographers engaged in this mode of intertextual practice are part of the discourse of history. As a mode of critical praxis, rework-ings pull out previously untold threads, layer and juxtapose new associations, and undo or unravel previous readings.

Stewart choreographed his first work in 1991, and his style is characterised by its fast, aggressive and 'no-compromise' approach. He took over the artistic direc-torship of the Australian Dance Theatre in 1999. Before this he danced with var-ious companies, including ADT, and was awarded a series of fellowships enabling him to study at the Susan Klein School of Dance in New York and to research dance and new technologies. These influences are evident in his current choreo-graphies and his ongoing interest in video effects and lighting, and are incorpo-rated into *BirdBrain* as developed with video artist Tim Grunchy.

BirdBrain uses the elements of design, video and physical virtuosity to pull the ballet apart to expand into 'the crevices of the narrative' (Percival 2003). Rather than retell the narrative (in the manner of Ek, Bourne and Morris), *BirdBrain*

Plate 8   Birdbrain (2001) by Garry Stewart
Photographer: Alex Makayev

operates through a fragmented, multilayered structure. Instead of the narrative developing in any logical or linear mode, narratives are sporadically inserted, located in the film, text, costume and music as much as, if not more than, in the performed and dance actions, such that the references to the ballet and its narrative occur in multiple allusions and in plural voices. Thereby this dance comments on and references ballet in general, and *Swan Lake* specifically, while all but discarding narrative in any traditional sense.

The dance begins with a single dancer entering the stage. On her T-shirt, which she wears with dark dance pants, is printed the word 'Overture'. Sitting downstage with an old record player, she plays a fast-forward version of the Tchaikovsky music score. As she does this the word 'B E G I N' is carried across stage behind her in illuminated and large-scale letters. Thereafter a high-energy, techno soundtrack by Jad McAdam and Luke Smiles takes over. It is to this techno score that the members of the '*corps*' enter – identified by the word 'corps' printed in bold type on their T-shirts. Taking ballet poses and actions, they turn these movements inside out and mix them with a stew of falls, rolls and twists which are styled by street dance and physical theatre. Standing in a row, they perform movements akin to *arabesques*, *cabrioles* and *attitudes*, all while hopping to the driving beat of the music and tipping and swinging their bodies off balance. As the group of dancers exit, a list of words are projected onto the screen, which is in the middle of the backdrop – heritage, manner, patron, craft, meaning, transcendence – the list goes on, words that typify the values and features of the ballet form.

Rothbart is the first 'character' to make an appearance. Dressed in period costume – a tweed waistcoat and trousers – Rothbart in this reworking is performed by a contortionist. He forms extreme and shape-shifting poses behind the

backlit projection screen, on which digitised images are shifting, and his movements are uncomfortable to view as he twitches his arms and claws with his hands.
As is the case with the other 'characters', Rothbart's role is not developed, or inte-
grated, into any clear narrative; rather, he appears as one of many fragmented
images through the dance. Similarly, later in the work the prince and his party –
again dressed in period costume – appear on stage and enact an archery 'scene',
recalling the hunting scene in conventional versions. These sections sit apart from
the high-energy dancing that forms the majority of the work.

While much of the choreography is not specific in its representation, there are
a few sections that clearly hark back to the ballet. For example, while an image of
a swan gliding on water is projected on the screen behind the '*corps*', their movements take on bird-like qualities: they project their chins forwards, isolate their
heads and use their arms as beaks and as wings. Likewise four dancers perform
Stewart's version of 'The dance of little swans', with their arms crossed and holding hands, and this becomes a piece of complex choreography in which the
dancers intertwine their bodies to lift and support each other. This is followed by
a sequence of thirty-two *fouettés en tournant* – in an imitation of the famous celebration of a ballerina's virtuosity in act III of *Swan Lake*. In Stewart's work this
sequence is not a solo effort; rather, the *fouettés* are executed by a line of four
dancers, each of whom perform a few rotations, while the number of turns is
displayed on the projection screen.

The role of Odette is evident at various points in the work via the printing of
her name on a T-shirt. Also, in a more embodied fashion, there is an extended
solo that powerfully suggests her transformation from swan to woman. This solo,
performed by Larissa McGowan, shifts from extreme contortions and intense
physical action, in which she throws herself to the floor, swings into shoulder
stands and flops her head and arms, to movements which progressively become
calm and smooth, as she performs complex bows and sends ripples through arms,
more akin to the grace of ballet.

In juxtaposition to the conventional emphasis in *Swan Lake* on romance and
illusion, *BirdBrain* focuses upon a raw physicality and a celebration of overt
strength and agility. The dancers break-dance, hip-hop and engage in breakneck
high-speed physical theatre as well as performing allusions to the ballet in groups
and in pairs. The dominant movement vocabulary is akin to the 'Eurocrash'
movement that developed out of contact improvisation and the work of companies such as DV8 Physical Theatre and Ultima Vez. Stewart's choreography, as in
Eurocrash, is aggressively performed as the dancers throw themselves, and each
other, dynamically about the stage.

This powerful physicality coming from an Australian context, a culture so
deeply ingrained in the athleticism of bodies, becomes an interesting reflection on
the extremes to which bodies can go. These extremes are evident across a range
of movement forms – from the contortions of yoga to the rotations of ballet, as
well as the flung vocabulary of Eurocrash dance. In addition, the bidirectional
gaze of reworkings means that a juxtaposition between the types of physicality

Plate 9 *Birdbrain* (2001) by Garry Stewart

Photographer: Alex Makayev

evident in *BirdBrain* and the vocabulary of a ballet version of *Swan Lake* becomes apparent. This juxtaposition is effective in redirecting meanings – foregrounding the tendency in ballet to valorise technical prowess over other concerns.

The relentlessness of the Eurocrash style, however, also dulls the senses. Although this style of work can be exciting, it has been criticised for its tendency towards unremittingly aggressive physicality. Similarly, in this reworking the Eurocrash movement style becomes an empty celebration of the physical. Thereby a tension exists in this reworking between Stewart's allusions towards critical commentary and the aggressive movement vocabulary that is driven by the techno music that continues throughout.

This tension often means that Stewart's point of view, the purpose of his deconstructive drive, is somewhat obscure. This is particularly evident in the use of printed and projected words. For example the T-shirts are printed with the names of characters, roles and locations, including 'corps', 'legend', 'hero', 'forest', 'Odette', 'Odile', 'swans', 'tragedy queen', 'lake' and 'the story this far', while others suggest emotions or a critical commentary upon ballet, such as 'peasant joy', 'royal distain', 'lust', 'despair', 'fucked up' and 'more irrelevant revelry'. This labelling reflects a Brechtian methodology and also resonates with fashion designer Katharine Hamnet's political T-shirts, yet, as with Hamnet's T-shirts, there is also a simultaneous containment by the aegis of commercialisation.

Outlining roles and key themes in the ballet, and remarking on the genre of ballet in the manner of bullet points, means that it comes to appear arbitrary and the references are reduced to empty signifiers. Recalling histories in this manner, Stewart, like other postmoderns as criticised by Fredric Jameson in 1993, leaves us condemned to live a present wherein the fragmentation of time becomes a series of perpetual presents which have little connection and for which there is no conceivable future on the horizon. While the history of the ballet comes to us in this work in a variety of guises, the potential historical commentary is drowned out by the overall drive of the aggressive high-energy movement and fragmented into such small moments that *Swan Lake*'s history is isolated, disconnected, discontinuous, as we float in an ever present limbo in which the celebration of ingenuity and athletic prowess rules. Stewart's reworking embodies a sense of emptiness, recalling *Swan Lake* with little sense of attachment or relationship beyond the obvious pleasure in intertextual playfulness, for here the ballet becomes a surface – empty and endlessly repeatable.

Questioning the critical position of *BirdBrain* gives rise to further questions about the nature of reworkings that overtly appropriate and reference their sources. These dances, as discussed in chapter 1, risk containment and contamination by the colonising forces of the canon. Addressing these concerns, Hal Foster traces Benjamin Buchloh's discussion of 'allegorical procedures' in art. He notes how this approach might turn '"splintering" into critical procedure'. Buchloh writes:

> The allegorical mind sides with the object and protests against its devaluation to the status of commodity by devaluating [*sic*] it a second time in allegorical practice. In the splintering of the signifier and signified, the allegorist subjects the sign to the same division functions that the object has undergone in its transformation into commodity. The repetition of the original act of depletion and the new attribution of meaning redeems the object.
>
> (Cited in Foster 1999: 92)

Acknowledging this argument, Foster asks:

> [W]hen does montage recode, let alone redeem, the splintering of the commodity sign, and when does it exacerbate it? When does appropriation double the mythical sign critically, and when does it replicate it, even reinforce it cynically? Is it ever purely one or the other?
>
> (Ibid.: 93)

He concludes that, while some practices used the mandate of appropriation to create 'innovative work concerning the making of meaning and value, identity and privilege, in dominant representations and cultural discourses', others were taken with 'the passion of the commodity-sign, its vicissitudes under advanced capitalism' (ibid.: 93, 96). In these works the commodity-sign becomes a fetish.

This double stance is a feature of all reworkings of Classical and Romantic ballets, for all these dances embody, to a certain extent, a passion for the 'commodity-sign' (when the ballet is acknowledged as commodity), directing the viewer via allusions and references. These choreographers, more than most, 'rely on the reader sharing these conventions and being aware of the codes and references they contain' (Adshead-Lansdale 1999: 17). Importantly, reworkings rely on the sharing of specific (if mythologised) codes and references (see chapter 1). They encourage an audience to be aware of the self-conscious references to the past. At the same time, however, they expose themselves and, to varying extents, direct the audience towards multiple readings, resulting in a move away from the illusion of the closed or coherent text.

Stewart's approach assumes knowledge of the traditional ballet and its story, for here the source, as obligatory intertext, is used and commented upon but not retold. So although the dance clearly still works with the pleasure of the recognition and distance from the ballet, Stewart undermines the idea that working with a canonical text requires a production to offer another (closed) reading of the ballet. *BirdBrain* focuses on how *Swan Lake* as an intertext might be embodied, and what it might mean in this new context. Since it holds the ballet at a greater distance, than, say, Ek's or Bourne's approach, the audience is provided with a plethora of references, which are arranged through fragmentation and juxaposition, on which to base their response; this permits space from multiple readings. Ironically and somewhat paradoxically, what is not altogether clear is the extent to which reworkings such as *BirdBrain* require an audience to be *more* familiar with the source text in order to recognise the appropriate signs. It may well be that readers are required to bring more of their own knowledge to the work in order to make an interpretation of it.

This referential approach, redolent with poststructuralist methodologies, is overtly intertextual and moves towards a deconstructive account of the ballet. The ballet is in evidence in numerous guises but is never 'whole', for the references are fragmented across *BirdBrain* in a manner which announces to the viewer that Stewart is entering an old text from a new critical direction. So while all dances can be read intertextually, this work uses intertextual play to create its meanings and convey Stewart's attitude towards the ballet that is its source – critical, reverential and otherwise.

If Stewart's work is closely aligned with a Western capitalism and the high-tech world of display and excess, Meryl Tankard's *Aurora* (1994) resonates with a post-colonial commentary through parody and the carnivalesque. *Aurora* is a reworking of the Petipa ballet *The Sleeping Beauty* (1890), in which the principal female role is that of Princess Aurora. The dance has been described as 'uncompromisingly contemporary and inflected in ways that are recognisably located within a newer tradition of Australian carnivalesque post-colonialism' (Kiernander 1995: 5). The choice to rework *The Sleeping Beauty*, Tankard says, was perhaps due in part to all the press attention surrounding the royal family and Lady Diana Spencer in particular (in Hallet 1994). The ballet is inextricably linked to traditions of monarchy and fairy tales and embodies a thoroughly European ideology. In an Australian context, which continues to have politically charged debates about monarchy and republicanism and, in particular, to the constitutional status of the British royal family, the links between this reworking and republicanism are unavoidable. Adrian Kiernander notes:

> While Tankard's piece does not intervene directly or polemically in the debate, its concerns are woven through this currently contentious area of national life, and many features of the work conspire to link the concept of monarchy with that of classical ballet, both of them conservatizing forces within the community.
>
> (Kiernander 1995: 5)

Further this dance points not only to current debates about republicanism through its specific use of *The Sleeping Beauty*, but also to ballet in general as a tool of imperial colonialism. As noted in chapter 1, ballet has spread across the globe and come to appear universal. This reworking, like others such as those by Iwana and Shakti (see chapter 5), re-envisage ballet from a particular cultural perspective and highlight the cultural specificity of the form while also risking reinscribing the ballet as a universal signifier.

Tankard trained initially as a ballet dancer and performed with the Australian Ballet. In 1978 she joined Wuppertal Tanztheater under the directorship of Pina Bausch. Tankard remained with Bausch's company until 1983 and created a number of significant roles in works such as *Café Muller*, *Kontakthof*, *Arien*, *Kenscheitslegende*, *1980*, *Walzer* and *Bandoneon*. Her roles at Wuppertal are noted as much for their brash and irreverent humour as for her dancing. After moving back to Australia in 1989 Tankard became artistic director of her own company. Four years later she was invited to become director of Australian Dance Theatre, for which she created *Furioso* (1993), *Aurora* (1994), *Possessed* (1995) and *Rasa* (1996), among others. Since turning freelance in 1998 her commissions have included *Bolero* (1998), for the Lyon Opera Ballet, *Merrylands* (2002), a work for Netherlands Dance Theatre 3, and *Wild Swans* (2003), a joint commission from the Australian Ballet and the Sydney Opera House, alongside an eclectic range of works for the Sydney Olympic Games, New Yorks's Museum of National History, and the for the sydney Olympic Games, New York's Museum of National History, and the Dalai Lama and Disney, for whom she choreographed *Tarzan* in 2006.

The theatre programme for *Aurora* suggests that this contemporary version of the ballet does not scorn, mimic or ridicule a style. Rather, Shirley Stott Despoja writes, 'what *Aurora* is about is disturbance – of our expectations, most obviously of a ballet about Aurora, the *Sleeping Beauty*; but also of other things, among them, scale, political correctness, and what we take as a dance presentation's "natural" progression' (Despoja 1994). Reworking the ballet in two acts and nineteen scenes, *Aurora* incorporates images that are playful and discontinuous. The choreography makes use of an eclectic range of dance styles, happily mixing traditionally disparate elements. The dance starts, for example, with a solo for Aurora, dressed in a bell-shaped skirt and fitted bodice in pastel colours; she is reminiscent of a typical fairy-tale princess. In the very next scene, however, troupes of limping gardeners push wheelbarrows, toss their caps and tumble about the stage. When the fairies enter, this playful approach continues. Dressed in puffball versions of tutus and wearing tap shoes, these male and female fairies carry Chinese lanterns and perform hybridised movement styles derived from classical ballet and tap.

> These impish and potentially violent fairies enter in savaged, short tutus, the men leaping barefoot and the women wearing tap shoes. Their tap routines are wild, anarchic and noisy, nothing like 42nd Street.
>
> (Kiernander 1995: 7)

Their routines are also nothing like the serene, harmonious ones of Petipa's fairies. These tap-dancing fairies perform steps akin to ballet and use earthy, freely flung movements. Rather than decorating the stage in circular groupings and commanding attention through their decorous dancing, Tankard's fairies are boisterous and claim attention through their loud, rather farcical behaviour. These carnivalesque bodies are then starkly juxtaposed with a total change in style and scale. Contrasting the colour and carnival of act I, act II opens with an extended series of large shadows. This is Aurora's sleep sequence, which passes not in passive slumber, but through traumatic dreams. The dancers' movements, which become fluid and full-bodied, are performed behind screens that cover the whole height and width of the stage and are strongly backlit. The emphasis, as the dancers fall, run and turn, is on shifting scales and surreal contrasts. Pulling away and towards each other, couples dance out difficult and painful relationships.

Later in the dance, when Aurora wakes up, Tankard shifts the style again, this time via an array of circus acts. These acts include juggling, conjuring tricks and flying acrobatics. The incorporation of elements from a different field of performance such as circus opens up the work even further. By mixing not only different dance styles but also different performance forms Tankard disrupts any sense of a unified body. The work presents multiple bodies in such a way that the 'vernacular' body (of tap and circus) collides with the 'elitist' body (of ballet). Neither physical form is given precedence and, in this way, the dance defies the divisions of high and low art and presents a plural, poly-vocal dance.

Although Petipa's ballet is also eclectic, in that it incorporates movement forms derived from the classical canon, social dance and various 'national dances', the ballet's geometry of form codifies this eclecticism and holds it within a unified approach. The body is a singular one that conforms to a standardised technique and strives to comply in order to establish the ideal of uniformity. The overall thrust of Petipa's *Sleeping Beauty* is univocal. As Sally Banes notes: 'the music, the costumes, the scenery, the pantomime, as well as the dance steps, all told the same story' (1994: 284). In contrast *Aurora* is fragmented and hybrid. This dance questions the benchmark of the audience's expectations and assumptions about a received interpretation of the ballet, replacing the codification of ballet not with another still single set of assumptions and skills but with multiple and fragmented ones. This work opposes the 'purity' of imperialism and authenticity.

Tankard's use of a number of different forms demonstrates a love of the perverse, the everyday, the vestigial and the messy, reflecting the thrust within postmodernism towards eclecticism. The particular mix of forms in *Aurora* is not, however, arbitrarily eclectic but incites intertextual readings, opening up the dance to a wide range of aesthetic and cultural concerns. References to the frog prince in act I, scene 6, echo Petipa's inclusion of multiple fairy-tale characters, while the references to feet in act I, scene 9, indicate both the tale of Cinderella and a more contemporary royal incident in the form of the then Duchess of York's (Sarah Ferguson) infamous 'toe sucking' saga, thereby bringing her references to the British royal family into view.[7] Tankard also incorporates elements and styles that form intertexts with an Australian sensibility and theatre heritage. Kiernander notes that the references to circus techniques, Chinese performance styles and physical disability resonate with the carnivalesque and multicultural influences in contemporary Australian theatre (1995: 7). For example, the gardeners in act I, scene 2, who, with wheelbarrows, brown clothing and cloth caps of various descriptions, grin and wheel themselves around the stage with exaggerated limps, reflect the postcolonialist approach of other Australian artists. Kiernander states:

> It is paradoxical that in a country whose stereotype is the physically perfect and near-nude surf lifesaver on a beach, many Australian artists and playwrights have focused on images of the grotesque or distorted as a way of writing back against European myths of classical perfection, sometimes as a response to the perceived inferiority of a marginal outpost relative to the metropolitan center.
>
> (ibid.)

This reworking represents *The Sleeping Beauty* in keeping with its new cultural context. Taking up the global cultural awareness of the ballet, Tankard represents a specifically Australian experience. Tankard's dance, like the work of other Australian artists, speaks back to imperialism. It is both implicitly critical and overtly carnivalesque, between Brechtian and Bakhtinian. Tankard's unruly overturning of received assumptions and her incorporation of disparate and fragmented elements, which belie the expectation of logical progression, elicit a radical approach purposefully obscured by the ostensibly fun and excessive performance. Following a dream logic, she evokes unfinished and disparate bodies, effectively decolonialising the hierarchical corpus of imperial culture.

While distinct in style and driven by different interests, these two reworkings by Stewart and Tankard both make use of overt intertexts and are formed through the use of an eclectic mix of radical juxtapositions. Each significantly embodies a poststructuralist intertextuality, and each exceeds and fractures the authority of the texts that it addresses. This strategy involves not just 'fiddling' with the canon, but cutting at it with a knife.

Conclusion

This overview of dances demonstrates how reworkings, in different ways, can be seen to test the boundaries of canonical ballet's value and authority, fracturing and entering from insurgent, and sometimes marginal, positions. The multiplicity of reworkings discussed here bring to the fore the fact that classics are not the authentic or hegemonic objects that the canon seeks to designate them; rather, they are specific representations of moments of cultural and artistic production.

Reworkings have, however, been shown to evoke a problematic double gaze, as they always risk, if not fetishising, at least recapitulating, the ballets at their source. A reworking does not guarantee an oppositional or discordant impulse. Whether a reworking exceeds the containing and constraining properties of the source, or whether a dance remains held within a frame of mainstream cultural concepts, cannot be assumed, but requires detailed attention to the specifics of each dance and its context. Tampering with the canon is clearly a dangerous ploy.

Judith Butler elucidates a similar problem in her analysis of the political signifier as the sedimentation of prior signifiers. She argues that the risk of drawing on prior signifiers is that, when they are reworked into a 'new' production, the 'new' 'is itself only established through recourse to those embedded conventions, past conventions, that have conventionally been invested with the political power to signify the future' (Butler 1993: 220).

However, the dangers of being held within the status quo notwithstanding (for surely some seepage is bound to occur), choreographers have found innovative and radical means through which to rework nineteenth-century canonical ballets. Questioning, resisting and on occasion subverting the weight of their source texts, these dances provoke different ways of thinking about performances of the past and current practices. Methods include recontextualising the dance, reformulating the choreography and the movement vocabulary, restructuring in order to form an eclectic juxtaposition of dance styles and theatre forms, and working within the gaps to play out previously unseen perspectives.

This overview reveals some different ways in which dancers' bodies have been reshaped, regendered, resexed and cultured anew – queering and querying tradition. The dances have been shown to embody the *potential* for liberation and transformation, creating unstable identities and radically revising established discourse. As such these reworkings, through the strategic refiguring of dancing bodies, have been shown to challenge the traditional representations of race, gender, sexuality and ethnicity within the canon. These themes are developed in the following chapters as I turn to discuss the consider specific dances in more depth. Organised around themes of gender and cultural revision, the dances intersect with queer, feminist and intercultural debates.

Part II

Refiguring the body and the politics of identity

Chapter 3

Female bodies and the erotic

Performativity, becoming and the phallus

Re-vision – the act of looking back, of seeing with fresh eyes, of entering an old text from a new critical direction – is for women more than a chapter in cultural history: it is an act of survival. Until we can understand the assumptions in which we are drenched we cannot know ourselves.

(Rich 1980: 35)

I found myself in the classic situation of women who, at one time or another, feel that it is not they who have produced culture ... Culture was there, but it was a barrier forbidding me to enter, whereas of course, from the depths of my body, I had a desire for the objects of culture. I therefore found myself obliged to steal them ... So that in a sense [culture] is always there [in the work], but it is always there in a displaced, diverted, reversed way. I have always used it in a totally ironic way.

(Cixous, in Suleiman 1985: 18)

Encounters between reworkings and feminism

Here I turn to reworkings by two women that self-consciously revision the ballet from feminist perspectives and, in doing so, explicate the potential relationships between the choreographic strategies employed in reworkings and feminism. The dances discussed in this chapter are *Lac de Signes* (1983) and *The Ballerina's Phallic Pointe* (1994) by Susan Foster, and my own choreographic installation *O (a set of footnotes to Swan Lake)* (2002).

Created at points over almost a twenty-year period, these dances reflect and participate in the feminist agendas of their eras and can clearly be positioned as part of the feminist project to rewrite history, deconstruct the canon and reclaim the body. As Rich and Cixous, quoted above, reveal, the commentary upon and reappropriation of dominant cultural productions by means of disruptive re-readings and rewritings have become integral to feminist strategies of resistance.

What becomes clear throughout this chapter are the ways in which the reworkings discussed engage with the critical task of refiguring the body. The insidious and persuasive construction of the body within the ballet canon, which tends to inscribe the body as object, makes the reworking of the body particularly urgent. The body (in particular the female body) is positioned as a potential site of resistance, a site that is never simply a passive object, but which maintains the possibility of counter-strategic reinscription. The body in these feminist reworkings can be seen to usefully alter the source text, embodying strategies of resistance.

It is significant thereby that both Foster and I work through our own bodies to engage with the ballet through a personal embodiment, questioning the representations of women that are evident in the ballet. The employment of our own bodies is an important feature of these dances, reflecting the views of Hélène Cixous, who suggests that women should write their own bodies. However, while Cixous has sometimes been accused of essentialism, the bodies discussed here are not essentialist or 'natural', but conditional and circumstantial.

In *Lac de Signes*, *The Ballerina's Phallic Pointe* and *O (a set of footnotes to Swan Lake)* the body and embodied gender signs are revealed to be fictive in nature. For in reworkings the deliberate reinscription of the body overtly marks gender as a construct. Because reworkings self-consciously 'repeat' the dances of the past, they bring the performativity of gender into the open – failing to reiterate, and thereby failing to produce, the bodily acts of their sources. The body's ability to fracture has been shown to provide a significant site for feminist counter-discourse. Rather than reinstating the highly coded bodies of the ballet canon, these reworkings have rechoreographed the body such that a wider variety of bodily incarnations are encompassed, allowing for divergence and multiplicity, as opposed to uniformity and sameness.

These dances refuse to cast all ballet as 'bad' or to create fixed monolithic presentations of women.[1] While some feminists have attacked ballet and stereotyped the representations of women within it, Alexandra Carter has argued, through problematising the previously universalising tendencies of feminist analysis, that 'we can now site ourselves within a web of identity which can accommodate conflicting personal responses, for we are not imprisoned by a unitary feminist ideology' (2001: 14). Further, she states that 'the ballerina does not always have to be a passive sylph or seductive siren any more, for sylphs can be powerful and sirens deeply moral' (ibid.). Complexities such as these are explicitly and self-consciously brought to the foreground in the reworkings that are the focus of this chapter.

Moreover, these dances rewrite and reclaim the erotic for women, and, given the body of the ballerina has historically been eroticised by viewers and choreographers,[2] this is another key strategy of resistance. However, the ways in which the erotic might best be reclaimed for women in reworkings are by no means straightforward or clear-cut. The problem is that women's bodies generally, and ballerina's bodies specifically, are saturated with sex, but conversely women have often been distanced from an erotic life. Women's sexuality has been deeply constrained by the discourses and practices of patriarchy, and the representation of female eroticism has been a contested area. As Gayle Rubin (2000) makes clear, the erotic life of women and its representation is a political issue. Reclaiming the erotic body as a source of creativity, which has all too often been repressed and marginalised, can be a resistive act. While different feminisms have taken contradictory stances towards the erotic and the sexual, over ten years ago Rubin argued that it was time 'to encourage erotic creativity' (2000: 354).

However, as Jeanie Forte (1992: 256), in a discussion of performance art, asked: 'How might it be possible for a feminist performer to express "female" pleasure, especially in terms of the female body, without resorting to essentialist categories?' Forte makes a useful and convincing argument when she suggests that the answer lies in the concept of erotic agency – that is, in women artists manipulating imagery to inscribe themselves in the discourse as erotic or creating an erotic sensibility. In doing so women may be able to transgress the limits of representation and construct a different viewing space, intervening in the cultural construction of woman as fantasy object, replacing it with the 'subject-performer' (Forte 1992). This erotic subject, Forte proposes, may or may not on the surface appear sexual, but expresses her own pleasure in and of her body, rather than referring to the arousal of the viewer (ibid.).

More recently the dancer and dance scholar Emilyn Claid (2001, 2002, 2006) has demonstrated that the successful reclaiming of seductive audience–performer relationships by female performers is possible. She writes that 'female bodies have re-emerged as seductive performers while maintaining their position as subjects of their own work' (2002: 41) and argues that seduction occurs in live dance theatre performance between performer and spectator, as, importantly, 'seductiveness in dance theatre performance becomes an interactive, interchangeable, pleasurable play of multiple desires and meanings between performer and spectator' (ibid.: 31). In this interaction, 'identifying who is seducing and who is seduced, who begins and who ends, is secondary to playing the game of seduction itself' (Claid 2001: 41).

Seductive strategies, Claid suggests, can be 'liberating tool[s] with disruptive, unfixing potential' (Claid 2002: 41). Key to the strategies for seductive relations is the oscillation between the dancer's real body and her performed surface, creating an ambiguity. This ambiguity draws the spectator to imagine, interpret and identify meanings that are continuously deferred. In seductive viewing the body is a teasing, desiring and knowing body that consistently evades capture, to remain fluid and ambiguous.

Discussing firstly *Lac de Signes* and *The Ballerina's Phallic Pointe,* and then *O (a set of footnotes to Swan Lake),* I consider the ways in which these dances appropriate and rewrite against the grain of the traditional narratives and embodiments of ballet and analyse the ways in which these works assert partial identities and different concepts of eroticism. Central to these works and the following analysis is the reconceptualisation of the ballerina's body and the female body *per se*. Representing the body for new contexts, these dances reappropriate the female body and the erotic as a force for women, and, in doing so, challenge conventional audience–performer relationships.

Destabilising the norm of viewing expectations derived from the classical ballet, the reworkings discussed here are (at least in part) able to present differing and ambiguous female bodies and assert seductive, materially sexual inscriptions that disrupt the gaze. In so doing, these dancing bodies signify radically revised notions of the female body and its potential for erotic agency.

Lac de Signes (1983) and The Ballerina's Phallic Pointe (1994) by Susan Leigh Foster

A dancer and academic, Susan Leigh Foster has published widely and has toured concerts of her own dances in the United States and Europe since 1977. Much of this work has focused upon revisions of the ballerina from poststructuralist feminist perspectives, and her writings have been highly influential in the field of dance studies.[3]

Here I am discussing a performance by Foster of *Lac de Signes* (1983) and *The Ballerina's Phallic Pointe* (1994) as presented in June 1996 at Highways, California, USA. This programme offers a radical reworking and divergent vision of *Swan Lake* and *Giselle*, for Foster's approach to both of these ballets has a particular emphasis upon the image of the ballerina. In these dances she does not attempt to follow the form, style, narrative or aesthetic of either *Giselle* or *Swan Lake*, so it is reasonable to ask how they are reworkings of these ballets. The answer is that they are reworkings in that they are fundamentally based on these pre-existing dances. Her dances exist because of them and remark upon them. While she doesn't attempt to reproduce the ballets, she does refer to them in the manner of an obligatory intertext, using characters, choreographic elements and fragments of music from them.[4] The signs of the ballets *Swan Lake* and *Giselle* are incorporated via parody into the very substance of Foster's work, becoming extended, trans-contextualised references. Working within the gaps and excesses of the ballet canon, and reflecting feminist criticisms of the ballet, Foster reworks elements of *Swan Lake* and *Giselle* to produce dances that operate as commentaries upon ballet rather than as new interpretations of the particular sources. It is via critique that she reinvests *Swan Lake* and *Giselle* with new meanings and reconceptualises the ballerina's body.

In her programme Foster presents her critique in three parts. Each part has a clear identity and each represents a different approach to reworking the ballet. The first part, a variation on her 1983 work *Lac des Signes*, begins with Foster dressed in black knee-length leggings, red trainers and a white tutu – held up by braces. Placed on the stage are a Grecian styled pedestal (downstage left) and a wooden board (upstage right). Foster enters and flutters her arms in a manner reminiscent of Odette at the moment Siegfried first sees her. 'Can't you see I'm trying to tell you something?' she asks. Clasping her hands together she makes a begging gesture, moving from side to side, and then falls sideways to the floor. Then, if we have yet to pick up the references to *Swan Lake*, she lifts her head and states: 'If the Swan Queen ends downstage right then the *corps de ballet* could come in upstage left and they could circle around her here and she could just get up and disappear.' Through this dance Foster refers repeatedly to well-known sections of *Swan Lake* via balletically styled sequences and through spoken text while radically transforming these references.

In the second part, *The Ballerina's Phallic Pointe* (first presented in 1994), Foster enters from upstage right and proceeds to shuffle across the stage in a *pas de*

Plate 10   The Ballerina's Phallic Pointe (1994) by Susan Foster

Photographer: Gretchan Hydler

bourrée couru motion to downstage left. She is dressed in a long-sleeved shirt and a knee-length tutu. The tutu is made from multiple pairs of pointe shoes, hanging on their ribbons from her waist. She is framed by her own headdress, for attached to her head is a T-shaped bar from which red curtains hang at each end. Displayed between her own curtains, Foster makes soft circular gestures with her forearms and announces her unattainability with the words, 'You want me. You can't have me.'

In the third part Foster is dressed in a black tunic and trousers. The stage is now bare and lighting defines the space. The sustained reference is to *Giselle*. In a fragmentary manner the ballet's libretto and choreographic form is evoked. Myrtha, Queen of the Wilis, is the central figure; she relates the narrative and comments upon the ballet. In a recurring image Foster strikes an *arabesque* pose and announces: 'I'm Myrtha, Queen of the Wilis.' Gesturing overhead, she states: 'With my wand of rosemary I forced Giselle to dance for Albrecht. She will lead him to his death ... death ... dea ... dea ... dea ...'

Throughout this third part Foster repeatedly cuts between movements that parody the ballet vocabulary performed by Myrtha, Giselle and Albrecht and an idiosyncratic (typically postmodern) style.[5] The movements from ballet (for example, *arabesques*, *développés* and *balancés*) are performed in a high-flown, overexaggerated fashion. These movements are whole-bodied and extended, in contrast to the pedestrian attitude to the body evident in the idiosyncratic vocabulary which emphasise the articulation of the joints and are small and internally focused. Isolated limbs stay close to the body as Foster performs multiple shifts and rotations of the head, neck, shoulders, elbows, wrists, pelvis, knees and ankles.

The dance ends with a shift in atmosphere. The music drones in a low tone and the lighting becomes muted. The mood becomes serious and Foster performs the longest purely movement section of the whole dance. This final section, which lasts nearly eight minutes, is an extension and development of the articulated, idiosyncratic, 'postmodern' dance style used previously. Full of actions which refer back to earlier images in the dance and incorporating awkward balances and repeated gestures, this extended dance sequence suggests a new reworked vision. Since it is presented at the end of the dance, it suggests possibilities for a new ending, for as Foster, speaking as Myrtha, states: 'I never liked that ending ... I can make another.'

What is it that Foster sets out to achieve via her radical reworking? Her political and personal investment is evident at the start of the dance when she asks: 'Can't you see I'm trying to tell you something?' This question is accompanied by arm gestures akin to the mimetic gestures performed by Odette when she first meets the Prince. The question refers to the narrative of *Swan Lake* – evoking Odette's attempts to communicate her humanity, hidden, as it is, by her Swan guise – but also serves to bring to the fore Foster's attempts to communicate with us. What is it she is trying to tell us? What is it, as Foster states shortly after, she wishes she could say/dance? Pushing and tensing in her arms, as if trying to remove something from the centre of her body, she says: 'If only I could say it. If only I could dance it.'

It seems to me that one of the things Foster is trying to tell us (if only she could say it ... if only she could dance it) is that ballet and the ballerina are in need of dismantling. Foster performs a critical commentary on *Swan Lake* and *Giselle* to present a reading of these ballets which reveals the layers of their construction and makes evident discontinuities that normally remain invisible. Via making explicit directorial comments such as, 'he could carry her around and leave her stage right', referring to Siegfried carrying Odette, the source texts are revealed to the audience to be manufactured by a particular director's vision rather than as 'natural'. Gender roles are also presented as mutable and contingent rather than fixed, for Foster dances both male and female roles and discusses the nature of those roles. Thereby that which is customarily taken for granted and seen as normal is in this reworking destabilised and denaturalised.

Looking-at-to-be-looked-at-ness: performance and spectacle

Central to the imagery in *The Ballerina's Phallic Pointe* is the theme of looking-at-to-be-looked-at-ness, and Foster, like other feminist performers,[6] demonstrates an interest in finding ways of evading and subverting the disciplining gaze. Foster explicitly makes the audience's gaze evident and engages us in a critique of the gaze. *The Ballerina's Phallic Pointe* alienates the way the ballerina is objectified and deautomatises the spectator's response to the viewing construct. To achieve this Foster uses a range of critical distancing techniques, making explicit the act of looking through the strategies of framing, fragmentation and parody. She draws attention to the gaze and refuses objectification. She also, in her construction of the ballerina-as-phallus (discussed later), offers an alternative and potentially subversive way of looking at the ballerina.

The relationship between the audience and the ballerina, cited by feminist dance scholars following Laura Mulvey (2001), is brought to the fore and challenged by Foster. In order to bring the gaze to the viewer's attention, and to dismantle it, Foster echoes the deconstructive devices of Brechtian theatre. There is potential in this method for, as Elin Diamond notes, Brechtian theory can offer 'a female body in representation that resists fetishization and a viable position for the female spectator' (2001: 79). Using contradictory signs in movement, spoken text, music and costume, Foster alienates gender and the figure of the ballerina and enables the viewer to see gender as ideologically constructed.

One example of Brechtian strategy in *The Ballerina's Phallic Pointe* is the framing of the dancer by a pair of mock stage curtains – forming a reference to the conventions of a proscenium arch stage. For, as discussed earlier in this chapter, Foster literally frames herself between a pair of curtains that are attached to her via a headdress. While wearing this headdress and travelling downstage in a *bourrée*, Foster teases the viewer, speaking the words: 'You want me. You can't have me. You desire me. It's futile.' This image demonstrates the objectification of the ballerina while at the same time gives voice to the ballerina's power. By presenting the ballerina as site/sight in this way Foster transforms the body from the site of looking to the speaking subject of looking-at-to-be-looked-at-ness.

The framed image of the ballerina is reiterated when Foster places a plastic ballerina doll within a miniature set of curtains. Spotlit by torchlight, this plastic object is placed centre stage. This repeated image makes explicit the pictorial aesthetic of the ballet genre and makes reference to the ballerina as an object of display. As an added twist the ballerina doll is strapped to Foster's pubis as a phallus/penis (the focus of desires?). The image 'over-displays' (Aston 1995: 95) the ballerina, showing the way in which the female body has been constructed as spectacle for male consumption.

Feminists have highlighted the ways in which 'the male gaze' places women into an impossible position. Rather than falling into a 'no-win situation' in which the status quo will always be asserted (Daly 1992: 243), Foster asserts a more empowering form of female performance/spectatorship in which she is both subject and object, deconstructing the binary model evident in Mulvey. In an attempt to reach beyond the boundaries of the stage, Foster asks us to meet her. Standing close to the front of the stage, she looks directly at the audience and says, 'Look at me. No. Me. Meet me.' In this moment the audience is reminded by Foster that we are looking at her; we are challenged not to look at her as object, but as subject. We are asked to meet Foster, the person, rather than gaze upon her body. This objectification of the body is highlighted further when Foster for the second time says, 'Meet me', for this time she also bends her knee up to her chest and taps her calf. The calf muscle wobbles and, in a play on words, we meet her body as meat. The suggestion is that in gazing upon her we are treating her like meat, a piece of desirable flesh.

The ballerina's traditional object status is also made explicit in *Lac de Signes*, as Foster, speaking as choreographer, positions and repositions the ballerina. Walking around the stage with her arms held up overhead, as if holding the ballerina on her shoulder, Foster states: 'He could carry her around and leave her upstage right.' This external commentary upon the choreography and placing of the ballerina on stage brings to the fore the manipulation of the ballerina. She doesn't position herself but is positioned by the choreographer, and that choreographer is presented as male, for Foster plays the male dancer's role as she carries the ballerina to the required spot. The directing of the ballerina's actions also, however, suggests that the choreography could be otherwise. Through presenting the stage directions as possibilities, that is, 'he could', rather than 'he does', Foster leaves room for us to imagine the choreography differently. Thereby *Swan Lake* and the ballerina, which are usually imagined to be fixed, become open to change and are revealed as potentially ever changing.

Foster challenges the audience, disrupting their viewing pleasures, and, in doing so, brings to the fore the very construction of the gaze. Shifting their gaze she establishes a de-eroticised image and reclaims the audience–viewer relationship to conceive a new language of desire. This language of desire is not based in scopophilia,[7] in which the process of looking arouses sexual stimulation and objectifies the person looked at; rather Foster evokes a fluid and unruly female image. Her direct engagement with the audience and her critique of the norm embodies the pleasures of resistance, for she presents a view of the ballerina that is against the grain.

Trans-contextualising bodies: postmodern parody and hybridity

Another way in which Foster undermines the operation of the gaze is to refuse the viewer's identification with any extended narrative structure; rather she cuts, slices and fragments images together, making overt intertextual references. The ways in which fragmented elements of *Swan Lake* are used and inverted in *The Ballerina's Phallic Pointe* reflect the discursive possibilities of parodic methodology. Foster references and uses fragments of *Swan Lake*, such as sections of the conventional Tchaikovsky music score, recognisable ballet positions, and the libretto, trans-contextualising these elements by positioning them within a new location. She also replays cultural and critical analyses of the ballet, particularly analyses established in feminist writings. These trans-contextualisations function so as to reveal the underlying agendas of the ballet form and to make evident the otherwise hidden constructions of the ballerina. *The Ballerina's Phallic Pointe* involves the viewer in a process of decoding, as old meanings are shifted and new meanings are generated. As Rose writes:

> the work to be parodied is 'decoded' by the parodist and offered again (or encoded) in a 'distorted' or changed form to another decoder, the reader of the parody, whose expectations of the original of the parodied work may also be played upon and evoked and then transformed by the parodist as part of the parody of the work.
>
> (Rose 1993: 39)

The ballet movements Foster incorporates via parody are performed with different qualities, as her movements are not extended and taut in the way that ballet is usually performed; her style is more relaxed. These parodic ballet steps are juxtaposed with movements from other contexts, such as shadow boxing, tap and everyday gestures. Foster also cuts into the norm of the presented ballet vocabulary by juxtaposing spoken text. Her opening section, for example, incorporates a balletically styled movement sequence that uses *arabesque penché*, *developpé écarté* and *pas de bourrée couru*. Having completed this sequence, Foster states: 'We can't go on like this!' Following the parodic performance of ballet steps, these words further dismantle the illusory appeal of the form. The implication is that we cannot continue to repeat the same movement patterns, that we need another vocabulary with which to speak. At the same time Foster also is cleverly referring to and subverting the narrative of *Swan Lake*, for the ballet sequence is presented as a reference to a *pas de deux* by Odette and Siegfried; as such Foster is double coding her words, for they could also refer to those that a modern Odette might say to her lover.

In another example Foster mimics the movements that Odette usually dances at the start of the *grand pas de deux*. This balletic vocabulary (including recognisable floor positions such as the body bent over towards the knees with the arms crossed over at the wrist)[8] soon gets undercut, as she starts to flex her feet and add movements such as jogging, tap shuffles and shadow boxing. Through such strategies (juxtaposing references in movement to the ballet with spoken text and contrasting movement styles) the coherence of the source texts is challenged and new associations are made. So in the above example the usually highly romantic and emotional image becomes instead linked to effort, fitness and competition. Images from *Swan Lake* are fragmented as moments are taken out of their original balletic context and placed into a new hybrid and inclusive text. This hybrid text, through its very hybridity, suggests a provisional stance. While, as discussed in chapter 1, to some extent all reworkings operate as hybrid forms, Foster's reworking is very overt in its hybridity, cutting across forms and making explicit references to both the ballets at its source and other intertexts. This parodic hybrid approach creates a double-voiced text that is not an imitation or monologic mastery of other discourses, but in content, form and structure represents a dialogic meeting with the discourse of others.

As discussed in chapter 1, Hutcheon argues that parody is a means of mastering and superseding influential predecessors and is thereby one way of coping with 'the anxiety of influence' (Hutcheon 1985: 96).[9] She writes:

> Intertextual parody of canonical American and European classics is one mode of appropriating and reformulating – with significant change – the dominant white, male, middle class, heterosexual, Eurocentric culture.
>
> (Hutcheon 1988: 130)

Foster's work, in its critique of preconceived norms, allows her and the audience to surpass the power of the ballet canon by revealing its construction. Reading against the grain of 'master-works' of Western culture, Foster offers new readings of these works, readings that are more acceptable to a feminist politic. Also, via the reflection back on the 'master-work', she reveals the ideologies embedded within *Swan Lake* and *Giselle* which hitherto were hidden from view. The mythic nature of such works is thereby challenged. They are revealed as specific and contextualised as opposed to neutral and ahistorical. Through parody, the passive consumption of the so-called master-works can be challenged as the viewer is made aware of their status and implications.

However, as parody operates paradoxically, the ballet becomes simultaneously insignificant and highly important: it is insignificant in that it becomes trivialised, and highly important in that *Swan Lake* and *Giselle* are the source texts, the very basis of Foster's work. This duality is part of the structure of parodic manifestations – for parody operates in a place in between the replaying of past images and the critiquing of those images. That which is parodied by Foster is not completely divorced from its original, but the images are placed in surprising new contexts and combinations. Here each sign becomes another sign but does not altogether lose its particular history and integrity; the juxtaposition of different discourses manipulates old signs to incorporate them with a new logic. As Hutcheon argues, in *The Politics of Postmodernism*, parody does not wrest past art from its original historical context and reassemble it into some sort of spectacle. Instead, through a double process of installing and ironising, parody signals how present representations come from past ones and what ideological consequences derive from both continuity and difference (1989: 93). Foster deconstructs the structures of authority within theatricality and exposes the ideological underpinnings of the latter without presenting an alternative 'truth' via an overt entering into of a purposeful intertextual discourse.

Pierre Bourdieu (1993), in his discussion of current artistic practices, suggests that there is no room for naivety, as every act, gesture and event is a sort of nudge and wink between accomplices. Through this 'game', argues Bourdieu, silent and hidden references to past and present artists are included in the works as silent traces which confirm a complicitous relationship in their interrelations and interactions. This game, it could be argued, is an elitist one – a game that can only be appreciated by 'those in the know'. In many ways all reworkings rely on the audience's prior knowledge as, arguably, much of the pleasure in these dances is generated by the awareness of the ways in which the source text is being reworked. However, if they rely only on the 'in joke' the efficacy of these works will be limited, alienating the general viewer. Foster's dance at times certainly feels this way, as knowledge of source texts is needed in order to appreciate the humour. Also, at other points, explicit 'in jokes' which relate to her specific audience are made. Foster integrates references to the ballet libretto and a reference to teaching staff at the university to which she is associated. Bursting with laughter and grasping her sides she says:

> Tell me … what happened next?
> I know he married the princess …
> He got a job – teaching ballet – at UCLA!
>
> He has a new show opening … in Orange County!

This elicits a wave of laughter among the 'in' audience, potentially excluding part of her audience. This interweaving of personal 'in jokes' with dance references highlights the nature of the parodic game. It requires an informed audience to appreciate the parody and its resultant humour. This is an elitist position, perhaps, but one that announces the provisional and context-specific nature of Foster's dance in opposition to the seemingly universalist stance of the ballets at this reworking's source.

Parodic comedy and the performativity of gender

In Foster's work much of the parody results in comedy. For example, the parodic reprise of Myrtha, Queen of the Wilis, is performed in an overly exaggerated manner, where the *arabesque* positions are not held or performed with customary care; rather, Foster throws her leg and arms into something approximating an *arabesque*. While performing these poses she speaks with a stereotypically operatic intonation. She is unruly; her movement and language are too loud, too large, and too absurd to be taken seriously.

Foster's parodic comedy is also evident in the ways in which she shifts the audience's expectations via juxtaposition. Dancing to the rock and roll song *(You're the) Devil in Disguise* (1963) by Elvis Presley, she transforms movements from the ballet lexicon into movements more akin to popular dance. Conflicting conventions are crossed and juxtaposed in a combination of traditional ballet steps and release-based movement, boxing and tap, rock and roll, jazz and Indian dance, causing the viewer to reconsider what should be thought of as high-art dance. Foster's disruption of the boundaries between forms, alongside the incongruity of the rock and roll music, surprises the audience and generates laughter.

The lyrics in the music are also amusingly transformed. In the context of a reworking of *Swan Lake*, Elvis's song becomes a reference to the disguise of Odile, the Black Swan, as she pretends to be Odette and deceives Siegfried. For, as the lyrics state:

> You look like an angel
> Walk like an angel
> Talk like an angel
> But I got wise
> You're the devil in disguise
> Oh yes you are
> The devil in disguise

The audience enjoys other unexpected twists. For example, having performed a *bourrée* across the stage and announced herself as 'the perfect figure of unattain-ablity', Foster pauses for a moment and then lifts her arms to reveal strands of fabric dangling from her armpit. She brushes her hand under each armpit and turns to face the audience with a knowing smile. This image touches at boundaries of the grotesque body, as armpit hair, represented by the fabric, is in the classical body removed, while here Foster takes pleasure in the presence of her overly long and wild armpit hair and so presents the audience with the opposite of their expectations.

While commonly associated with parody, comedy has been denigrated as a limited and limiting view of the effect of parody. This negative attitude towards the comic in parody has been especially evident within postmodern descriptions. Linda Hutcheon (1985, 1988) is one such postmodern critic. She seeks to distance parody from comedy in order to highlight the metafictional and critical nature of parody. The perceived relationship with comedy, argues Hutcheon, limits the function and purpose of parody, reducing it to a frivolous technique. However, Margaret Rose (1993) argues that postmodern parody is at its most complex when it is considered to be *both* metafictional and comic.

Whatever the definitions of parody, the use of comedy by a female performer can present a subversive stance. Women, and especially women in dance, are rarely associated with comedy. It seems to me that a female performer, in a dance that speaks of the ballet form, using comedy, is a wonderful inversion of expectations. Foster refuses to take seriously the supposedly serious matter of the cultural object to which she refers – that is, the ballet. She applies strategies of humour and the absurd, making explicit her refusal to take ballet too seriously.

Using parodic comedy to re-present past representations of women, Foster imbues Odette and Giselle with a strength and 'attitude' that their traditional counterparts do not have, and extends the underdeveloped potential of Odile and Myrtha. Through strategies of excess, irony and fragmentation, past representations are trans-contextualised and disrupted. This confrontation with the dominant representations of women in ballet reveals these representations to have particular political resonances as opposed to operating as 'true' or 'real'; the traditional image of women is uncovered as only a partial or even a mis-representation.

The difficulty of the comic effect of parody, to which Hutcheon points, is, however, also evident in *The Ballerina's Phallic Pointe*. The high-flown parodic imitation of the ballet lexicon may additionally be seen to propound a stance of ridicule. This sense of ridicule trivialises the ballet and undermines Foster's potentially efficacious commentary. Overall she uses the comic effect of parody to stress the critical, for the playfulness involved does not exclude a seriousness of purpose.

The parodic approach used by Foster to rework the ballet enables gender to be presented as a learned performative act encoded by the gendered vocabulary of ballet. Via the parodic and comic performance of both male and female roles she highlights the gendered nature of ballet. For example, performing the male dancer's role, she walks in a direct fashion around the space, stands still while holding the imaginary partner's waist and performs a series of angular gestures which cut and dissect space, whereas when taking the female dancer's role she curves through space, hops in an *arabesque* and sways side to side in a *bourrée*. As the male dancer Foster 'discovers,' 'supports' and 'promenades'. As the female dancer she is 'fragile,' 'sexy,' and repeatedly 'effortless', 'effortless', 'effortless' (*The Ballerina's Phallic Pointe*, 1996). As she interweaves these gendered vocabularies, forming a seamless dialogue between the two, Foster asserts a continual shifting of identities. The two languages are, she implies, self-consciously posed, not fixed but existing only on the surface, and open to contestation and change. Gender roles in the ballet, insists *The Ballerina's Phallic Pointe*, are only performative, and as such the codes of each can be altered, mixed or discarded.

Foster's representation of gender as performative relates her work to that of Judith Butler (1990, 1993). Gender as 'performance' places a question mark over the 'authenticity' of what is offered, for performance is conventionally something constructed. Butler's concept of performativity uses this distinction between what is authentic and what is constructed in a specific way through the nuanced term 'performativity'. Performativity, as a performance of identity, operates in an everyday sphere and problematises authenticity, identity and origins. Butler is careful to distinguish her concept from conventional concepts of performance, and she writes: 'performativity must be understood not as a singular or deliberate "act", but, rather, as the reiterative and citational practice by which discourse produces the effects that it names' (1993: 1).

In her discussion of parody, Butler writes that parody 'reveals the original to be nothing other than a parody of the idea of the natural and the original' (1990: 31). Using this concept, it is thereby possible to conceive of Foster's parody of the ballerina as a copy of a copy of a copy, leaving no 'original' at the source. This is a dance, like Baudrillard's simulacra (1993), of incomplete copies. Foster presents the ballerina image as an overt overdisplay of what it is to be female and reveals that what it is to be female is itself already a parody of a non-existent original. For, through Butler's concept of performativity and parody, it is possible to consider femininity itself as parodic. By adopting one parodic mask after the other, Foster exposes the fact that there is no essential feminine but only the performance of it. The public spectacle of a woman's body enacts and stylises an embodied presence of what it is to be female rather than its being a core gender identity.

Through a series of embodied presences, Foster calls into question the idea of any pre-existing authentic self, for, via parody, a distance between Foster and the ballerina as performer and the image appears. As parodies they expose the constructed nature of femininity, as any coherence between the identity of the performer and the artifice of the performance collapses. Thus parody dislocates image and refuses integration thereby; the image becomes open for women to manipulate and interpret – thus allowing women to shift position.

Foster opens spaces and creates fractures, eschewing the traditional hermeneuticism of the ballet form and its attendant political ambivalence. Via its use of 'low' and 'high' art forms, comedy, wit and theoretical commentary, Foster's deconstructive work is anarchic and counter-canonical. Using parody, she recycles past images, transforming and inverting them in such a way that the viewer is made aware of their sociological implications. She asserts a self-reflexive discourse that is inextricably bound to social discourse, foregrounding the historical, social and ideological context in which ballet existed and continues to exist, and her parodic play gives the viewer the opportunity to see how history is plundered in ironic commentary, not in nostalgic recall.

The phallus, the penis, the dildo and the ballerina

The Ballerina's Phallic Pointe is particularly interesting in its challenge to the way the ballerina is perceived. In this vision, as discussed in a written essay also entitled 'The ballerina's phallic pointe', the ballerina is, 'in a word, the phallus' (Foster 1996a: 3).

Foster's definition of the ballerina-as-phallus follows Lacan and the feminist reappropriations of his work.[10] Lacan sees the phallus as signifier of the law that divides the symbolic from the imaginary. The imaginary is conceptualised as the period during childhood before a sense of self emerges. As a child distinguishes itself from others and develops a sense of self, becoming subject, it enters into the world of the symbolic. This is the world of culture and language systems, and through these systems the child begins the process of socialisation, with its prohibitions and restraints. The phallus, as central to the symbolic, anchors the free-floating signifiers of the unconscious. Representing the law of the father, and underlining the patriarchal nature of the symbolic system, the phallus is the centre of order and control, limiting play and fixing meanings. According to Lacan no one, neither men nor women, has the phallus for, while it seems to represent masculine access to social power, it in fact represents absence or lack. The phallus is a cultural construction which holds symbolic power, and while men have a penis, this does not mean that they possess the phallus. It is only through another's desire that man can feel he has the phallus.

The ballerina-as-phallus is visually represented in a variety of ways. Foster wears a plastic ballerina and a pointe shoe as a phallus; she uses phallic terminology, describes the vocabulary of ballet in phallic terms, and rubs and rhythmically pumps a pointe shoe, as if a phallus. The pointe shoe provides a clear visual representation of a phallus as the symbolic sign of the penis. With its length and breadth, smooth pink surface, hardened form and slightly bulbous end, the pointe shoe is a model phallic object.

Foster wears her pointe shoes not on her feet, but on her hands, and also has a shoe tied around her waist so that it hangs on her pubic bone. She performs exercises such as *pliés* and *développés*, while stating: 'Try harder, hold it longer, do it faster, get it higher.' She proceeds then to push her pelvis forward and rub at the pointe shoe hanging at her pubis, simulating masturbation. This ends with Foster repeatedly and aggressively punching a pointe shoe into the ground. In a frustrated tone she repeatedly shouts: 'Harder, faster, longer, higher, harder, faster, longer, higher.' Through the combination of the pointe shoe as phallus and exercises from a typical ballet class, the repressive phallus is linked to the control and, as Foster perceives it, the constant violations of the dancer's body in ballet. As Foster writes, the ballet dancer must 'learn to do more and more – harder sequences, faster steps, longer balances, higher legs – with less and less body' (Foster 1995a: 111). The pointe shoe and the ballerina's geometric body as phallus become the symbols of repression.

The ballerina's lifted, aerial and upright thrust is, Foster's danced and written texts suggest, the foundation of the conceptualisation of the ballerina-as-phallus. The movement vocabulary of ballet is referred to throughout in phallic terms. Movements are 'hard', 'long', 'extended' and 'inflated'. The ballerina demonstratively embodies the hardened and extended phallus. As if standing at a *barre* taking a ballet class, Foster extends her leg out to the side *à la seconde* and says, 'Hard'; the leg is then bent up at the knee and Foster, touching her relaxed calf muscle, says, 'Soft'. This is in one sense descriptive of the muscle tone required for each action, but it also makes reference to the phallus – the extended leg becomes a literal image of the phallus. The movement continues as Foster performs *port de bras*, *développés*, *retiré* and *grand battement*, bringing the audience's attention to the shape of these actions with her spoken text – 'circle', 'line', 'triangle', 'angle', etc.

These images reflect the potency of Foster's concept and significantly give rise to a phallic identity that is much more than a simple metaphor. It is through the coded and ordered form of ballet that the ballerina 'gives figure to signification. In her, the chaos of body transmutes into rational form. The years of bodily disciplining have refigured fleshy curves and masses as lines and circles', writes Foster (1996a: 14). Further, she states: 'Via this geometry her movements turn mess into symbol' (ibid.).

As symbol, however, the ballerina-as-phallus paradoxically resists phallocentric cultural symbolisations. Rather than operating as a veiled phallus, the ballerina-as-phallus makes her status within the symbolic system overt and thereby her position is revealed. This revealing occurs via making manifest her theatrical construction. The ballerina is disrobed (literally, as Foster removes her curtain headdress and skirt), the movement training that forms her body is made visible, and her body is located in discourse.

Asserting a challenge to the construction of the subject, Foster uses and abuses the imagery of the symbolic order and turns it on itself. There is also a sense in which Foster asserts a desire to exit from the symbolic order. She regally and ironically exits from the symbolic frame – picking up her curtain headdress, her very own proscenium arch stage, and waving, or perhaps wafting her wing, she steps behind the curtain, and so leaves the stifling frame.

Foster argues that the ballerina can be considered a phallus because of the classical routing of the viewer's gaze. She suggests that imagining the ballerina-as-phallus promotes an examination into the 'female viewer's attention' (1996a: 3). This inquiry emphasises that the female viewer must look through the eyes of the male dancer at his partner or that she must empathise with the ballerina as an object of male desire (ibid.).[11] As phallus she takes on the power of the symbolic rather than continuing to exist as 'lack'. If she is the phallus, remembering that the phallus is possessed by no one, she cannot be 'had', cannot be 'owned', for while she may be desired she is an illusion. For those who see her illusion her cultural construction is revealed and the delusion of the phallus as power is broken.

Like Butler's rewriting of woman and the Lacanian phallus, the ballerina-as-phallus is a masquerade. Butler argues that, if 'being' the phallus is masquerade, for women cannot have the phallus but only the appearance of being phallus, then the phallus has no being of its own. It is always a mask, a surface. She maintains that if this is the case, like the parodic copy, 'then it would appear to reduce all being to a form of appearing, the appearance of being, with the consequences that all gender ontology is reducible to the play of appearances' (1990: 47). Significantly, however, she also proposes that another reading of phallic masquerade is possible. She states:

> on the other hand, masquerade suggests that there is a 'being' or ontological specification of femininity *prior to* the masquerade, a feminine desire or demand that is masked and capable of disclosure, that, indeed, might promise an eventual disruption and displacement of the phallogocentric signifying economy.
>
> (Ibid.)

This releases woman from the Lacanian model based on lack and indicates a masked desire – a desire that can thereby be reclaimed. Foster, extending her concept of the ballerina-as-phallus, suggests that it has the potential which 'all monsters afford, to forge from the cataclysmic energy of their aberrant parts a new

identity that meets the political and the aesthetic exigencies of the moment'
(1996a: 3). Foster proposes that:

> Perhaps, via the ballerina-as-phallus, her power can reconfigure so as to sus-
> tain her charisma even as she begins to determine her own fate. Perhaps the
> ballerina-as-phallus can even reclaim for ballet, long viewed as a neutral
> parade of geometrized forms, a certain sensual and even sexual potency.
>
> (Ibid.)

To what extent then does Foster's vision of the ballerina – her representation of
her as phallus – proffer a more sensual or sexual potency? To what extent does
the ballerina's new guise resist symbolisation, resist fixity, and thereby give rise to
a reconfigured, self-determined fate? The phallic ballerina is certainly a more sexually overt one than her traditional counterpart – for this is a woman who is confident in her sexuality and who brings the sexual connotations of the ballet to the
fore. However, as she masturbates the pointe shoe tied to her pubis, she grimaces
and pushes her pelvis forward, pleased with her own grotesque mannerisms. The
references are to the penis and to the dildo.

This image of masturbating the pointe shoe and, later, the strapping on of the
plastic ballerina doll to her pubis, suggests connections to the dildo and its har-
ness. The image of the dildo and its associations with lesbian sexuality further
opens up and problematises the construction of the ballerina by placing non-
normative sexuality into the context of *Swan Lake* and *Giselle*, both of which are
intertwined with compulsory heterosexuality. As Banes notes, *Swan Lake* perpetuates a deeply romantic notion of a transcendent love match while *Giselle* 'is pro-
marriage, asserting that one must have a partner' (1998: 35), and that partner be
of the opposite sex. Inserting same-sex eroticism via reference to the dildo into
this context, Foster questions the nature of desire. She asserts that bodies do not
always line up into expected categories as sexual practices proliferate.

Further, Foster enjoys the material fleshiness of her own body. She brings our
attention to her fleshy calves, repeatedly tapping them while arching her head
back and moaning in an orgasmic fashion, finally pressing her calves together, like
Irigaray's labial lips, in a 'kiss'. In thinking beyond desire based on lack, Foster
represents a rejection of male-dominated definitions of woman and calls the
whole gender system into question. 'In other words', writes Braidotti, 'she is neither "nonman", nor "nonwoman", but, rather, radically other' (Braidotti 1994:
271). Foster's reference to lesbian sexuality can be said to go beyond identity as
based on the phallus to suggest instead a female eroticism that threatens normative bipolarised sexuality.

Sexual references continue throughout. Towards the end of the middle section
Foster performs a parodic series of movements akin to the extensions and linking
steps of ballet. Foster accompanies these steps with the words 'inflate', 'deflate',
'inflate', 'deflate', spoken in high-flown tones. These terms relate the vocabulary
of ballet to the image of the phallus but also suggest the more mobile penis,

shifting between its erect and flaccid states. Foster extends this language of the penis to parodically evoke the interaction between the male and female dancer. He inflates, deflates and supports; she is fragile, delicate and sexy.

The image of the penis genders and problematises the symbolic construct of the phallus. Foster's representation of the penile phallus intersects with feminist revisions of the phallus. Feminists have argued that the phallus, when constructed as gender neutral and as unconnected to the male penis, perpetuates patriarchal inequalities. Feminist revisionists have thereby sought to unveil the phallus in a gesture which 'reveals the fallacy of the phallus' (Bernheimer 1992: 117). Charles Bernheimer usefully reinstates the place of the penis within Lacanian phallic theory and argues that:

> The most evident effect of penile reference on the transcendental phallus is the onslaught of temporality and the consequent variability of the penis between its rigid and limp states.
>
> (Ibid.: 119)

As a phallus the ballerina, it could be argued, is 'inert, insensible, unresponsive to variations in context and circumstance. The phallic penis is impersonal and unchanging, always erect, impervious to differences in desire – whether the other's or one's own' (Bernheimer 1992: 120). However, when the phallus is connected to the materiality of the penis it can be imagined as a changeable, mutable form. Thereby the ballerina-as-penis may have a little more room for manoeuvre. This is not to conflate the penis and the phallus, for, as Heather Findlay writes in her discussion of lesbian dildo debates, the collapsing of the difference between a symbol (the phallus) and a real body organ (the penis) is one of the assertions of patriarchy (1999: 470). What I am arguing here is that, while the ballerina-as-phallus suggests a powerful reclaiming of feminine desire via masquerade, she is still fixed by the rigidity of the phallus. Reworking her as penis, however, she becomes a more material body, a body that is imperfect and leaky.

The ballerina, like the phallus, encompasses the illusion of universality and transcendence. Locked into the symbolic system, the ballerina-as-phallus refers to no particular body, whereas imagining the phallus, and the ballerina, as penis removes the transcendental illusion and insists on an awareness of gender and specificity. The penis, unlike the phallus, has a bodily experience and belongs to a specific body – a body that has a race, class and sexual orientation (Bernheimer 1992: 118).

Problematically this body is male, and the penile phallus (whether used in symbolic, metaphorical or 'real' ways) is still highly gendered, as is the theory; however, this conception of the ballerina could give rise to differentiated bodies. Perhaps the ballerina-as-penis could construct an indecipherable and shifting dance – one in which her subjectivity, race, history and gender are represented fluidly – a dance in which, while not whole or essentialist, she is not constructed as lacking.

Overall, this deconstructive work challenges the ballerina's objectification, and Foster's innovative allusion of the ballerina as phallus gives rise to a more fluid body in which the erotic is reclaimed. In this (re)construction the ballerina becomes an unstable subject who challenges the symbolic order. Foster indicates the body's materiality (soft fleshy and wobbling calves) and threatens its boundaries (extending it via the attachment of the phallic ballerina). The phallic extension of the body is not fleshy, but plastic, a dildo. This gives rise to the possibilities of a lesbian reading that threatens normative sexuality. Reclaiming the ballerina's sexuality, rather than becoming the object of a male sexual gaze, Foster in a radical step offers ownership of the phallus to the ballerina.

O (a set of footnotes to Swan Lake) (2002) by Vida L. Midgelow

O (a set of footnotes to Swan Lake) (2002) is a video, solo dance and sonic art installation. The space is darkly lit, the atmosphere cool. On translucent screens there is a projected image of feathers falling. A voice is heard; a dancer makes a sharp turn of the head, an isolation of the shoulder ripples out through to the hand; 'swan, woman, woman, swan', states the text projected from a laptop computer.

The choreographic installation *footnotes* (as I shall refer to the work) is conceived and performed by me, with video editing by Jane Bacon and Robert Daniels and a sound score by Oliver Ryles.[12] Inspired by the writings of many feminist dance scholars, in particular those of dancer–academics such as Susan Foster and Ann Cooper Albright, this installation is an engagement with these writings, and others, in practice. Yet rather than theory being causal, the processes of making performance means that this reworking follows its own logic, its own trajectory – for it is not a demonstration of a pre-theorised position. Still, discussing and critiquing one's own work is a hard thing to do. This analysis attempts to frame the work critically, placing it within theory, while also remaining open to the recognition of its more problematic aspects. Following the theoretical constructions of the female body evident in the writings of Irigaray, Deleuze and Guattari, I discuss *footnotes* in terms of hybridity, plurality and becoming, yet also problematise these unstable bodies by inserting into this frame a body which is 'real'. The 'realness' of this body, of this person, brings to the fore the potential risk of discourse in which the body might be lost altogether.

Footnotes is the latest in a series of works in which I have explored different modes of reworking. These dances, *Awaking Aurora* (1995–6), *The Original Sylph* (1997–8), *O* (2001),[13] plus aspects of *The Collection* (1999) (with Mulchrone),[14] progressively depart from their source texts. This departure has involved selectively leaving behind more and more central structural features or invariants (see chapter 1 and Suvin 1988). For example, *Awaking Aurora*, a reworking of *The Sleeping Beauty* (1890), used core sections of Tchaikovsky's music score and followed a linear narrative while reconceiving the role of Aurora and rechoreographing the movement in order to bring to the fore the darker and older aspects of the fairy

Plate 11   O (a set of footnotes to Swan Lake) (2002) by Vida Midgelow

Photograph: author's own

tale. *The Original Sylph* (as discussed in chapter 1) highlighted the fragmented and provisional nature of history, aligning this with a discordant representation of Giselle as both exceedingly knowing and rather fey. The dance used small fragments of Adam's music score and made references to the ballet in movement and costume while having a non-linear form. *footnotes*, as shall become evident through this chapter, is informed by theoretical concerns and the analysis of other reworkings. The installation incorporates no direct invariants of *Swan Lake* (1895) but consistently invokes the ballet through sound, image, text and movement.

Four screens hang in the space. Two large translucent screens (one plastic and one fabric) form a right angle. On these screens are two intersecting video projections. Linking these screens is a floor covering of plastic 4 metres square. A third smaller screen, placed to the edge and slightly back of the main right angle, has written text projected onto it from a computer. A final long thin screen, mirrored by a floor covering, is to the opposite side of the space. I dance solo in the space, shifting between the screens, the floor areas and a stool. The performance is improvised and I form movement around some previously explored, and some totally spontaneous, images. Shifting out of an overtly performative mode into a more functional mode, I come to and from a centrally placed computer. At this computer I am able to select from a list of fragments of text in order to project this text onto the small third screen.

Sound plays continuously throughout. The score contains a collection of fragmented elements and has an insistent tone. Shifting through sections of sound in a seamless manner, the music weaves its way through the voices of past and current ballet dancers, derisive laughter and distorted digitised sounds. The sound operates in layers within which partial references to *Swan Lake* are present; for example, Natalia Markarova's voice is heard telling moments of the libretto, dancers discuss their experiences of performing as cygnets, and a child tells of watching the ballet. These elements are, due to the effect of layering, parts of a total soundscape which creates an intense atmosphere.

On the long, thin floor covering to the side of the space I take halting steps. My heels are raised as high as possible – held up by my hands. I step, lifting each foot into place. On the large plastic screen fragmentary images of me rolling and sliding, dressed in a white tutu and pointe shoes, are playing. On the fabric screen feathers are falling. 'Every story tells a story that has already been told', states the projected text. These images evoke possible moments and together can be taken to suggest various meanings. However, as the connections between elements, and a particular audience member's angle of vision to these elements, is in no way fixed or fixable, these descriptions (as the descriptions throughout this chapter) give only a feel for the type, rather than the definitive collection, of images, sounds and movement in the space. Further, members of the audience are able freely to enter and exit the installation throughout the performance, which also works against any impression of single experience.

Working through the gaps and silences of the ballet *Swan Lake*, this work kindles a sense or resonance of the ballet but does not embody it within its own substance. Transgressing traditional binaries between absence and presence – a model in which presence is valued over absence – *footnotes* evokes *Swan Lake* as an absent presence. The sound and images (video, danced and written) in the space are only partial; they are pared down and offer an impressionistic representation rather than a detailed retelling. Fragmentary images and sounds provide a trace of half-remembered images, but the connections between them, and from them back to the ballet, are never fully realised. The gaps in *footnotes* have to be filled in by the viewers, who are required to exercise their own associations and memories in order to make 'sense' of the work.

To differing extents all reworkings operate through the audience's degree of awareness of the source text. These dances evoke, at the very least, a bidirectional gaze (see chapter 1), for the audience simultaneously enjoys the new work and the relationship with, or contrast to, the source text. The normative mode of viewing in reworkings that maintain conventional structures asserts a hierarchical relationship between the source and the reworking, a mode that privileges the source. In *footnotes* this hierarchy is challenged as the boundaries between absence and presence become blurred. While the ballet is present, for it is resonant throughout *footnotes*, the bidirectionality of this reworking is shifted such that no particular moments in *Swan Lake* and *footnotes* coalesce. It becomes almost impossible to conceive a *direct* relationship between the two works. I avoid the explicit device of parodic quotation in the manner of *The Ballerina's Phallic Pointe*, as discussed above. This choreographic installation plays with and interweaves many fragments and is left open enough to encourage the audience to inscribe their own meanings,

Plate 12   O (a set of footnotes to Swan Lake) (2002) by Vida Midgelow

Photograph: author's own

their own intertexts, rather than relying on notions of 'origin' or 'influence'. In this way *footnotes* is an ambiguous text which has the capacity to generate multiple, shifting and potentially contradictory meanings.

The reference in the title of the work to footnotes attempts to suggest two directions: firstly, to the paratextual information conventionally placed at the end of a written page; secondly, to bring playfully to the viewer's attention the feet and the act of dancing. As footnotes, this is a dance that operates from a marginalised space – a dance in the wings, or perhaps even further off centre, from beyond the stage door.

Linda Hutcheon (1989) argues that the paratextual role of footnotes in novels and history writings asserts a double narrative, inserting intertextual references to other texts and the external world. Footnotes are used to supplement, support and lend authority to the main body of the text. This marginalised space is also often where opposing views are dealt with. Importantly, footnotes disrupt linear reading in such a manner that the creation of a coherent narrative is fractured. The presentation of the footnotes only (as is the case in this reworking) might be seen to disrupt the normative balance between the primary text and the secondary paratextual footnotes even further. Seizing on unregarded details, *footnotes* performs a strategic reversal, emphasising that which is hidden rather than that which is to the fore. Ironically *Swan Lake*, as a dance text, does not come with a set of prescribed footnotes. These notes are not only unregarded details but details that are not even present. This work evokes imaginary footnotes, the footnotes that are missing, footnotes that might be added by the feminist viewer suffering from the anxiety of pleasure and distaste.[15] In line with postmodern thought, the master narrative of ballet is questioned and the marginal and ex-centric is called to the viewer's attention. Through this paratextual strategy *footnotes* reminds the viewer that the primary text, *Swan Lake*, is fictive. Its role as a masterly discourse of Western culture, its centrality, is revealed to be illusory.

Footnotes are often intended to elucidate the meaning of the primary text. In *footnotes*, however, the traces, or 'meanings' (such as they are), are disseminated throughout the work across sound, text, video and dance. This dissemination of meanings increases the likelihood that much of it may drift. 'Meanings' are constantly 'deferred' and also 'differential'. This fluidity of meanings can be usefully illuminated by Jacques Derrida, who coined the term '*différance*' to indicate the 'restless play within language that can not be fixed or pinned down for the purposes of conceptual definition' (Norris 1987: 15). For Derrida, meaning never arrives; it is always subject to semantic slippage and therefore remains out of grasp. In *footnotes* the collections of signs evident do not coincide in a clear, coherent manner; traces are suggested but never complete. Also, as the work is improvisatory, no meanings can be fixed as relationships between elements are constantly shifting.

Reading *footnotes* as a dance in which *Swan Lake* is absent yet present requires, through a Derridian perspective, that the ballet and the work *footnotes* are pursued beyond their lexical systems to the various sub-units or components in order to enter a chain of substitutions. As this chain cannot be satisfactorily completed, it becomes evident that in *footnotes* I am less interested in breaking through traditional, limited, readings of the ballet in order to offer yet another (closed) reading, and more interested in opening up possibilities. This places in doubt the notion of making *a* reading in the first place.

Evoking *Swan Lake* as an absent presence risks that, in becoming so absent, *Swan Lake* will not be recognisable at all, thereby mitigating what might be seen as necessary for a reworking to have efficacy. That is, the audience perhaps has to be able to perceive the subversion taking place in order to experience the pleasure of proliferating identities. This may well be the case. However, *footnotes*, as an installation that operates in between absence and presence, attempts to circumvent the difficulties of a parodic process and also to disrupt traditional feminist agendas which have operated in terms of binary judgements.[16] This in-between place perhaps lacks the dramatisation of political force and may seem too ambiguous to harbour a feminist mobilisation for change. However, as Homi Bhabha notes, in-between places can be productive places which shift forces and fixities (1995: 34). The in between, as animated by a marginal voice, such as my choreographic one, can be mobilised in order to rethink identity.

Open texts – enacting becomings

Footnotes is made of shifting fragments and multi-perspectives and is improvisatory. The work is made up of a spectrum of possibilities. The order and relationship between the elements in the work are not repeated or repeatable. Structured in the form of 'spontaneous determination' (to use Yvonne Rainer's term, in Banes 1995: 100), *footnotes* uses a combination of fixed elements that change in combination, predetermined options and free improvisation.

The work is intended to operate as an open text, the notion of which practises a concept developed by Barthes (1975). He argues that the open or writerly (*scriptible*) text encourages the reader to produce meanings, as opposed to the closed or readerly (*lisible*) text, which turns the reader into a consumer. To encourage 'scriptiblity' the installation is ever changing. In this context, therefore, by open text I mean a text in which the movement and the relationships between movement, video, sound and space alter from moment to moment throughout the performance, and from performance to performance. Operating around shifting relationships between media, no elements remain in the same relationship at any point, thereby leaving space for a viewer to create meanings.

Both the sound and the two video images are looped. The relationships between the sound and the video, and between the two videos, shift throughout the performance as each runs at a slightly different pace, the result being that, while images and sounds recur, the same combinations never do. The movement performed live is improvised, and the improvisations are formed around clusters of images. There are also ten slides of written text, any of which can be projected at any time. The selection of movement images and text, in relation to video images and sound, is not pre-determined but decided in the moment of performance. I also intercede to disrupt the fixity of the video image by shifting the location of the projection onto my body – effectively blocking the screen image and rearranging the space.

The live dance improvisation is the most open element of the work, and this is continuously shifting and goalless. The movement improvisations are conceived in 'image clusters' (to use a Skinner releasing term).[17] Images such as swan/woman, topography of the ballet body, pointe shoes, posing at the edges, whipping turns and moments of drowning guide but do not shape the improvisations. For example, the topography of the ballet body improvisation tends to, but does not always, take place standing on the stool. Shifting through the body, the internal sensations of realigning the body in accordance with the principles of ballet are juxtaposed with an opposite organisation of the body. As the body moves from pose to pose, the back elongates and pitches forward at the pelvis, one hip pushes out to the side and then rotates around. Both knees bend and the leg is turned in and out from the pelvis. An arm extends out to the side, reaching away from the centre of the body. Pose. The shoulder rotates; the arm drops and swings from the shoulder. Improvised movement such as this develops in the moment of enactment. As the body forms shifting textures and landscapes, the viewer is encouraged to focus on the detail of these landscapes, as no logical external composition ever occurs.

Letting go of the assurance of pre-choreographed work allows the focus to be placed on transformation. In *footnotes* the improvised dance promotes a constantly shifting identity, as each time a new image cluster is performed or revisited the identity of that image is determined anew. The work invites an alternative way of looking, a looking which focuses on the detail of moments and interconnections within moments, rather than the consideration of grand composition – for the grand composition is never complete. Through these transformation processes the identity of the body comes to be in constant flux, militating against fixity and singularity. The improvisations stage their own disappearance while also, in a Deleuzian sense, simultaneously becoming.

Sarah Rubidge suggests that the open work is a challenge to notions of identity and authorial integrity. The identity of a work, she argues, coheres around our ability to recognise its instantiations, the relative closeness to notated scores, the originating impulse, and the work's original form (2000: 205–6). She writes that, 'when individuating dance works, we rely on the identification of essential, … perceptible properties, that is, features which are observable in the presentational form across several performances' (ibid.: 208).

The 'identity and form of the open work', states Rubidge, 'is, more than another kind of work, constantly deferred, demonstrating what Andrew Benjamin (Benjamin 1994: 24) calls an "ontology of becoming"' (2000: 210). Benjamin, in his discussion of fine art, argues that, rather than a being-object, the object *for* interpretation is an aspect *of* interpretation, thereby redefining the art-object as a temporal matter. The ontological status of *all* works of art is such that they change over time; the work of art is a 'becoming-object'. The object is incorporated into the process of becoming in such a way that it comes to be evident that any work is subject to its own history, and the history of the world in which it is presented. This argument brings into the fine arts issues of provisional identity and absence of an 'original' object that have long been grappled with in the ephemeral art of dance.

Following Benjamin, Rubidge notes that:

> If this is so for any work it is even more so for the open work. An integral, even essential, part of the identity, the 'nature', of the open work *is* that flux, *is* the shift in form, *is* the work's 'becoming'.
>
> (Rubidge 2000: 211, emphasis in original)

As an open work, *footnotes* is a challenge to the ontology of invariance – a philosophical argument in which the essential nature of a phenomenon is fixed. This is an inherently unstable performance text. The work shouts of its lack of fixity, and, in its determination to remain uncapturable, refuses the structures of viewing which seek to pin it down and make it harden into myth.

This lack of fixity is somewhat ironic, for as a radical reworking *footnotes* is intimately intertwined with its source, a source that appears fixed, a source that might be called the 'original'. On the other hand, as an open text, it is formed in such a manner that no 'original' text is produced, no moment which can be said to be 'the work', the 'authentic' performance. This radical reworking of *Swan Lake* is thereby at odds with the ballet. *Swan Lake* has a clearly defined identity and is, *seemingly*, unchanging; *footnotes* challenges this assumption. The lack of boundaries and fluidity in *footnotes* reflects an oppositional stance to the *perception* of sameness and authorship of the source text.[18]

Footnotes is a work that enacts becoming. Only identifiable as it occurs, each image cluster has a life only at that very moment; each action, each becoming, is valued free from any end point. This is not a becoming of some being. Deleuze and Guattari's (1988) conceptualisation of becoming means doing away with the opposition between being and becoming. This involves destabilising patterns of organisation and suggests new possibilities for self-transformation.

Once the body has taken a pose, the fingers mark out time and then the body slowly crumbles out of its position: starting from the centre, the torso, then the shoulders and pelvis, knees and elbows cave in. The body moves from one position to another in a constant process of mutation, each position being realised out of the internal collapse of the previous one. Varying and changing without a pre-given purpose or goal, the enactment of becoming is revealed through time. But this enactment does not resolve or complete; rather, it continues in a state of flux. The body continues to form, dissolve and re-form, such that no formation is ever the complete form.

The video images also enact becomings. The camera often moves with, around or in opposition to the dancer, creating no single point of reference. These shift-ing, moving images are freed from an ordering point of view. The images cut from one place, one image, to another, creating a montage, and this montage is extended by the simultaneous layering of montages being made with live dance, text and sound. This montage effect is not reducible to each single image. Rather each movement, sound, text and video image transforms the whole, thereby creating new becomings.

Bodies in the act of becoming, and female bodies in particular, are then never complete; they are never finished. In *footnotes* the unfinished body, as it can never reach a point at which it can be fixed into a binary opposition, can fluctuate in between. The bodies which inhabit this open text imply that the body can be rein-vented, distorted, collaged, dismembered and fictionalised. *footnotes* operates counter to any 'authentic' or 'originary' notion of the body

Hybrid body – plural bodies – my body

The female body evoked in this work is hybrid and plural. The bodies in *footnotes* suggest a shifting fluid presence as I 'mutate' between animal and human forms and play out multiple identities, disrupting any sense of a coherent singular identity. The hybridity and plurality of bodies evoked resists the commodification of the body, as no single image is maintained, no one image exists. However, in what may seem like a contradiction, the body in *footnotes* is specific, marked and singular.

A repeated improvisation in *footnotes* explores and expands the image and concept of Odette – the queen of the swans. Odette is part bird and part woman. The improvisation evokes her as a hybrid being – a swan woman in constant mutation – a woman out of whom the bird seeps. She has wings, a twitching head and webbed feet. Working from an internal sensation, the improvisation evolves as a relationship between swan and human features which are embodied singularly. While the torso remains upright, the knees lift and the feet shift, taking long strides, creating awkward angles in the hips and knees. As the legs return to a more everyday alignment, the head makes a sharp turn to the side and then lifts upwards. The eyes are glazed. Deep from between the shoulder blades the shoulder reaches out to the side. There is a sense of a lost wing, a wing that tries to unfold, but instead an arm extends and a hand comes to the face in a very human gesture. Seen through the eyes of Deleuze and Guattari (1988), it can be said that she is a becoming-animal. By becoming hybrid she can perceive otherwise, as she has the potential to create lines of flight. Freed from the 'human', she suggests the possibility of the 'transversal'. Transversal becomings, for Deleuze and Guattari, are the key to the openness of life. Through the hybrid improvisation there is not an attempt to become a swan, or even to behave like a swan. Rather, through constant transformation there is a sense of feeling a swan's movement. The actions are not directed towards repetition or replication, rather each action is performed without a pre-determined end. Indeed, the movement is such that what is 'the action' and what is 'the transformation' become indistinct. Through this becoming, the multiple, mutating swan woman asserts intersections that expand perceptions.

This recurring body is not quite whole. Hybrids are indistinct and cannot be easily classified. The hybrid disrupts the boundaries between the human and the animal, the natural and the constructed. Embodying the ambiguous feelings we have towards our own bodies, they tantalisingly suggest the power and strength of different animals – but at the same time also a lack or absence in the human body. In its relationship to animal bodies, the hybrid body flaunts classical views of the body. For the hybrid body is not ordered and harmonious but real and fleshy. It is often a grotesque body – it is exaggerated, inflated and embellished in unpredictable and fanciful ways. In the ballet, however, Odette's ambiguous, even subversive, potential as a bird woman is controlled by the coded geometry of the ballet vocabulary. She is held within the classical view of the body, and the swan side of her nature is presented as a torturous pain.

The magic of the hybrid has often also been associated with the healer or the shaman who can transmute himself/herself and draw on animal forces. However, in *Swan Lake* Odette has no such power. This time it is the narrative that thwarts the subversive potential. She has been transformed, and is controlled by, the evil Rothbart. Her transformation between swan and woman takes place within set hours of the night over which Odette has no control. The swan form is represented as a tragic oppression.

Part human, part bird, the swan woman also connects to many such hybrids in folklore and mythology. Marina Warner (1995) writes that bird features, such as webbed feet and the long beak, have denoted female power and deviancy. For example, the deathly sirens were, in the classical tradition, bird-bodied. These hybrid women were in addition highly sexual creatures who defied the 'natural' order. In *footnotes* the hybrid swan woman becomes a phenomenon of endless transformation. She is continuously mutating in such a way that the bird and the woman are simultaneously evident, making manifest, and extending, the subversive (but unexplored) hybrid potential of the ballet swan woman, Odette. In line with mythic readings of bird women, she also embodies an erotic quality, and I will return to this later. The improvisation emphasises that bodies only exist in a process of constant transformation, for, as Cathy Griggers notes, 'there are only hybrid bodies, moving bodies, migrant bodies, becoming bodies' (1994: 128). Through improvisation and hybridity, *footnotes* avoids notions of essentialism and fixity, recognising that identities are heterogeneous and diverse.

To add to these already complex embodiments there are also multiple fragmentary bodies – screen bodies, live bodies and shadow bodies – extending the hybrid body into a plurality of interconnected bodies (for one dancer performs all the roles) which are in constant states of becoming. These interconnected pluralities, which the ballet's dual swan women already suggest, indicate that unity is an illusion. Risking the accusation of reinforcing binaries between women, and without wishing to suggest a schizophrenic body, *footnotes* incorporates a multiplicity of bodies: live and recorded, ballerina and showgirl, functional and danced, shadow and real. These various bodies blur boundaries and confound expectations.

These multiple bodies are dispersed across different elements of the installation. The video images incorporate two dancing girls – one dressed in tutu and pointe shoes, the other dressed in pink boa and silver sequins. Another embodiment on the screen is the naked body: unadorned, a woman's body comes in and out of focus. In the live performance two other bodies are enacted: the 'dancerly' performative body and the everyday functional body. These two bodies are marked through the usage of the body. The 'dancerly' body performs extraordinary movements – complex turns, usual shifts of weight, off-centre poses. This body's organisation is rearranged between improvisations so that, while clearly a single body, it can at any point enact a transformation. This 'dancerly' body also takes up movement images from the screen bodies, in an echo or precursor of the screen bodies; she poses like the pink show girl and totters like the ballet body – further blurring identities. The functional body is carried in a casual fashion: she walks in a matter of fact manner and sits slightly stooped in order to operate the computer mouse. This body constantly cuts into the 'dancerly' body's actions, asserting its presence and thwarting any continuous engagement of fantasy.

The interaction between bodies in this dance of absent presences blurs the dualisms of the material body/immaterial mind and visibility/invisibility. The shadow body, which is cast onto the screen when the live dancing body intercepts the light of the video projector, marks itself into the video image. This dark, hard-lined body cuts into the video, creating gaps in the image. The shadow image is ironically perhaps the most present of the various bodies inscribed throughout *footnotes*. It appears manifest, for it is clearly marked but it is also only a semblance, a reflection which requires a real presence to be formed and has no substantive form of its own. The shadow creates absence yet requires a presence as an inseparable companion. In these ways the shadow/live body is absent and present, visible and invisible. Reflecting current feminist thought, these plural bodies attest to the impossibility of viewing or conceptualising 'the' body, as bodies are revealed to be unstable and fleeting (see, for example, Riley, Grosz and Butler, in Price and Shildrick 1999).

While anti-essentialist thinking has usefully warned against an identification of woman with the body, making clear that 'the body' cannot be conceived as a pre-given entity, for there is no body which has not already been marked by (male) discourse, this has also led to a position in which there is almost no body, no experience of the body at all. The plurality of bodies in current discourse (feminist and otherwise), and the becoming bodies of Deleuze and Guattari, which *footnotes* conceptually reflects, risks making the body disappear altogether. Through these lenses it often appears that the day-to-day real body, real person, is absent.

However, in *footnotes* there is an actual 'real' body, an actual 'real' person in the space, and this body has a history. This body is not fixed or biologically essentialist. Gatens argues that by granting the body a history it may become possible to locate experiences and restrictions on and of the body without resorting to biological essentialism (1999: 228). The body in *footnotes*, my body, is present, is specific. It is a white, middle-class, English body – a body marked by the practices of release-based dance, modern dance and ballet. This body is currently slim and has experienced injury, pregnancy and breast-feeding. It also experiences sitting for hours in front of a computer screen, driving long distances, standing in front of people in classroom situations and performing.

Through a self-reflexive process I experience this body, and reciprocally my experiences are shaped by it. As Trinh T. Minh-ha so succinctly puts it, 'we do not *have* bodies, we *are* bodies' (Minh-ha 1999: 258, emphasis in original). My corporeal experiences are not necessarily explicit in *footnotes* (although the audience is made aware of the 'academic' body and the 'dancerly' body, and these are contextualised via the projected text as working bodies); however, the realness of the body and its close proximity allow the viewer to see bodily scarrings and stretch marks, removing any illusion of an ideal unmarked body.

Breaking the gaze – inscribing a haptic presence

The disciplining structure of the gaze and the subsequent visual objectification of the ballerina is, I have suggested, examined and undermined through parodic overdisplay by Susan Foster in *The Ballerina's Phallic Pointe*. Here, by emphasising the kinaesthetic, and the sense of touch through a haptic system, the audience–performer relationship is also reconceived.

Deleuze and Guattari's concept of haptic vision distinguishes between haptic and optical space. Haptic space uses close vision, while optical space requires long-distance vision. This distinction usefully reflects the different viewing experiences of *footnotes* (close vision – haptic) and a conventional *Swan Lake* (long distance – optical). *Swan Lake*, as a ballet performed behind a proscenium arch, reflects and perpetuates the primacy of the visual within Western culture as noted in relation to Foster's reworking. The drive to find a more kinetic mode of viewing is particularly relevant in the light of this. *footnotes* asserts a different sense, a different mode of visuality and more tactile representation, and as such implicitly positions itself contrary to *Swan Lake*. This is important for a feminist reworking, for 'the critique of visual mastery', as Marks notes, 'speaks from an awareness about the deathful and truly imperialist potential of vision' (Marks 1998: 347).

The notion of a haptic system, a system in which we experience bodily rather than visually, writes Jennifer Fisher, comprises 'the tactile, kinaesthetic, and proprioceptive functions'. This describes 'aspects of engagement that are qualitatively distinct from the capabilities of the visual sense' (Fisher 1997: 6). Functioning by contiguity and touch, the haptic sense is most resonant in the perception of weight, balance, pressure, temperature, space and presence. Fisher notes that early research on haptic perception considered the haptic sense as a proximal sense – a sense which required the actual contact with, or use of, the body (ibid.). However, haptic perception is not totally discrete from visual perception. A haptic system of visuality asserts that the eyes function like organs of touch and, as such, the viewer's body becomes more obviously involved with the process of seeing. Haptic perception accounts for the way we experience touch both on the surface and inside our bodies.

In *footnotes* the installation is arranged in such a manner that the process of seeing is brought to the fore. The viewer has to make choices about which angle to look from, where and how to locate their own body – whether to sit, stand or lie – whether to look at the live, screen or shadow body. How the viewer's eye/body shifts over the video image/live presence becomes multi-sensorial rather than solely visual, similar to the processes of haptic preception. As Laura U. Marks writes, in an essay entitled 'Video haptics and erotics', the haptic video 'does not invite identification with a figure so much as it encourages a bodily relationship between the viewer and the video image' (1998: 332). Haptic images are, she suggests, textured and emphasise touch.

Footnotes isolates touch from narrative. As a feature of the haptic, this dissociation of touch and narrative needs to be differentiated from the alienation of visual presence and storyline discussed by Mulvey. In Mulvey the presence of woman, connoting a to-be-looked-at-ness, 'tends to work against the development of a story line, to freeze the flow of action in moments of erotic contemplation' (2001: 188). In *footnotes* the tactile body (live and video) evokes identification with touch itself, surpassing any identification with character. The sense of touch evoked by the fragmented and textured body becomes the narrative, becomes the subject itself.

The viewer of *footnotes* is distanced from any external narrative and from identification with character in a number of ways. Long periods of the video are given over to the creation of textures rather than characters, and when figures do appear the video constantly shifts in and out of focus, or becomes so close that a figure can no longer be identified; also as characters they are not contextualised or developed. The live presence shifts between locations and improvisations in seemingly random ways such that no linear narrative develops. The narrative of the source text *Swan Lake* is only ever evoked as a fictive presence, never as an identifiable force. Images, text and live bodies are fragmented and never coalesce. In this work the viewer interacts with the creation of meaning rather than entering into an illusory fantasy.

The images on screen in *footnotes* are a flow of tactile impressions. In extended sections, images of feathers falling, water rippling and shifting colour emphasise the experience of texture. Close-up pink images slowly cross-fade between one texture and another. The actual objects are never made clear. Rather, the focus is upon the depth of colour, the subtle changes in tone and the materiality of the image. The falling feathers are filmed such that no location is evident: they fall and drift across the screen. As the downy feathers pile up from the base of the screens they form a white mass, and the screen's surfaces appear to change – taking on a more dense quality.

These textures are put alongside those of the woman dancing in a white tutu, in a pink feathered 'show girl' costume, and naked. Images dissolve and resolve in layers and are textured in a number of ways. Through close-up shots the skin becomes a landscape, and the shifting lens, which skims across the body, brings the images in and out of focus. Also the body has been digitised, given a pixelated quality, which protects the body from the viewer's gaze, obscuring the video image. In addition, the effect of being projected onto translucent plastic and fabric screens gives the images a ghost-like quality. The images, as they are not fixed within the dense frame of television, become floating traces. They are, at once, present and absent – present in that they can be clearly seen but absent due to their fictive status; the images are disembodied plays of light. The traces offer no resistance as bodies pass through them, but they also mark their presence on the surface of the skin.

A haptic visuality 'implies making oneself vulnerable to the image, reversing the relation of mastery that characterises optical viewing' (Marks 1998: 341). In *footnotes* the viewer is encouraged to make herself/himself 'vulnerable' on account of not only the video image but also the context of that image. Images cannot be viewed safely from one's seat as the space is made to be walked around. The viewer may at any point also be the viewed. The presence of the live body also provides the potential that the 'image' might at any point 'look back'.

The large projected images which leak past the screens also implicate the viewer, for the textured screen images are cast onto the viewer as she/he walks around the space. Conversely the viewer also becomes part of the video image as she/he casts shadows onto the screens. These interactions are such that the viewer becomes 'commingled' with the image. As Deleuze and Guattari write:

The first aspect of the haptic, smooth space of close vision is that its orientations, landmarks, and linkages are in continuous variation ... Contrary to what is sometimes said, one never sees from a distance in a space of this kind, nor does one see it from a distance; one is never 'in front of', any more than one is 'in' (one is 'on' ...).

(1988: 493)

Thus in *footnotes* the watcher–watched relationship of the audience and performer is altered and implicitly critiqued.

Eroticism and the politics of touch

As noted at the start of this chapter, Emilyn Claid (2002) suggests that it is the interplay between fixed points that forms the seductive relations established between the viewer and the performer in performance. She writes that the 'oscillation between the real body of the performer and her/his illusive surface image is the trigger for seductive relations between performer and spectator' (Claid 2002: 2). Just such oscillations exist in *footnotes* as I shift from the performative illusory presentations in the extended dance improvisations to the functional, and from an internal gaze which allows the viewer's eyes to travel over me to a gaze which interacts and 'plays' with the viewer.

In *footnotes* the ideal relationship between the viewer and the performer/video is one of mutuality. The viewer is encouraged to lose her/his sense of proportion as the eyes, as organs of touch, caress and are caressed by the live body/video image: *footnotes* thereby evokes an erotic relationship. As Marks writes, 'haptic images are erotic regardless of their content, because they construct an intersubjective relationship between beholder and image' (Marks 1998: 341). She argues further that 'haptics move eroticism from the site of what is represented to the surface of image' (ibid.), eroticism arising from the *way* of looking rather than the images themselves. In *footnotes*, however, the way of looking *and* the images themselves might be said to be erotic. The body is presented naked and in semi-translucent, revealing clothing and movements have a sinuous sensuality. While *footnotes* is not graphically sexual and its purpose is not to incite arousal, it does evoke a desiring, desired body.

The debates about the boundaries and relative efficacy or commodification of erotic and pornographic representations of women are beyond the remit of this discussion, but it is useful to consider the different modes of seeing evident in pornography as opposed to *footnotes*.[19] Pornography suggests the visual inscription of the orgasmic body and the viewer's visual mastery of the body. The limited visibility of the body in *footnotes* – the video effects and shots, the textures upon the body, the ghostly rendition of the body as projected on a translucent screen and the body as hybrid – attempts to undermine the viewer's mastery and hinder sexual gratification. The body is not generally 'put on display', and when it is, such as when posed on the stool, it is not posed but changing and mutable. The body is not ever fully in view (as while the live body can be fully seen it is never completed and always in between), therefore the viewer, in order to complete the process of viewing, has to become involved in that process. This involvement is self-aware and implicates the onlooker, for haptics 'is based more upon interaction than voyeurism, haptic visuality is erotic' (Marks 1998: 342).

The image caresses the viewer as the viewer's body becomes involved in the process of seeing. The physical and erotic involvement of the viewer is not denied. Rather, as Ramsay Burt argues, 'through our visceral response to performance, dance teaches us about the body, defining and in some cases contesting its socially constructed limits' (2001: 220). The pleasure of touch provides another level of delight as it deprivileges the visual, emphasising the corporeal. This pleasure, when doubled with sensuous images, multiplies the erotic contact with the viewer.

This erotic haptic body, with its emphasis on surfaces and touching, temptingly relates to Irigaray's female tactile body. Irigaray's woman 'has sex organs more or less everywhere. She finds pleasure almost everywhere … the geography of her pleasure is far more diversified, more multiple in its differences, more complex, more subtle, than is commonly imagined' (1985b: 28). The body described by Irigaray exists in the constant touching of surfaces. It is a fluid body and a sexually female body with vagina, vaginal lips, and breasts. As its surfaces rub, this body blurs boundaries and distinctions.

A close-up shot of a naked body: a breast, an arm, and a shoulder, perhaps. Indistinct and fragmented, the angles of the camera on the body are difficult to discern, disrupting the viewer's perspective. As the camera shifts even closer to the body, the screen is filled with moving skin, muscle and bone. The texture of the skin and the plays of light and shadow on the body become the focus. The camera and the body are in motion, meaning that few of the images become clearly defined. Fleeting moments reveal folds of flesh, legs brushing together, the crease of an armpit and a hand touching the neck. The body slowly becomes more recognisable as hands hold feet and, in a kneeling position, rest on the top of the thighs. Following an image of the body rolling across the screen is a close-up of the face. And lastly, from a close-up shot of breasts, the camera pulls back, revealing the fully naked body, standing in an everyday pose. The hands are on the hips, only moving to rub the neck and brush hair back behind the ears. This section of video presents a fluid body full of touching surfaces as the body folds and creases.

The use of a semi-clad/naked erotic body is dangerous for the politically motivated artist. For while the naked and semi-naked body in *footnotes* suggest a pleasure in and of the body, it is important to ask: Whose pleasure is this? And, How is that pleasure viewed? The pleasure in and of the body evident in *footnotes* is unlike the topography of the ballet body. *Swan Lake* suggests sexual union and the dancer's intimate touch, but the ballet's narrative and the codification of the form veils these erotic possibilities. In *footnotes*, however, the body becomes a site of pleasure, the body is desiring and desired, for as subject and object it at once resists and invites the viewer's objectification.

Perhaps the most overtly erotic section of *footnotes* is found during a repeated collection of images in the video which focus on the mouth and feet and use costumes as fetishised objects. In the foreground lie a pair of pink, somewhat worn-out pointe shoes. I am to the back of the image, naked. Dipping my head into the white tutu in front of me, I crawl forward, with the tutu casually hanging at my waist. Reaching forward, I grasp the pointe shoes in my mouth, shaking them from side to side. The fetishistic treatment of the pointe shoe reflects stories of Russian balletomanes who held a banquet at which the main course was a dish including one of Marie Taglioni's used ballet shoes. More generally, it also refers to the image of the dancer *per se* who has become the site of fetishist speculation.

The fetishist and naked images on the screen are juxtaposed with the live presence and projected text. Through the live dance I intersect with the video image. I stand on the stool with my hands on my hips (a stance that also appears on the video screens). While standing in this pose I look about the space and view the viewers. At times I catch the eye of a viewer, and their 'safe' viewing is disturbed. At another point I sit in front of the projector, casting the image directly onto my body and effectively blocking the screen while also being marked by my own image. I become both seer and seen, entering into a network of relationships. I am watched while I view myself on screen, while I also watch the viewers of my viewing! In this there is a constant emphasis on my bodily presence, and in this dual role there is an inherent refusal to give up the object status while at the same time claiming the viewing subject position. This has the potential to make both positions unstable.

As a work which recalls *Swan Lake* as an absent presence, *footnotes* operates in the margins, evoking never fully realised resonances in such a manner that 'meanings' disseminate and drift. The relationships between this reworking and *Swan Lake* are constantly deferred and the conjunctions between the elements within the work (movement, sound, video and projected text) are constantly shifting. This slippage, I have suggested, makes it difficult to read *footnotes* and indeed places into doubt the possibility of making *a* reading in the first place, creating instead an ambiguous text in which multiple and contradictory possibilities exist. Using improvisational structures within a changing landscape of video projections and sound emphasises transformation and provisionality in a manner that relates to concepts of becoming. I have argued that the recurring improvisational dance that explores the image of Odette as a hybrid swan/woman is particularly potent as, by becoming animal, she has the potential to create other lines of flight. This is an important challenge to previous constructions of woman as coherent and singular, for as a hybrid, she embodies multiple identities. However, *footnotes* also emanates from a specific body – that is, my body. This 'real' body, 'real' person, problematises the instability of feminist/poststructuralist bodies and emphasises the risk of losing the body altogether within discourse.

The haptic form of *footnotes* also problematises the structures of optical, erotic viewing. In opposition to the long-distance vision of proscenium arch stages – commonly the viewing arena for ballet – the installation format of *footnotes* implicates the viewer such that she/he becomes part of the work and is engaged in a seductive relationship with me as the performer. Evoking a tactile and embodied response rather than an optical one, *footnotes* enables the illusion of reality to be challenged and pushes the viewer back to the surface of the image, militating against identification, narrative and legibility. The representation of the nude body and the erotic images in this work operate as a feminist strategy rather than an essentially feminine form. Given the repression of the erotic in the ballet *Swan Lake*, perhaps the embodiment of it in *footnotes*, while risky, implies a critique, and alleges a transformation. The erotic properties also connect the swan woman to other bird women – to hybrids that have a more sexual nature. As such she becomes a deviant subversive creature, countering the more conventional, fragile image of her predecessors.

Conclusion

These reworkings of *Swan Lake* and *Giselle* embody feminisms from the 1980s to early 2000s. Foster's critique is explicit as she unwraps and demythologises the ballet. Recontextualising and critiquing her sources, she creates hybrid texts that are an explicit example of the shift in art towards the self-referential and reflects postmodern/poststructualist attitudes towards the past. Participating in changing concepts of the body, Foster takes the ballet on through parody in an overtly performative manner. She embodies the roles of Myrtha, Giselle, Albrecht, Odette and Odile to critique the ballet, and through humour and irony comments upon the ballet and the frames through which it is observed and analysed.

Whereas I am not as explicit in my feminist agendas, *footnotes* operates ambiguously, crossing binary frames to suggest a feminist sensibility without making overt statements. Through imagination and reinvention, this ambiguity embodies crucial questions about bodies and their representation, visuality and the erotic, giving rise to a politics of desire in which the female body can be refashioned in the flux of identities that speak in plural styles.

Participating in feminist discourse, these reworkings enable us to dismantle the fixed architecture of canonical discourse, for they enter into and change canonical ballets, radically reinscribing them rather than endorsing the ideologies of the source texts. For these feminist reworkings reconstitute the canon – becoming vehicles for alternative values and newly refigured bodies.

Chapter 4

Princely revisions
Stillness, excess and queerness

'[Q]ueer' represents, among other things, an aggressive impulse of generalization;
it rejects a minoritizing logic of toleration or simple political interest-representation
in favor of a more thorough resistance to regimes of the normal ... For both
academics and activists, 'queer' gets a critical edge by defining itself against the
normal rather than the heterosexual, and normal includes normal business in
the academy.

(Warner 1993: xxvi)

Masculinities, the male dancer and reworkings

In line with Warner's call for a 'thorough resistance to regimes of the normal', the
reworkings of *Swan Lake* by Javier de Frutos and Raimund Hoghe, the focus of
this chapter, work to reveal the hegemony of the canon – querying and queering
the ballet. As concepts of masculinity, sexuality and the male dancer are intertwined, and the ways in which they impress on each other are investigated, the
reworkings by de Frutos and Hoghe reveal variously refigured male bodies, masculinities and sexual identities. Marked by internal contradictions and historical
disruptions, these reworkings present images of men that have the potential radically to reconfigure the status quo, for the borders have been breached and the
masking cloak removed.

By de-emphasising conventional choreographic forms (as evident in both ballet
and modern dance), Hoghe and de Frutos bring attention to the materiality of the
body. For these two choreographers, in contrast to the disembodied ideals embedded in *Swan Lake*, locate the materiality of the body, with its history and experiences, identity and flesh, fully intact. Using their own (queer) male bodies they
bring to the fore the specificity of bodies, and the hierarchical value placed upon
differing bodies, by locating the idiosyncratic and non-normative at the centre.
This, in tandem with the spectre of the feminised theatrical space that they
occupy, troubles the foundations of masculinity.

Echoing the plurality of femininities that are now the subject of feminisms,
masculinity, once unquestioned and invisible, has given way to masculinities.

Dance has participated in this revolution, providing a place in which that which had previously appeared to be highly differentiated and fixed can become acknowledged and recognised as fluid. This awareness of pluralities of genders and sexualities is exemplified in dance scholarship by Jane Desmond's book *Dancing Desires* (2001). In this edited collection Desmond suggest that: 'Just as earlier work in dance studies during the 1980s and 1990s revised dance history by bringing to bear the analytic tools of feminist theory and critical race studies, so too it must be transformed again by making sexuality a central component of critical analyses' (2001: 5).

Reworkings – as forms of critical praxis – have provided a site for shifts in the perception and representation of bodies to occur, as, by the default of repetition but with significant difference, masculinity (singular) has proliferated in these dances. This proliferation is not straightforward, however, or even necessarily 'straight', for embedded within ballet and the dances that rework them are complex cultural scripts of masculinity encompassing both normative representations and non-normative associations. It is also clear that, as in everyday contexts, not all masculinities are necessarily equally valued.

While acknowledging that normative scripts of masculinity (what men 'ought' to be) are historically and culturally specific, and thereby not fixed, current normative or hegemonic scripts of masculinity in European and American contexts are often found in media studies in discussions of John Wayne's 'shoot-out' American westerns, or of movie stars in related genres such as thrillers or war movies (see, for example, Donald 2004 and Lehman 2001). These visible bearers of masculinity may or may not reflect the reality of specific lives and identities, yet that which is culturally dominant in society maintains hegemony. So while normative definitions are what men must measure up to in order to be counted as men, Connell asks: 'What is "normative" about a norm hardly anyone meets?' (2004: 33). He goes on to argue that, while few men may 'measure up', the majority of men 'gain from its hegemony, since they benefit from the patriarchal dividend' (ibid.: 40).

Significantly masculinity is most often, and most resolutely, denoted as 'not femininity' – thereby it becomes known through opposition and via the refusal to embrace female 'otherness'. In this definition 'masculinity is the unmarked term, the place of symbolic authority. The phallus is master-signifier, and femininity is symbolically defined by lack' (Connell 2004: 33). Also discussing definitions of masculinity, Jeffrey Weeks writes, 'masculinity or the male identity is achieved by the constant process of warding off threats to it. It is precariously achieved by the rejection of femininity and homosexuality' (Weeks 1985: 190). As (hetero)sexuality has been one of the central facets of male identity, gay male identities are one of the places in which the authority of normative scripts is being challenged and rewritten. Gay identities offer counter-expressions of masculine performance that bring into question the naturalness of gender division as standards of gender become undermined and contested. Yet the disruptive power of homosexual identities is also problematic, for homosexual men have historically been too easy to dismiss as 'other then male', as blurred with femininity, and thereby rendered harmless. As Connell notes:

> Oppression positions homosexual masculinities at the bottom of the gender hierarchy among men. Gayness, in patriarchal ideology, is the repository of whatever is symbolically expelled from hegemonic masculinity. ... Hence, from the point of view of hegemonic masculinity, gayness is easily assimilated to femininity.
>
> (Connell 2004: 40)

This 'danger', this blurring with femininity, has meant that dance has been a complex site for men, for it requires them to occupy, and risk being tainted by, the feminised space that is the theatrical stage. To explain further, theatricality and, specifically, dance are overly determined sites of the feminine. These sites require a display of the body and a submission to the spectator's gaze, in opposition to the 'ideal' model of masculinity. Thereby the theatrical stage threatens to emasculate those men who enter. As Amelia Jones writes, theatricality itself 'suggests the participant in the spectacle of theatre is feminised, democratised, and uneducated ("idiotic") – and thus definitely opposed to the refined, firmly "erect" masculine elite of high culture' (Jones 1998: 111). In Western phallocentric culture men are not 'allowed' to be openly vulnerable or submissive. Further, patriarchal constructs insinuate that the expressivity of men dancing signifies femininity, and, as femininity is submissive, men dancing may disrupt 'the fragile erection of phallic significance' (Claid 2006: 170). This for men is both the promise and the danger of dance.

As if to counter any suggestion of deviancy, Classical and Romantic ballets tend to emphasise a stereotypical image of men that reinforces patriarchal ideologies. For, as Susan Foster notes, ballet has been 'partially salvaged [from homosexual associations] through references to chivalric codes and aristocratic comportment' (Foster 2001: 150). In Petipa's ballets, for instance, narratives tend to be told from the lead male character's perspective and to focus on heterosexual partnering – conforming to what Sally Banes has called the 'marriage plot' (1998: 5) (as discussed in chapter 2). Typical features of a male dancer's style, in line with hegemonic norms of masculinity, involve engulfing space and performing large spectacular jumps, marking out the male as virile and authoritative, in direct contrast to the female. While of course on close inspection it is quite possible to see nuances in the choreographies that suggest less homogeneous images of men in the ballet (not the least of which is the knowledge that many male roles within Romantic ballets were originally performed by women *en travesti*), overall Classical and Romantic ballet celebrates difference between men and women in clear sexual divisions of labour.

In contrast, under Diaghilev, ballet became 'a form that in effect created and supported the idea of the artistic homosexual man and defined a homosexual aesthetic sensibility' (Burt 2001: 214), shifting conceptions of artistic subjectivity. In lavish displays Diaghilev created closeted yet acceptable gay male ballets by linking genius and homosexuality.[1] As such, ballet has come to encompass mythologised and hegemonic images of masculinity, interlaced with more multifaceted yet restricted representations of men, placed alongside closeted homosexual erotics. As Foster notes, dance has been 'one of the most remarkably open closets of any profession' (Foster 2001:199). Although it attracts a gay audience and is a profession for a significant number of gay dancers/choreographers, theatre dance has rarely been explicitly homoerotic, for the stage has remained, until more recently, firmly closeted. While, as in Nijinsky's ballets, some dances have been double coded (embodying (homo)erotic images for those who cared to look), dances such as *Swan Lake* by Bourne have revealed with 'astonishing clarity just how little sexual desire, much less homosexual desire, the modern dance has ever staged' (ibid.: 149) (see chapter 2).

However, since the 1960s, and increasingly to the present, unequivocally queer dance works have appeared (Burt 2001). Sexuality is now often used in productive ambiguity or explicit subversion to challenge normative masculinity, presenting diverse masculinities and sexualities on the stage. On account of the invisibility of queerness, however, this is a difficult process, for while, as I discussed in chapter 2, there are possibilities (and dangers) in drag, the gay man who desires to express his sexual otherness without recourse to female impersonation can do so only through complex systems of signification (Claid 1998: 121). Queering the ballet and the canon has involved framing dance and sexuality in terms of desire, power and pleasure. Paying particular attention to these intersecting areas, queer choreographers, such as the ones discussed here, have sought to tease out underlying structures and meaning-making mechanisms. Queering canonical ballets opens the possibility for the public staging of desire and pleasure that exceeds normative models, giving rise to transgressive acts.

Over ten years ago Eve Sedgwick traced the changing meanings of the word 'queer' in 'Queer and now' and in doing so offered an embracing understanding of its contemporary possibilities:

> 'Queer' can refer to: the open mesh of possibilities, gaps, overlaps, dissonances and resonances, lapses and excesses of meaning when the constituent elements of anyone's gender, of anyone's sexuality, are made (or *can't* be made) to signify monolithically.
>
> (Sedgwick 1993: 8)

While her work grows out of gay and lesbian studies, Sedgwick marks out a territory for queerness that is also distinct from those studies. She points towards diverse and shifting practices, emphasising the disruptive, the fractured and the contingent, in resistance to the 'norm', that is, to hegemonic institutions and the practices of heterosexuality. Expressing queerness in this way, Sedgwick echoes Michel Foucault's (1980) call for a general economy of pleasure not based on sexual norms, highlighting a world of instabilities. And instability is at the heart of queerness.

More recently dance scholars have begun to address the ways in which dancing bodies might intersect with queer commentary, for, as Desmond writes, 'queer commentary can do the epistemological work of revealing the historical contingency of heterosexuality. It can expose heterosexuality as an unmarked yet hegemonic category of social formation, one intricately and inextricably linked to other modes of social differentiation, including race, gender, and nationality' (2001: 11).

Echoing this approach, the reworkings of Hoghe and de Frutos are discussed in terms of the ways in which they embody queerness at an intersection with other atypical bodily markers, promoting kinaesthetics of sexuality and disjuncture. Through the intersections between the process of reworking, queerness and the (non-normative 'disabled') body of Hoghe and the (excessive) body of de Frutos, they challenge the very concept of dance and what it is to be a dancer. For these two dancers/dance-makers undermine the hegemony of the canon – intersecting with, and queering, the gendered codes of ballet in complex ways: they point backwards towards mythical norms of authoritative masculinity, tussle variously with the feminisation of the theatrical space and slide forward towards the destabilisation of norms, for here the male body, so often unproblematically unmarked, is revealed and unmasked. Through the project of reworking Hoghe and de Frutos proliferate masculinities, queering the *Swan Lake* of convention, for, as Burt notes, 'queerness is characterized by a determined resistance to regimes of the normal' (Burt 2001: 215).

Javier de Frutos and *The Hypochondriac Bird* (1998)

Strains of Hawaiian folk music are playing. The brightly lit stage is surrounded by a glowing blue ridge – like the edges of an inflatable pool. Upstage, in the far left corner, de Frutos lies on top of a splayed Jamie Watton. In time with the grating repeats of music – like a stuck record – de Frutos presses his pelvis onto Watton's raised buttocks. This simulated sex, this 'dry humping', hints at the depiction of the playful yet uncompromisingly painful homosexual relationship that de Frutos stages in *The Hypochondriac Bird* (1998).

Based in the UK, the Venezuelan dancer, Javier de Frutos studied at the London School of Contemporary Dance and at the Merce Cunningham studio with Barbara Mahler and Sara Rudner in New York. He performed with the Laura Dean Dancers and Musicians from 1989, then returned to London in 1994 establishing the Javier de Frutos Dance Company, for which he created twenty-four pieces, including *Grass*, which won a South Bank Show award – one accolade among the many his choreographies have received. He has also created works for a diverse range of companies, including the Rotterdam Dance Group, Ballet Shindowski, the Rambert Dance Company, the Royal New Zealand Ballet and Candoco and is currently artistic director of the Phoenix Dance Theatre.

His choreography is notable for its evocative and passionate theatricality, his direct defiance of norms and his nude performances. De Frutos is, writes Roger

Plate 13   The Hypochondriac Bird (1998) by Javier de Frutos

Photographer: Chris Nash

Salas (2000), 'a born confrontationalist, a militant with a lot to say as one who uses nudity as a slap in the face, not just a provocation.' Indeed it was his performances in the nude and his idiosyncratic movement style that brought de Frutos to public attention in the UK, with works such as *Transatlantic* (1996), *Carnal Glory* (1996) and *Grass* (1997). *Carnal Glory* recalls Vaslav Nijinsky's fawn from *l'Apres-midi d'un faune*, recovering Nijinsky's celebrated body to reinsert a gay body into dance history. The dark *Grass* begins as a dance of courtships that descends into an emotional and gruelling duet. With blood smeared around their mouths and anuses the dancers fuck each other to death. De Frutos's dances are full of torment, brutality and passion, whilst also revealing a fascination for history and the instincts of a showman.

The Hypochondriac Bird (or *Bird* for short, as I shall refer to the piece) was commissioned for the Expo '98 Festival in Lisbon, whose organisers asked that de Frutos consider water in his choreography.[2] In response de Frutos created a duet for himself and Jamie Watton in which references to water and oceans become embodied in the colours and textures of work as a context for an exploration of pleasure, play and coupling between the two men. De Frutos engages the audience through his play with masculine and feminine desire, consciously counteracting notions of union and transcendence from sexual desire (Claid 1998: 32), for in *Bird* he presents a very 'real', explicit, sexuality.

Bird is structured in two distinct halves and ends with a coda. The first half – the foreplay – enacts (manipulative) flirtations and shifts across a frivolous surface to reveal the complex relationship that exists beneath that surface. It is played out in a series of associated sequences – rather than developing in a logical or coherent manner – in which de Frutos variously seeks to entice and compel Watton to enter his sexual games. The second half – the sexual intercourse – is a dark and intense enactment of lovemaking. Here the movements are continuous, as one roll, fall or embrace tumbles seamlessly out of the previous ones.

The Hawaiian music, to which the opening images of 'dry humping' (described above), alongside rippling, swan-like arm gestures, are performed, is followed by chords from Tchaikovsky's score. De Frutos and Watton rise up from the floor and hold hands. Their heads twitch, and their torsos pulsate, as they dance out their conflict and desire. This sequence becomes progressively more agitated until de Frutos turns on Watton and, with his protruding chest, begins to push him to the floor. Watton repeatedly falls backwards, returning to his feet, his body jerking and shuddering – only to be pushed again.

Watton continues to be the focus of de Frutos's manipulations as, in the next sequence, performed to the music of *Swan Lake* played as if through a telephone, de Frutos undoes Watton's trouser zipper and mincingly places his hand inside. Curving and rotating in his torso while fluttering his fingers and making repeated prancing steps, de Frutos lifts his knee and rotates in his hip socket. Later in this same sequence he performs a series of small beats with his lifted foot, in a playful mimic of Odette's shimmering actions.

Having moved to a different spot on the stage, de Frutos reaches for Watton's crotch again. This time Watton flicks his hand away and pulls his pelvis back. De Frutos repeats his attempt until, at a sharp change in the music, Watton's hand goes to de Frutos's neck, and de Frutos jumps up and down – feet flexing. Like a sulking child he beats at Watton's chest with his fists, gesticulates his frustration, and beats his chest again. Watton remains impassive throughout, aloof and determinedly unaffected by his partner's antics.

As the evocative music of Odette and Seigfried's adagio begins, de Frutos stages a dance of kisses. Again Watton stands unresponsively, allowing his body to be touched and manipulated, for de Frutos rotates his head in order to place a kiss on his lips, ears, neck and arms. The kisses soon become caresses, grasps and clutches, as de Frutos, in time with the rhythms of the music, grapples Watton's chest, as if cupping his breasts, and holds his penis. Watton eventually returns these attentions, only to walk away.

Following a series a small stepping motions, complete with hip rocks and whipping rotations, the lights lower to a dark flickering blue and the sounds of rumbling water and crashing waves fill the space – the second half of the performance has begun. De Frutos performs heart compressions and the kiss of life on Watton's supine body. Progressively these compressions become strokes across his chest and the kisses become more intimate as de Frutos presses his mouth on Watton's penis in simulated oral sex. Watton's back arches and his body writhes – as if in orgasmic bliss.

For the rest of the dance the two men roll across the floor together, their bodies and legs intertwined, embracing and supporting one another. De Frutos rests his torso onto Watton and raises his legs up into the air. Smoothly they maintain physical contact with each other, their actions tender and intense. As the sound of waves crashing increases, as if lapping around their bodies, the lovemaking becomes a period of forgetting, as they immerse themselves in the pleasures, and pains, of each other's bodies.

Suddenly the stage is flooded with light and they return to their previous roles. Watton's movements are jerky and spasmodic, while de Frutos rotates around him fussily. As they repeat their destructive behaviours the atmosphere becomes more frenzied, the couple more desperate. The pain of their disintegrating relationship climaxes as Watton screams and repeatedly falls while hitting his own body with his fist. The work ends as Watton, in a reversal of their earlier interaction, turns de Frutos's head towards him, places his mouth on de Frutos's mouth and then leaves the stage. De Frutos gestures towards him – to no avail.

Bird is a highly erotic dance of desire. While queer embodiments are generally invisible (unlike those of race and gender, for instance), here de Frutos interlaces a performance of homosexual sexual intercourse, homoerotic display and parodic effeminate gestures in such a way that queerness is overtly staged. Further, I will argue, de Frutos creates an interplay between surface and depth, exterior and interior, such that the work brings to the fore the potential risks of queer theory, while still revelling in queer erotics.

Raimund Hoghe and *Swan Lake, 4 Acts* (2005)

In contrast to the explicit and excessive dance by de Frutos, Raimund Hoghe's *Swan Lake, 4 Acts* (2005) is an austere reworking that operates through stillness and duration, creating a sense of ritualistic acts that reference and radically reconceive the ballet *Swan Lake*. Via his pared-down approach and the centrality of his own (non-normative) body, a body marked by a hump caused by a severe curvature of the spine, Hoghe reconfigures what we mean by dance and what kind of bodies can dance.

Plate 14   Swan Lake, 4 Acts (2005) by Raimund Hoghe

Photographer: Rosa Frank

Hoghe, who was born in Wuppertal and lives in Düsseldorf (Germany), is a respected and well-established journalist/dance writer and a dance-maker. Throughout the 1980s he was dramaturge for Pina Bausch and her Wuppertal Tanztheater, which became the subject of two of his books. Throwing his own body into the fight (to paraphrase the title of his 2000–1 performance lecture), he has for the last ten years been in the vanguard of the arts,[3] performing throughout Europe and creating dance, performance and theatre pieces for various dancers and actors. He produced his first solo for himself, *Meinwärts* (1994), which, together with *Chambre séparée* (1997) and *Another Dream* (2000), made a trilogy of pieces for the twentieth century. Describing *Another Dream*, one critic notes that Hoghe 'invites us into his world of on-stage play, ritual and enjoyment of music and memory' and that he takes these performance principles, 'whittling them down to their barest form' (Phillips 2005: 25). As is typical of Hoghe, he uses the stage as a canvas to be filled with (fragile) memories, his and ours, as he allows us to read ourselves into his work. Using intimate material that draws on historical events, his own life and the unique characteristics of his body, Hoghe explores themes of love, loneliness, xenophobia and racism. While they are formed with an economy of means, his works are meticulously crafted, involving ritualistic, minimal movement with almost ceremonial rigour, as they resonate with emotion. Gerald Siegmund writes:

> Raimund Hoghe's Tanztheater manages to be explicitly political without neglecting form. The ritual severity of Japanese theatre combines with

American performance art, German expressionism and his own interest in human feelings and socio-political states to create his minimalist pieces ... He formulates his memories so that the historic events are called to mind through subjective and purely private moments. His body, which due to his hump does not correspond with society's norm, holds a place for us all and our personal memories. He opens up spaces between things, words and songs for personal reminiscences and affective moments. They are moments for reflection but also for laughter.

(Siegmund 2006)

Using unforgettable music – from the classics to the popular – Hoghe draws on the archive of collective memories, for, as he states: 'People know them and have memories associated with them: for example, they remember the life of the singer, or the moment when they first heard a special song for the first time' (cited in Johnson 2005: 339). Several of his dances have also referenced ballet – for example, *Tanzgeschichten* (2003) opens with music from *The Nutcracker*, the second part of *Another Dream* (2000) uses Stravinsky's *Le Sacre de printemps* following a series of popular songs, and *Sarah, Vincent et moi* (2004) contains images from *Swan Lake*, as do *Dialogue with Charlotte (1998)* and *Tanzgeschichten*. These references have been extended in his most recent dances that use music from *Le Sacre de printemps* and *Swan Lake*.

Hoghe's reworking of *Sacre* is a duet with his collaborator Lorenzo de Brabandere, a young untrained performer. Together their contrasting bodies pulsate with a tender, touching intimacy. Yet, while complex and desirous strings resonate between them throughout, the relationship never becomes remotely sexually explicit or homoerotic. Their connection is unself-conscious, undramatised, as they mirror each other's simple movements and balance against each other, establishing a remarkable equivalence, despite their differing physicalities. De Brabandere and his connection to Hoghe are also central to *Swan Lake, 4 Acts*. Here too their relationship has an aura of intensity, while remaining similarly ambiguous throughout the duration of the performance.

As the members of the audience enter the performance space for *Swan Lake, 4 Acts* they see a row of chairs placed at the back of the stage, between which there is a smaller area that reaches further back; this recess, through which all entrances and exits are made, forms another location for performance. Strains of the lush rich music of Tchaikovsky's *Swan Lake* are heard. This music, used throughout by Hoghe, provides the most direct and extended reference to the ballet. However, the music is cut, reordered and played on tape, as if at times from a scratched vinyl record, giving a small hint of the stark uncompromising reworking that is Hoghe's vision. For in this work all references to the ballet have been radically altered to give way to Hoghe's strident asceticism and minimal movement.

As Hoghe enters and illuminates a miniature theatre placed at the very back of the stage, act I has begun. The overture continues and Hoghe comes to sit on one of the chairs. In time three other performers – Ornella Balestra (the only female dancer and a consummate ballerina), Bynjar Bandlien and Nabil Yahia-Aissa – slowly enter and

Plate 15   Swan Lake, 4 Acts (2005) by Raimund Hoghe
Photographer: Rosa Frank

similarly sit on the chairs. They sit apart from each other, avoiding contact with each other, their hands resting in their laps as they look blankly towards the audience. They remain in place until Hoghe, who acts as both stage manager and protagonist, rises to stand in front of each of them in turn – giving them permission to rise and walk forward to the front of the stage. There they perform the smallest actions of the eyes, the head and the arms – an arm ripple, a head tilt, a glance to the side. These actions are related to the recognisable gestures of the swans and the coded mime of the ballet, yet isolated from any emotional resonance. Nor do they have any narrative purpose. Hoghe then returns to stand by the side of each dancer and walks them back to the row of chairs, where they sit, in half darkness, and continue their small, hardly visible gestures, while Hoghe goes back into the recessed space at the rear of the stage. After a time Hoghe is joined by another man – de Brabandere – with whom he swaps T-shirts – white for black. There is an ambiguous connection between these two men that stretches out across the space as Hoghe steps backwards towards the audience. The act ends as Hoghe, seated back and centre, reaches his arms forward and then pulls them both behind his back – the first of several times he will perform these gestures that are so reminiscent of the ballet swans.

Act II begins with Hoghe laying out on the stage floor a series of identical paper cut-out swans. The placement of each of these paper swans is precise, and Hoghe takes his time as he arranges them into neat rows – a row of three, a space in the centre, and another row of three – with two further rows placed directly behind – nine swans on each side of the stage in all. Having completed this task he kneels centre stage and brings his arms steadily overhead and then forward to the floor, opening out behind his back – echoing the swan gesture performed previously.

While Hoghe remains on the floor, Balestra enters wearing a brown trench coat, which she removes to reveal a black tutu. She then proceeds to perform as if she were the embodiment of Odette/Odile – her arms rippling as they rise and lower at her side. The light quickly dims on her actions, such that we can only make out her movements as if in twilight. As the music ends and silence falls she pulls her coat back on and exits.

Following this solo Hoghe returns to a standing position and proceeds to cover each of the paper swans with a white tissue – shuffling across the floor on his knees to each one. Following a repeat of his 'swan' gestures and a solo of simple ballet exercises by one of the other male dancers, Hoghe removes the paper swans and goes to lie on his back. Placing one of the tissues on his face, he exhales, blowing the tissue into the air. This action is repeated by each of the other performers, who lie blowing and replacing the tissue in their own timing.

Later, Hoghe ties his jacket onto his back and, lifting out the arms – as if they are wings – he walks in a meandering fashion across the stage while waving his arms up and down. He ends facing de Brabandere. Intimately each places their hands on the shoulders of the other. As the music ends, in a hushed silence, they again raise their arms to each other's shoulders, reverse the action and repeat twice more. The lights lower, ending act II.

Act III begins with Hoghe, again, placing objects. This time it is ice cubes that he places around the edges of the space. Again he performs the task in an unhurried and somewhat careful manner. Once the task is complete he takes an ice cube and uses it to trace the line of his arms and shoulders. This action is repeated in turn on the bodies of all the performers, and one performer to another. As each marks the line of their body with the melting ice, the differences between bodies is marked as both insubstantial and significant.

Balestra, Bandlien and Yahia-Aissa each lie again on their backs. This time they perform small arm and leg gestures from ballet – *port de bras*, *développés* and *petits battements*. Yet here, as in the rest of this work and in contrast to ballet, it is the horizontal not the vertical that is celebrated. As each dancer continues their floor sequences, Hoghe joins them. Lying on his back is clearly difficult and, as if trying to fit – trying to find someone to match or be comfortable with – he lies next to each one in turn, only to move on after a time. At the end of this section, when the others have left, de Brabandere enters and approaches Hoghe. They proceed to dance a duet of ice kisses. Placing a piece of ice between their bodies – forehead to forehead, cheek to cheek – they lean into each other, supporting each other's weight and maintaining the connection between them as each piece of ice melts away.

Hoghe begins act IV scattering what appears to be powdery white sand. The powder forms beautiful arches as is it thrown, settling to cover the back recess area, its whiteness a stark contrast to the otherwise black dance mat. When he has finished Hoghe kneels and repeats his 'swan' gesture – this time facing the back corner. After a time de Brabandere joins Hoghe, echoing his pose until they both rise to stand – mirroring each other's movements, raising their arms, rotating, walking and cradling each other's necks. This quiet interaction continues as Hoghe and de Brabandere tentatively lean and support each other. The moment ends with a stretched out de Brabandere placing all his weight on top of Hoghe and that already weakened back.

The space becomes charged as Hoghe rips up the flooring – half reversing the black dance mat to reveal its white underside. The other dancers, oblivious to the disorder, walk downstage, one forming *port de bras*, another swinging his legs. The work ends as de Brabandere covers Hoghe in the white powder, blowing it over his naked, prone body.

In the gaps and absences

While contrasting in tone and atmosphere, the reworkings of both de Frutos and Hoghe operate within the gaps of the ballet – bringing to the fore those things which are absent in order to create works which speak from a position not so much of 'What can I do with *Swan Lake*?' but, rather, 'What does *Swan Lake* mean to me? And 'How can this material, this cultural artefact, be useful to me?'

Both of these reworkings reference the ballet through their titles (Hoghe explicitly and de Frutos more laterally), the music, and the use of reminiscent images and gestures. Throughout *Swan Lake, 4 Acts* Tchaikovsky's score is played in a seemingly random order and is at times distorted. While it provides an important reference in terms of coming to understand the dance, it is in the main ignored by the performers, who move without reference to the tempo and rhythms of the music – working instead at their own internal, or task-derived, pace. In addition to the music, the ballet *Swan Lake* is present through the use of the paper cut-out swans and ice cubes (like miniature lakes). These objects frame the space and encapsulate Hoghe's compressed approach. In addition, Hoghe's repeated arm actions, together with the movements of the other performers (such as an arm flutter at the side of the body and small beats of the feet) and the costume and danced references of Balestra (who at various points wears a knee-length black tutu and pointe shoes), connect us to the ballet – as does the simple but carefully executed exchange of one black and one white T-shirt, which sparingly connote Odette and Odile, the black and white swans. Unadorned and bearing little elaboration, these elements hark back to the ballet forming the mainstay of the work. Yet, they are performed as if recalling distant memories, and are so small that they appear lost, for Hoghe engages us in a recuperation of the loss of history and a revisiting of the loss of meaning.

While for Hoghe the resonance of *Swan Lake* forms the main counterpoint for his work, for de Frutos the ballet is used within a broader context of (homo)sexual coupling and water. However, again it is Tchaikovsky's music that provides the most extended and obligatory reference, though there is no attempt to follow a parallel or linear logic in the order of the music or the dance. The sound score flits between different scenes from the ballet. For example, the music goes from Odette and Siegfried's *pas de deux* from act II (played as if heard through a telephone) to Odile's famous thirty-two *fouettés en tournant* solo from act III (played at speed and with repeats), and then, following a short burst of Hawaiian folk music, the ballet's final sections of music are directly followed by Siegfried's second entrance and a refrain of the *pas de deux* in act II. Interestingly, the dance has not been discussed (unlike the dances of Hoghe, Bourne, Morris and Ek, for example) as a reworking, and little attention has been paid to the *Swan Lake* references. One commentator who does note the musical references writes:

> Tchaikovsky's music – interpolated with sound effects and folk songs – confers an intriguing special tint on the entire work, lifting the apparent crudeness of the subject matter to a higher and, at moments, almost lyrical level.
>
> (Poesio 1998)

While I concur that the music adds an 'intriguing' and 'special tint', this review problematically reinforces the canonical status of music. The *Swan Lake* music, the review implies, confers its transcendental status upon the work and improves what might otherwise be only crude (sexual) subject matter. However, de Frutos uses the signification of *Swan Lake* for his own ends, not to lift an otherwise vulgar work, but to insert queer sexuality into what is otherwise a heterosexual dance.

De Frutos also inserts movements and gestures akin to *Swan Lake* throughout. Within the first few moments, lying behind Watton, he sends rippling waves through his raised arm. The action is immediately recognisable as a swan gesture and is interwoven into the luscious movement developed by de Frutos. Later the *Swan Lake* references become more overt. Dancing to the evocative and dramatic music from the end of act II, the dancers' heads and torsos twitch and undulate, and, while they are not the delicate swans of convention, their actions are clearly bird-like and resonate with the music. Similarly de Frutos incorporates a small shaking action of his foot, forming another direct connection to the ballet. Like Odette and her famous quivering beats in front of her ankle, de Frutos lifts up his knee and sends a repeated pulse through to his pointed foot. These actions, together with the music, locate *Bird* within the gaps of the ballet. Yet, like *Swan Lake, 4 Acts*, this work full of complexity and ambiguity – in which *Swan Lake* exists through these explicit references, yet also resonates through absences.

In these dances *Swan Lake* is appropriated *and* erased, as layers of meaning and signification are written, and written over, palimpsestuously. Playing between absence and presence, the ballet is always in the process of simultaneous manifestation and dematerialisation. While, as discussed in the previous chapter, structures of presence (that which is visible) and absence (that which is invisible) tend to value presence over absence, here the two are conflated. For, while both reworkings make visible references to *Swan Lake*, it is the invisible ghost text that resonates most strongly. For example, neither reworking stages the famously virtuosic thirty-two *fouettés rond de jambe en tournant*, yet our cultural knowledge of this choreography affects our reading of their dances. We note the absence. The choice not to include this celebrated act leads to an awareness of what replaces it or, rather, what does not replace it.

In *Swan Lake, 4 Acts*, the paring away of such overt virtuosity and the locating of the only recognisable extended movement in the supine position is an important deviation. Using a shared cultural knowledge of convention, Hoghe stages a dance that is full of unfilled expectations and expressions of horizontality – creating a resonance of loss and sadness – not because these things are themselves 'losses', but rather because we experience the presence of absence, for Hoghe points us to this absence in order for us to dwell on the implications of our desires. Similarly, de Frutos replaces the coded forms of *pas de deux* with an explicit representation of sexual intercourse. Reversing the verticality of ballet, the two performers roll and tumble across the floor and hold each other's bodies close, while they intimately touch and kiss.

Thereby, full of reference and denial, Hoghe and de Frutos both establish ambiguous relationships to *Swan Lake*, for here the ballet exists in deconstructed bodies and our hazy memories. The play between absence and presence, visibility and invisibility, engenders an empathic force for a past that is missed but never to be recuperated fully. For this past is never taken whole (for that is not possible or desirable); rather it is cut up, examined, turned over and questioned, speaking across time without evoking a nostalgic or mythic sense of past. Instead, past and present productively collide. For reworkings transform the past while repeating it in a continuous playground of recollection and reaction. Revealing a complex relationship to history, Hoghe and de Frutos embody the desire to revisit history, not to recuperate it, but to live alongside it or perhaps in the face of it. Through this process we come to understand the past, not to repeat it, but to understand it from a new perspective.

Referring to a pre-existing work, these dances do not to repeat the steps, form, costume or even resonances of the source, but disclose the difference between themselves and that source. For here it is evident that at the core of repetition is difference. This approach echoes Deleuze's discourse in *Difference and Repetition* (1994). He has made clear that it is impossible to repeat history, repeat the past, for only through difference do we experience repetition, and real repetition maximises difference. He asks, 'does not the paradox of repetition [lie] in the fact that one can speak of repetition only by the virtue of the change of difference that it introduces in the mind which contemplates it? By virtue of a difference that mind *draws from* repetition?' (Deleuze 1994: 70).

The process of reworking, as evidenced *Swan Lake, 4 Acts* and *Bird*, echoes what Deleuze (1994) calls 'minor literature.' Deleuze suggests that this mode of literature 'repeats' the voice and law of tradition in order to reveal the specific style of voice. In other words, repetition is not in order to maintain tradition, but to transform tradition. It is in minor literature that repetition is experienced as the virtual power of difference rather than the banal repetition of the past. Minor literatures, as collective assemblages, are formed in styles that allow bodies to form new territories – and in these territories bodies may dislocate any sense of a universal or general subject. In this sense these reworkings, like minor literatures, evoke provisional identities, for rather than expressing something that 'is', these dances are hybrid complex sites that repeat the past and the present in order to create a future.

Such 'repetitions' do not express what went before but use the power of repetition and simultaneous difference to disrupt the identity and coherence of the canon. Thereby, after *Swan Lake, 4 Acts* and *Bird*, we can no longer view *Swan Lake* as just a nineteenth-century ballet. Rather these reworkings change and transform the past, making it impossible to consume the ballet innocently. Operating in two directions, reworkings use the past to rethink the future and through this process unfold the illusory fixity of the source – or, in Deleuzian terms, they disclose the power of the source *to become*.

This repeated turning over unsettles the dualisms of past/present, visible/invisible, absence/presence to queer history and *Swan Lake*. Inserting their own queer bodies into history, Hoghe and de Frutos reveal *Swan Lake* as provisional and open to contestation. The ballet's potential queerness (for there is clearly a perverse queerness in the tale of a man's sexual desire for a bird), which normally remains hidden, is brought to the surface and the heterosexual contract embedded in the ballet is challenged and destabilised. For these reworkings assert the ballet's representation of sexuality *per se*, and unitary heterosexuality, specifically, is a fiction.

Excess: de Frutos and homoeroticism

Javier de Frutos foregrounds homosexuality and the homoerotic and de-emphasises conventional choreographic forms. Claiming space for a determined (ef)feminisation and homosexual masculinity, he overtly inserts into *Swan Lake* a gay presence. The potential of his dance is that it may allow us to begin to reimagine sexuality as distinct from gender and enable the refiguring of a cornucopia of contingent and shifting identities to move significantly beyond the heterosexual matrix.

As discussed above in *Bird*, *Swan Lake* references are inserted as part of a collection of images and sounds to do with pleasure, sexuality, water and fluidity, such that the dance operates as an associative series of images while following the relationship between two men. Like Petipa and Ivanov's ballet with its heterosexual partners, *Bird* evokes a fragile couple exploring their (homo)sexuality. Similarly the relationship does not always go smoothly. However, this relationship is not from the realms of fantasy, nor is it coded as escapism. De Frutos and Watton dance out a homoerotic discourse of instability and disintegration. As the dancers manipulate and are manipulated by each other, de Frutos presents conflict and non-conformity in such a way that the provisional and plural nature of sexual identities is acknowledged. The sexuality embodied does not refer to women or to heterosexuality. De Frutos asserts instead a gay sexuality that destabilises normative associations.

The two men are in stark contrast – Frutos is dark, willowy, exotic and manipulative, while Watton is fair, stiff and passively resistant. De Frutos, naked under a long pale blue and white flowered skirt, has a fluid, flamboyant and significantly other-worldly quality. Watton, dressed in a white suit and blue ruffled shirt, uses small and agitated gestures, and holds himself in a stoic fashion. While they come to resemble the Swan and the Prince from the ballet, they also significantly revise these roles such that no direct parallel is formed, lessening any simple transference from ballet to reworking.

De Frutos creates queer rifts in his dancing through his disruption of the conventional aesthetics of the male dancing body. His own thin and muscular body is long limbed (almost disproportionate), his head is shaven, his chest is hairless and his penis dangles unrestrained. His dance exposes an awkwardness of the body (and interestingly he has commented upon his own discomfort with his body in post-show discussions) while also celebrating his own kinaesthetic pleasures. Throughout *Bird* he uses his very mobile face and large lips to create facial expressions that are exaggerated, as he grimaces and raises his eyebrows to play between the flirtatious and the grotesque. He also uses his arms and hands in an embellished fashion. Holding his skirt up on his hip, he lifts his hands out from his elbows to expose his wrists, making circling gestures and scooping his arms towards his body, and overhead he flutters and splays his fingers.

De Frutos's flamboyant use of the arms and hands are coded in excess and signify an 'effeminate' practice. Yet these gestures do not appear to reference a female physicality; rather they are eccentric and idiosyncratic. David Gere's discussion of the heroism of effeminacy is useful here, as he notes that 'effeminacy is never … a reference to the feminine. … It is never equivalent to the female but it is reversed, rather, for the male rendered "not male"' (Gere 2001: 358). Importantly Gere argues that 'effeminacy has emerged as a bold strategy to resist arbitrary societal restrictions, as a "not male" category' (ibid.: 359).

This type of excessive movement has also been related to camp performance, and in many ways Gere's notion of effeminacy resonates with Moe Meyer's (1994) concept of camp. As part of what has been traditionally coded as a gay aesthetic, camp performance has been 'used to enact queer identity' (1994: 5), providing a form for social visibility. Using Linda Hutcheon's (1985) definition of postmodern parody, Meyer suggests that, when embedded with a critical function, camp represents 'a suppressed and denied oppositional critique embodied in the signifying practices that processually constitute queer identities' (1994: 1). As Hutcheon (1985, 1989) has noted, however, there is always in parodic methodologies the risk of reappropriation, as that which is parodied may reassert itself through its recapitulation. Further, the association of parody and camp with frivolity and trivialising means that this approach is a risky one.[4]

However, de Frutos operates self-reflexively. He incorporates this playful camp approach but also ensures it resonates queerly by using camp as process, not as form – for there is in this dance recognition of the 'at-playness' of sexual desire. In this way de Frutos's embodiment of 'effeminate' movement codes can be seen as subversive and as queer – he avoids identity becoming fixed and maintains mutability. These effeminate acts are further complicated by his racial otherness, for as a nonwhite gay man he is doubly emasculated. Bearing the traces of feminisation through lack, his sexual identity intersects with his racial identity to mark him as exotically, and erotically, 'other'. He uses and exploits the expectations of this otherness to parody Latino flamboyance, evoking a queerly hyperbolic masculinity. For here, effeminate and eccentric gestures are performed by de Frutos's skilled, muscular and athletic body such that his masculinity is not threatened by the play of pleasure as vulnerable object. Rather he uses the position of object – taking pleasure in it instead of being taken by it – as he plays in an ironic fashion between phallic aggression and camp wiles. In doing so his homoeroticism shifts between pleasure and power.

And what of Watton? Throughout the first section of the dance he retains an impassive distance. He allows himself to be subjected to de Frutos's attentions while remaining stoically non-reactive. Viewing this, it would be easy to locate Watton in the passive, weak (typically female) sexual role. However, his action (or rather his non-action) is so pronounced as to warrant a second look. Watton's passivity is aggressive in its extremity, and as such it is interesting to view it as a position of power. In sadomasochistic contexts the power expectations of active and passive roles are reversed. In allocating agency to the submissive role, SM 'allows bodies to submit to pleasure as a statement of power, without fear of its associations with the demeaned signification of "female" weakness and passivity' (Claid 2006: 171). Now it is not that I am suggesting that Watton and de Frutos are engaging in SM practices during the work, or that the dance plays out an SM relationship (although there are hints of this); rather I am suggesting that the acknowledgement of the reversals of power possible in SM sexual politics enables us to view his role otherwise. Submitting to the manipulations on and of his body, Watton turns his submission into power – subverting norms.

Sexual desire is the driving force of queer theory, and the erotic can be seen as desiring in practice, for eroticism is based upon the sexual impulse. Indeed, eroticism can be seen as the infinite variety of practices and representations that humans have woven around the sexual impulse (Featherstone 1999: 1). Teasing out the erotics in *Bird* reveals the ways in which Watton and de Frutos subvert the norms of the *pas de deux*. Their male–male duet challenges expectations, refusing to cohere to established patterns of activity and passivity, dominance and submission. As the dance takes us on a journey of erotic exploration, the sexual practices between these two men is elaborated at length. Through this journey the erotic images shift from an emphasis upon surface and skin to one of depth and penetration, from exterior to interior. Skin, lips and hands are in the foreground through the first half of the work, as de Frutos strokes and kisses Watton's body. Dancing to Odette and Siegfried's *pas de deux* music from act II, de Frutos choreographs a dance of kisses. In time with the music he starts to kiss Watton on the neck. Like small pecks these kisses travel down Watton's arm, becoming quick caresses at his fingers. This dance, de Frutos says, validates kissing as a movement of the same value as a lift of a leg or any other movement from more traditional dance vocabularies (Shaw 1999 [see videography]).

Of course, while watching his dance of kisses, the viewer is reminded by the music of the stylised romance of the ballet. De Frutos's dance, although very different, is no less seductive or delicate, but perhaps less innocent and more self-knowing in its playfulness. These images emphasise looking and touching. We are invited as viewers to know de Frutos's pleasures. Flirtatious, coy and manipulative, he regularly looks from Watton to us, and even while kissing Watton holds us in his gaze, implicating us in his sexual play. Yet his gaze is neither the inviting open smile of the female pin-up nor the stare of the male pin-up (Dyer 1992: 109). Instead de Frutos engages us in a game of naughty and cheeky gazes – simultaneously desiring and desired, vulnerable and authoritative, we are embroiled in his manipulations, as he claims power by self-consciously allowing our gaze and looking back. This duality enables him to retain his subject position while performing as object of gaze. As Claid remarks, de Frutos takes charge, submitting his body to the pleasures of moving and being watched, turning submission into power by using the submission of his body as a politically subversive tool (Claid 2006: 171). As such his game of gazes brings into question the previously assumed authority of heterosexual male artists, for foregrounding the effects of his body on display and taking overt pleasure in allowing the penetrating gaze of the audience places his performance in opposition to hegemonic masculinity.

Thereby *Bird* destabilises normative ways of viewing. Burt writes that this is a potential feature of gay male dance:[5]

> Gay male dancing bodies signify the possibility that men can dissolve in pleasure within the leaky boundaries not of women but of other men. This blurring of masculine subjects and objects destabilises notions of male objectivity and rationality that, within Enlightenment thought, guaranteed the disinterestedness of the rational unitary subject.
>
> (Burt 2001: 211)

Discussing the ways in which queer male dancers may destabilise notions of the masculine and disinterestedness, Burt evokes his own, and others', visceral responses to (queer) dance. These visceral responses, he suggests, break the bounds of disinterestedness, causing the viewer to become involved in the performance, such that the distinction between object and subject blurs. Thinking this through in relation to *Bird*, it is clear that by explicitly bringing attention to the eroticized surface of his body, and by crossing the audience/performer boundary with his gaze, de Frutos avoids the dualism of object/subject. Rather de Frutos plays ambiguously, overtly acknowledging the dynamics of the theatrical space he enters, and brings to the fore what Amelia Jones calls 'the corruptive effects of theatricality' (1998: 112) – corruptive because theatricality is located as feminine. In doing so, de Frutos refigures the masculine – taking up the theatrical spectrum of femininity and deflating masculinity's claim to originality to articulate a subject that is particularised rather than normative.

Similarly challenging is the way in which both de Frutos and Watton refuse to perform the required dynamic display of masculinity. Their movements lack bravado and overt virtuosity, for when kisses become dance movements a schism occurs and masculinity fails to cohere, so that it turns into a performance of masculinity that is open-ended and contingent.

In the second half of *Bird* the dance becomes an extended sequence of sexual intercourse. As described above, de Frutos and Watton dance to the layered sounds of the ocean crashing against the shore, breath bubbles escaping a diver's mask, and the wind gusting, interspersed with folk songs and the strains of Tchaikovsky. The lighting is low and it flickers like water rippling across the stage. The whole dance takes place on the floor as they tumble and roll, lift and fall over each other's bodies. This dance is tender, passionate and erotically beautiful, as well as being pitiless and emotionally violent.

Here de Frutos reminds us of the reality of homosexual intercourse, presenting a body that opens a negotiatory spectatorial relation accommodating homoerotic and other forbidden desires, threatening heteronormative masculinity that prohibits male–male sexual bonding. Through links to his earlier work *Grass* (made and performed by de Frutos just one year before *Bird*), he foregrounds the anus as the locus of sexual pleasure and the site through which male creativity takes place. Far from being phallic and so 'transcendent', the anus is an especially vulnerable orifice. Orifices, Mary Douglas has pointed out, are boundaries marked by the grotesque, for 'Matter issuing from them is marginal stuff of the most obvious kind. Spittle, blood, milk, urine, faeces or tears by simply issuing forth have traversed the boundary of the body' (1966: 121). These bodies are abject, for the abject body is one that embodies reactions to the disavowed (the socially unacceptable) yet desired. These reactions are physical and visceral – 'retching, vomiting, spasms, choking – in brief, in disgust' (Grosz 2001: 145). The promise of the abject is that it makes clear that 'what must be expelled from the subject's corporeal functioning can never be fully obliterated but hovers at the border of a subject's identity, threatening apparent unities and stabilities with disruption and possible dissolution.' Further: 'it is what disturbs identity, systems and order, disrupting the social boundaries demanded by the symbolic. It respects no definite positions, or rules, boundaries or socially imposed limits' (ibid.: 144–5).

De Frutos's overt display of his penetrable orifice enables other boundaries to be crossed also. For in contrast to the impenetrability of masculine heterosexuality (an impenetrability that secures hegemonic masculinist identities) his penetrable body deflates 'masculine's claim to originality' (Butler 1993: 52), to articulate instead a postmodern subject that is particularised rather then normative. Further, Amelia Jones (1998) argues that the unveiling and dematerialization of the phallic body of the modernist artist/genius would be a dislocation of the entire mythology of creation as ejaculation. Thereby also undone is the notion of interpretation as a 'disinterested' reading of transparent meanings and the work of art as a static repository of the artist's intentionality. As such de Frutos's homoerotics destabilise the illegitimacy of authorship and originality – concepts already significantly undermined within reworkings *per se*. De Frutos purposefully fails to embody the authorial voice of the artistic genius, instead wallowing and relishing his own (flawed) corporeality.

Bird and *Grass* (with its images of sex and blood and therefore AIDS) bring to the fore the relationship between the erotic and death.[6] While it is not as violent or direct as *Grass*, the sense of disease and pain is still evident in *Bird*. Throughout, de Frutos appears distracted by his own body, checking for signs of disease. Watton is stiff and skittish and performs nervous uncomfortable gestures. As they tumble and roll together in passionate embraces the atmosphere, which by convention should be romantic, is instead dark and morose, the bodies intertwined in a mutually destructive bond. In the era of HIV/AIDS the associations between erotic practices and death become intense and very real. Reflecting this very tangible context, the erotic practices in this work are thereby specific and non-transcendental in nature, expressing a deep-rooted interiority. Offering the creator, and the source ballet, up for unromantic inspection, *Bird* constitutes a site of resistance against the dead weight of conformity to normative heterosexuality, as de Frutos explores pleasure and desire anew.

Stillness and (dis)ability: Hoghe and the ontology of dance

In *Swan Lake, 4 Acts*, concepts of dance, masculinity, homosexuality and disability collide, creating an extraordinarily rich site of investigation. Hoghe inserts his own non-normative body into a dance of stillness and repetition, casting aside established ontologies of dance. Eschewing all familiar virtuosity and expectations of the body, Hoghe, through his non-action (rather than action), breaks expectations of 'dance' – for dance has been related to action.

Hoghe challenges conventional aesthetic values, the flow of ballet being replaced by an economy of motion as images are repeatedly stretched out over duration. For extended periods he and his performers kneel or lie, waiting upon the floor. At other times they stand facing each other, or facing the audience, their bodies motionless and expressionless. Further, objects, having been steadily and carefully arranged, are left for us to contemplate. These acts of stillness are significant, for, as André Lepecki has convincingly argued, 'the insertion of stillness in dance, the deployment of different ways of slowing down movement and time, are particularly powerful propositions for modes of rethinking action and mobility through the performance of still-acts, rather than continuous movement' (Lepecki 2006: 15).

Lepecki writes that the 'still-act' can usefully reconfigure the 'unquestioned alignment of dance with movement' (2006: 16); this is important, he suggests, for 'dance ontologically imbricates itself with, is isomorphic to, movement' (ibid.: 2). This break of dance from movement, from mobility, enables a rethinking of the body and might blur divisions between 'the sensorial and the social, the somatic and the mnemonic, the linguistic and corporeal, the mobile and immobile' (ibid.: 15).

Hoghe's use of expanded duration and stillness, perhaps because of our expectation of dance to involve movement rather than performers standing still, is uncomfortable, even excruciating at times. This sensation is heightened by the contrast with Tchaikovsky's score, which continues to run onwards while little 'happens' on the stage. Yet this feeling of discomfort increasing becomes precisely the point of Hoghe's approach. Our expectations, it seems, are purposefully unfulfilled. For, if we can surpass our frustration, Hoghe suspends our usual experience of time – in particular theatrical and metered time. Requiring us to slow down, the work provokes us to enter into a more contemplative level of engagement through which it is possible, in self-reflexive manner, to note that which is unfulfilled, yet craved for, and consider the value systems at work within those very desires.

'Thus', Lepecki writes, 'the still-act … requires a performance of suspension, a corporeally based interruption of modes of composing flow. The still *acts* because it interrogates economies of time, because it reveals the possibility of one's agency within controlling regimes of capital, subjectivity, labor and mobility' (2006: 15). Interrupting flow, *Swan Lake, 4 Acts* allows the passing of time and the layers of historicity to come to the present in a foregrounding of the haunting forces of dance history.

Lepecki relates his ideas to those of Gaston Bachelard to suggest, through stillness, through shifts in temporality, we might come to experience a 'slower ontology' (Bachelard 1994: 215). This connection is useful for understanding the impact of duration in *Swan Lake, 4 Acts* as, for Bachelard, notions of stillness and silence are not passive. Rather, in creating a space of silence in and around a text, a sense of contemplation emerges, enabling a critical listening that may liberate energies and connections in the text which may lead outside of it. Bachelard's notion of 'slower ontology' then compellingly relates to Hoghe's focus upon the hidden and the miniaturised – for it is through the small gestures and objects that the inside/outside voices are merged, beyond sensory divisions and sensual speculations and sensuous delimitations.

When Hoghe places ice cubes in a square around the edge of the stage, positioning these items with meticulous care, he simply uses the time it takes to fulfil the task. As we wait, the ice cubes are left slowly to melt into small puddles. With time to gaze upon the objects, it is the waiting, the lack of action, which enables us to enjoy the poignant simplicity of the image and to ponder. Allowing the images to reverberate long enough for the range of intertexts and tangential thoughts to emerge and intertwine, we lose ourselves in our own subjective experiences.

Thereby the images Hoghe creates resonate precisely because of the slowness of unfolding and the attention to the micro, taking on the force of political action by delaying and withholding gratification. For in contemporary society, which tends to focus on movement, action and consumption, our capacity to concentrate on stillness, to be in the moment and to experience duration are qualities that embody radical potential. Shifting experiences of the temporal and relocating our attention to the small, the quiet and the unspoken, Hoghe challenges his viewers to reconsider their expectations and values. The power of this challenge to established ontologies of dance is that Hoghe's use of stillness is not a negation of dance; rather, his approach is affirmative, for as Una Bauer writes, 'when he moves, Raimund Hoghe is not trying to say: "Look at me, I am not dancing", but precisely the opposite: "Look at me, *I am dancing*" '(2006: 145). In doing so, Hoghe expands concepts of what it is to dance and what we mean by dancing.

The extended dialogue with objects by Hoghe is another way in which he expands notions of dance. Be it ice cubes, paper cut-outs of swans, miniature theatres or items of clothing, Hoghe's use of these things imbues them with special importance such that they become agents of meaning. All is arranged, performed and presented with methodical care, giving rise to the intense qualities of ritual. Yet in ritual we look for purpose and for the import of every gesture and each action. Hoghe denies us this resolution of meaning, as individual moments confound and confuse.

Arranging the '*corps de ballet*', of eighteen small paper cut-outs of swans, Hoghe lays them out with mathematical precision in rows across the stage. The placement of this paper '*corps*' takes time and emphasises his own controlling, yet at the same time timid and vulnerable, presence through the work. As the paper cut-outs are laid in place, juxtapositions are evoked between the detailed choreography of his arrangement, its understated simplicity, and our memories of swans as danced by a large *corps de ballet*. The two-dimensional quality of the paper cut-outs foregrounds the stereotypical three-dimensionality of the *corps* as represented in the ballet, for Hoghe takes the illusion of disembodiment, which is the foundation of conventional representations, to its logical extreme. At the same moment, and somewhat paradoxically, the conventional *corps de ballet*, which is normally experienced as an ethereal yet highly structured group, comes to appear fleshy and chaotic by comparison. Owing to the doubleness of reworkings, the inherent messiness of bodies is allowed to seep through, for Hoghe's cut-outs are so thoroughly and starkly disembodied that we enjoy the broken illusion.

Simultaneously, however, the qualities of ritual and the heightened sense of 'specialness' with which Hoghe infuses his simple objects endows them with the same status as the idealised, highly trained bodies of the ballet. Becoming 'extraordinary' and precious, these paper swans are not empty, they are not pared away to an aestheticised minimalism; rather, these simple objects become an intimate politics of beauty and history. Imbuing them with agency, Hoghe slides between a disidentification with the ghostly figure of the ballet and the ballerina and a quietly stated identification. Yet the mode is melancholic: he covers each paper swan with a white tissue as 'she' is laid to rest, and as he mourns the death of the icon, yet makes no attempt to resuscitate her.

Replacing the conventional swans with paper cut-outs and centrally locating his own body, Hoghe uses his diminutive stature, spine curvature and resultant hump to unmoor expectations, and his body does not go unnoticed. Critic Katja Werner (2003) describes him thus: 'Raimund Hoghe, small, hunchbacked, the perfect impersonation of loneliness', and Sanjoy Roy (2007) writes, 'Hoghe is a tiny, middle aged, hunchback', while Ramsay Burt (2005) notes his 'twisted spine and disabilities'. For these reviewers, and I would think most of the audience, Hoghe's body creates a disjuncture, a jolt to established expectations.

Taking this disjunction as a point of departure, I am going to consider for a moment the implications of Hoghe's homosexual 'disabled' body when it is placed into *Swan Lake*, and thereby at an intersection with all those idealised bodies that conventional versions contain. For it is pertinent to consider, as Ann Cooper Albright asks, 'what happens when disabled people move into the role of dancer, the very same role that has been historically reserved for the glorification of an ideal body?' (1997: 57).[7]

Albright asks this question in an insightful discussion about dance and disability which she begins with a description of the Romantic ballerina Marie Taglioni by Théophile Gautier. Emphasising Taglioni's lightness, delicacy and transcendence, Gautier provides 'a tantalizingly elusive vision of the spectator's desire' (Albright 1997: 56). Albright goes on to note that this is, of course, all about creating illusion and that it elides the dancer's sweat and pain. She uses this starting point as a foil through which to question the ways in which dance has equated 'physical ability with aesthetic quality' and suggests that, through the 'disabled' body, it might be possible to re-envision 'just what kinds of movements can constitute a dance, and by extension, what kind of body can constitute a dancer' (1997: 57).

Hoghe provides a site for just such a re-envisioning. As a dancer with a physical deformity, he purposefully and meaningfully challenges concepts of the body, specifically the dancer's body, and, in this process, reassesses aesthetic values. For, as Johnson writes, Hoghe's body 'interrupts the canonical exclusion of the non-normative body from the traditions of dance and theatre, to claim these spaces anew for atypical bodies' (Johnson 2005: 37). Establishing complex questions about the body, normality and beauty, his humped back and resultant somewhat stiff and awkward physicality creates a poignant contrast to images embedded the ballet – destabilising and refiguring aesthetic concepts.

Avoiding the studied illusion of ethereal transcendence in conventional *Swan Lakes*, Hoghe makes no attempt to disguise or surpass his hump; rather, we are made acutely aware of it. Kneeling centre stage, his body bent forwards, he extends his arms forwards over his head, and then reaches them around behind his back. His arms and hands twitch – like a half-remembered mimic of Odette or a swan that can no longer fly. This 'swan motif' occurs repeatedly, and each time he kneels down or raises his arms his hump and his stiff awkwardness are clear. As the stigma of his body is reiterated throughout – less we should forget – Hoghe uses the framing of theatre and the expectations of spectacle (which are never fulfilled) as a context for us to experience his disabled body, and this experience is palpable.

His repeated performance of the swan – which never complies with expectations – unsettles notions of completion, for each repetition disrupts the previous manifestations of the same gesture, such that, rather than making it clearer by repetition – the 'message' is magnified to such a point that we really start to note the detail – the detail creates complications and complexities. Through this repetition Hoghe destabilises conventional ways of seeing and expressing dance, as his body emerges as the consistent subject. And this body is a site of abnormality – a site of dissonance.

If this were not enough, Hoghe steadily exposes his body through the duration of the work: first he removes his jacket, then his t-shirt, until at the end he lies on the floor fully naked. These actions are in no way gratuitous; he removes his clothing cautiously, gradually revealing to us his deformed (seemingly) vulnerable back. And, as Johnson writes: 'Hoghe refuses to apologise for putting his body on stage, for the discomfort you might feel, for showing you up for not being accustomed to the encounter' (Johnson 2005: 37).

Albright (1997: 58) suggests we are forced to watch with a 'double vision' when viewing 'disabled' bodies dancing – for the negotiation between theatrical representation and the actuality of physical experiences is made acute. It becomes possible to note that 'while dance performance is grounded in the physical capacities of a dancer it is not limited by them' (Albright 1997: 58). Hoghe, through his non-action (for he tends to stand rather than 'move') and his (disconcerting) body, places a gap between expectations and that which confronts us – refusing to 'fit in' to discourse of normative bodies. By doing so he goes against aesthetics that are often located in ideals of beauty and/or athleticism, for dance, specifically ballet, has tended to reiterate the 'classical' body and action.

Performed by Hoghe's non-normative body, the 'swan motif' evokes images of a swan that is uncomfortable, isolated and vulnerable. The specifics of his body doing the choreography create a resonance with Odette's desire for transformation back into her human state, and even more strongly with her experience of imprisonment in her swan body. Hoghe's physical difficulties in kneeling and extending his arms backwards bring this to us anew such that that which is usually hidden by the beauty of the swan is here exposed as excruciating and frustrating. The insertion of his own body into *Swan Lake* in this way thereby brings about a reconsideration of Odette's experience.

This reconsideration of Odette is heightened further by the contrast established between Hoghe and Balestra. As Hoghe lies on the floor, Balestra performs the coded choreography of Odette. Her body, marked by years of ballet training and performance, is the embodiment of the ballet Swan. Her rippling arms and shimmering feet are in stark contrast to Hoghe's uncomfortable postures and stillness. Yet the poignancy of the contrast marks both performers – for we are reminded of the vulnerability of Odette and Hoghe, and we note the beauty of them both.

Hoghe highlights such differences, then, not to maintain them but rather to point to the similarities between bodies – between his body and those of others about him – his co-performers and us, as members of the audience. As he and de Brabandere stand face to face they mirror each other's actions and support each other's weight. The contrast between them couldn't be more pronounced. Hoghe, short, slight in build, middle-aged and humped, de Brabandere, average height and build, young, healthy. Yet the differences between them are blurred. Their touch is sensitive and tender, for neither body attempts to occupy the space of the perfect body. Rather, performing each action without artifice, Hoghe emphasises the individuality of everyone's body – theirs and ours.

In these ways Hoghe brings about a rethinking, challenging us to reconsider representations of the body and bodily ideals. For, as Hoghe suggests, being confronted with a body that does not conform to conventional ideas of beauty requires us to question our own experiences of the body (Hoghe, cited in Johnson 2005: 37). The possibility of his radical reconfiguration lies, then, in our connection to his disabled body as it resonates within our own bodies. Working to elide the all too easy binary between able and disabled bodies, Hoghe challenges the narratives of (dis)ability. This is an important task, for Shildrick and Price note: 'So long as "disabled" is seen as just another fixed identity category, an identity that we might carry with us into all situations, then the boundaries which separate us, one from the other, are left undisturbed' (1996: 96).

Through extended periods of stillness and the specifics of his own body, Hoghe provokes a reconsideration of what it is to act or to take action and, fundamentally, what it is to dance. For his is a dance in which the relationships between kinetic/non-kinetic, absence/presence, abled/disabled, passive/active are blurred. Through *Swan Lake, 4 Acts*, the experience of temporality is profound, enabling the audience to 'time-travel' – into personal reveries and histories – as the resonances of images and shifts in the body are brought to the fore. Yet, lest we should forget the individual uniqueness of every body, Hoghe quietly observes the importance of flesh and the proximity of our bodies to theirs (the performers) and our gaze on his stigmatised body.

(Auto)corpography and (beyond) queer theory

While *Bird* is explicit in its sexual content, *Swan Lake, 4 Acts* is more circumspect, yet both, I suggest, are fundamentally queer. We seem to have come along way from these discussions, however, and so (re)turning to questions of queerness I want to consider (at least briefly): How do these dances embody/question queerness? How might the processes of reworking register and gain efficacy in queer terms? And how might they suggest a movement beyond queerness or, more properly, beyond queer theories?

While talking about what is 'beyond' queer theory may seem somewhat premature, for in the lived sense of everyday queer lives it doesn't seem as yet possible or sensible to do so, there are, however, senses in which these choreographers are able to challenge queer theory from within the practice of reworking. Although queer theory offers exciting ways of unfixing sexualities and problematising normative structures, the risks of queer theory are its ever shifting and provisional approaches, in which 'real' lives, 'real' voices dissolve and vanish.

Indeed, critics of queer theory have pointed to the fact that much of this theorising has articulated an absent (no)body and argued that, 'even if we are all composed of a myriad of sexual possibilities, of fluid, changeable forms of sexuality, nevertheless these still conform to the configurations of the two sexes ... it *does* make a difference which kind of sexed body enacts the various modes of performance' (Grosz, cited in Desmond 2001: 10). These thoughts are echoed by David

Halperin, who argues that the difficulty of queer theory is that it is 'anchored in the perilous shifting sands of non-identity, positionality, discursive reversibility, and collective self-invention' (1995: 122).

In contrast, Hoghe and de Frutos assert the specificity of their own bodies – for each in his own way locates the materialites of his own body, his own life, as the locus of his practice. These bodily insertions, or (auto)corpographies as I want to call them, mean that these reworkings are as much 'about' Hoghe and de Frutos's own corporealities, own (auto)biographies, as they are commentaries upon *Swan Lake*. Participating (at least implicitly) in the debates around queer theory, they emphasise a 'new realism' of the body. In doing so they reinforce the importance of acknowledging the personal within the political (to repeat an old feminist adage). As it not desirable, or possible, to revert to a position in which sexuality is represented as a 'truth', it is also necessary to note the specificity of experience – in this case the experiences of particular queer male dancers.

Hoghe stages his homosexuality quietly through an enactment of a male–male relationship. But Hoghe is not overt, and certainly not homoerotic. Since he refuses artifice or effeminate coding, his homosexuality is rendered almost, but not quite, invisible, for, while the intimacy between him and de Babandere is in no way demonstrative, it is nevertheless clear. As they mirror each other's movements, slowly raising and lowering their arms, rest their hands upon each other's shoulders, and use ice cubes to trace over each other's bodies, their relationship is enacted through a series of slow and studied caresses. Their performance, while avoiding camp or homoerotic coding and remaining uninflected and unselfconscious, is still (or perhaps because of this ambiguity) readable as queer. For the ghost of the ballet and the ballerina – her feminising presence and *Swan Lake*'s emphasis upon romance – in combination with their staged intimacy, drive towards Hoghe and de Brabandere's pairing, as they dance a dance of unconventional erotic relations, both real and imagined, that evokes a queer queerness.

Further, the specificity of Hoghe's bodily disability gives rise to important questions as to the ways in which his disability interacts with his male, homosexual body, and in turn extends, or at least presses upon, queer theory. For, in a parallel manner to the ways in which earlier feminisms were challenged by questions of how gender intersects with other social characteristics, disability too complicates our understanding of gender, race and sexuality. Disability studies have just begun to raise these debates, asking, for instance: 'How does disability affect the gendering process?' and 'How does it affect the experience of gender?' (Gerschick 2000: 1263). As bodies are central to the recognition of gender, for gender is enacted through the body, Gerschick usefully highlights the ways in which 'the bodies of people with disabilities make them vulnerable to being denied recognition as women and men' (ibid.: 1264).

In line with Gerschick's observations, Hoghe's homosexuality, disability and profession combine to emasculate him. In other words, Hoghe is a man rendered not-male, for here masculinity collides with disability to elide masculine privilege. Further his disability is combined with his homosexuality and located within the stigma of the feminised stage space. Yet disability and homosexuality emerge as contradictory figures that haunt the recesses of the 'normal', and it is these deviant bodies that combine to remake the world – to nurture a profound alterity and articulate the future. Hoghe's bodily deviance unmoors the territories of broken and whole, beauty and grotesque, homosexual and heterosexual, existing in between to challenge the aesthetic values inherent in normative definitions of the body and of dance. He reappropriates his not-male status to contribute to the creation of alternative gender and sexual identities, and his queer queerness reveals both that gender and sexuality are provisional and that bodies do not always (or indeed generally) comply to match easily defined categories.

While less visible, de Frutos also insists on foregrounding the specificity of his (sexual) body, his homosexual life. He has commented that *Bird* is 'an autobiographical page' and, further, that within it he is 'defending his right [as a gay man] to have sex' (in Shaw 1999 [see videography]). Insisting on an embodied queer presence, he locates this within a lived (homo)sexuality. Further, he stages a dance which foregrounds the reality of intercourse in an era of HIV/AIDS. As de Frutos and Watton roll and tumble together, we cannot help but carry the twitching concerns they danced previously, and cannot forget the harsh images of blood smeared around mouths and anuses in *Grass*, their previous duet. Thereby the queerness of *Bird* is located specifically in late twentieth-century Western homosexual culture. It is this particular context, and the very directness of the sexual relationship displayed, that destabilises normative associations and brings about the radical reconfiguration of sexuality on stage.

Queer theory, in line with poststructuralist legacies, has construed the body as an inscribed surface, tending towards exteriorised models of corporeality in which the inscribed body carries socio-historical forces as if on the surface of a page. Yet Hoghe and de Frutos require us to consider their lived experience in and of the world, for, as dance historian Alexandra Carter explains, while 'the body may be in one sense surface, inscribed by ideologies of gender ... it also has depth and consciousness' (1999: 97). The works thereby reflect the shifting sand of queer theory, but this is importantly located in the reality of disability and sexual intercourse in an era of HIV/AIDS.

I am suggesting, then, in a movement beyond queer theories, beyond the mercurial of fluidity of discourse, these reworkings require the dance-maker's personal and bodily materialities be considered too. To be clear, however, I am not suggesting that their (auto)corpographies are statements of truth or reality in any unmediated sense. These reworkings do not speak of singular realities or reinforce unhelpful concepts of fixed identity. Rather I am suggesting that these (auto)corpographies, these self-representations, locate queerness in the materiality of their makers' own bodies, that they speak of the fleshy, intersubjective, and sexed experiences in and of their bodies. This is how they choose to portray themselves as queer men.

It is evident therefore that, while de Frutos and Hoghe assert the importance of using their own bodies, these bodies are not singular, but complex, for they carry the webs of historical, cultural and social experiences. This complexity is heightened by the palimpsestuous, self-consciously intertextual nature of reworkings. For here their corporealities connect to and extend the ghostly presence of the ballet and the ballerina. *Swan Lake* as the obligatory intertext variously asserts itself, giving rise to complexities as questions of feminisation through association. Rising to this challenge, Hoghe and de Frutos interrogate the safe categories of male identity to play between absence and presence, power and desire, projecting non-normative male bodies into theatrical and thereby feminised positions.

Undertaking the process of reworking – with its citational properties, its multiple registers and its referentiality – Hoghe and de Frutos contrive to disturb and resist norms. Enabling one thing to point to (many) others, they queer their canonical reference, for in these dances mythologies of time, originality and single authorship are revealed as provisional and open to contestation. Hoghe and de Frutos destabilise these myths and turn the canonical status of *Swan Lake* against itself. Challenging the emphasis upon reproductive continuity that is inherent in canon formation, these queer reworkings reveal not only the way that the canon excludes, but also the way the reproductive model of the canon reflects, heterosexisms.

Conclusion

These works have reconfigured masculinity on stage, dismantling the narrative and forms of Classical ballet, to stage alternative masculinities through their non-normative bodies, stillness, display, homoeroticism and queerness. Staging their atypical bodies – excessive, untrained, immobile, deformed and diseased – the choreographers displace not only the specialised (dis)embodiments of ballet, but also normative notions of the body *per se* – disturbing ideas and aesthetic norms. Further, I have suggested that de Frutos and Hoghe's (auto)corpographies reveal divergent modes of queerness, grounding the shifting sands of queer theory.

Staging politics of desire, de Frutos and Hoghe work to engage with society and, while not making explicit political statements, challenge (hetero)normative assumptions about the body and sexuality. These shifts are of course also evident in other dances by these same choreographers and in the work of others, yet, as reworkings and the operations of the bidirectional gaze, these dances are more explicit in their manoeuvres than others. Through 'mis'-repetitions and 'mis'-representation they foreground difference and draw attention to the processes of meaning-making. Queerly bidirectional, these reworking suggest that, far from being the norm, heterosexuality and its institutions are always threatened by the polymorphous nature of desire itself.

Chapter 5

Intercultural encounters
Flesh, hybridity and the exotic

When we experience ourselves through another cultural lens, we are enriched. When we interpret another culture through our own lens, we bring the difference the other can bring – sometimes the same things that insiders see, but more often aspects that bridge the known with the strange. And it is the strangeness of the unknown (how it can re-arrange our perceptual field) that calls us to travel across the bridge of difference, after all. Then, when familiar territory is given up, the traveler can stand in a new familiar, in the place where worlds (and they are whole worlds) meet.

(Fraleigh 1999: 17)

Reworkings as intercultural discourse

Given the cultural origins of ballet in Europe and the implicit 'whiteness' embodied in its history – a history which has exercised an almost comprehensive exclusion – it is not insignificant that non-white, non-Western dancers have turned their attentions to it. The dancers discussed here have reworked the ballet to form intercultural dances that bring to the fore questions of race, alongside those of gender and sexuality, inserting themselves and their 'otherness', intervening and disrupting the ballet.

Patrice Pavis suggests that intercultural performance can be understood in the relationship between the 'source culture' and the 'target culture', whereby the 'source culture' is made intelligible to audiences from a 'target culture' (Pavis 1992). By this definition all reworkings of existing historical dances can be said to be intercultural (or at least intracultural), as they take something from a distinct past culture and consciously alter it to present it in a new culture. They mix two cultures (at least), two time periods, and often two theatrical worlds. Via this 'mixing' or cultural exchange, variously hybrid and bidirectional texts are formed (see chapter 1).

This type of hybrid bidirectionality is echoed in Marvin Carlson's model of intercultural performance in which he proposes that 'the foreign and familiar create a new blend' (Carlson 1990: 50). While various types of 'blending' are a characteristic feature of all reworkings, the dances discussed in this chapter – *The Legend of Giselle (Jizeru-den)* (1994) by Masaki Iwana and *Swan Lake* (1998) by Shakti – are complicated by, while also in their turn complicating, existing intercultural models. For, in these reworkings, what might be considered the source or the target cultures, and what blending or assimilation takes place, is not straightforward or singularly located. Rather these dances evoke an array of networks, trajectories and ghostly resonances traversing the already densely saturated fields of interculturalism and reworkings.

Intercultural performance, write Julie Holledge and Joanne Tompkins, 'could be said to be inevitable as cultures attempt to define themselves by exploring their boundaries: once cultures push that exploration beyond their borders, they intersect and/or clash with other cultures' (2000: 7). While interculturalism is perhaps inevitable, the question of which cultures intersect and/or clash, and the mode of this coming together, has given rise to significant debate. In particular, critics of interculturalism have tended to focus upon Western 'borrowings' or 'appropriations' from the ethnic 'other', for intercultural texts have commonly been formed by Euro-American artists 'borrowing' from the East. For example, the well-documented and much cited performance by Peter Brook of *The Mahabharata* (1985) was criticised by Rustom Bharucha, who argued that this performance represented a cultural theft, in which the non-Western, in this case Indian, 'partners' of this intercultural meeting were manipulated and not necessarily in any way enriched by the exchange (Bharucha 1993). Bharucha's writing is located by the discourses of globalisation, orientalism and the postcolonial experience. These forces make clear that inequality continues to exist in political and economic terms between cultures, and inequalities, according to Bharucha, continue to be reflected in the unequal exchanges between cultures in intercultural performance.

In addition, interculturalism risks fixing cultures into simplistic codes of cultural difference – 'reducing culture to a stageable sign' (Holledge and Tompkins 2000: 12). Through such fixing, postcolonial countries, such as India, are lodged with 'an over determined matrix of submission and resistance' (Bennett 1996: 74). Bharucha argues that, to avoid the desire, evident in some intercultural performance practice, for a stable past and present, we must first play to 'historical contradictions' (1993: 250). As Phillip Zarrilli writes, 'performance as a mode of cultural action is not a simple reflection of essentialized, fixed attributes of a static monolithic culture but an arena for the constant process of renegotiating experiences and meanings that constitute culture' (Zarrilli 1992: 16).

Articulating a different perspective, Craig Latrell asks:

> why should we deny to other cultures the same sophistication and multiplicity of responses to 'foreign' influences that we grant to ourselves in viewing non-Western works? … Why not start with the assumption that other cultures are not just passive receivers of Western ideas and images, but active manipulators of such influences, and that intercultural borrowing is not simply a one-way process, but something far more interestingly dialogic?
>
> (Latrell 2000: 44)

Latrell, somewhat dangerously, underplays the political and economic implications of intercultural performance to usefully foreground the potentialities of such borrowings and empower non-Western cultures. Citing the hybrid practice of the Minangkabau traditional music ensemble in West Sumatra, he writes:

> Far from abandoning or tainting formerly pure local forms, the Sumatran musicians are assimilating new influences, and in the process interpreting what they borrow. Such complicated interactions between borrower and borrowed are the rule rather than the exceptions, and narratives of passivity and neo-colonialism have little place in this land of creativity.
>
> (Ibid.: 47)

The dances by Shakti and Iwana discussed here demonstrate that not all borrowings are one way – not all are done by the West to 'others'. For these two dancers rework the European narratives and forms of ballet, creating complex and hybrid crossings between cultures which cannot be decoded from one single, legitimate, point of view. Reversing the uneven flow of appropriations in art and performance between Western and non-Western cultures, these dancers use the European ballets *Swan Lake* and *Giselle* for their own reasons and in a creative fashion. As such their borrowings represent an active manipulation of influences in the manner of a dialogue, assimilating *and* interpreting what they adopt (Latrell 2000).

However, it is clear that in these intercultural reworkings, whether positively framed or the subject of criticism, issues of power and control tacitly remain, and the resulting debates are heightened by the nexus of interculturalism, globalisation, colonialism and orientalism within which intercultural performances reside. Operating within these clearly political structures, one must address the presence and presumption of power and the pervasiveness of commercialisation. For, as Daryl Chin notes, 'interculturalism hinges on the question of autonomy and empowerment' (1991: 94), and as such it is important to attend to the extent to which these reworkings of the ballet represent an increasing hegemony or cultural disruption.

These opposing forces run throughout the discussion that follows. While, on the one hand, Shakti's *Swan Lake* and Iwana's *The Legend of Giselle* provoke a reperception of both the canonical ballets at their source and the source cultures from which they arise – for strangeness of the other sharpens the familiar – on the other hand, they also risk reinvesting meaning in Western canonical works, reinforcing them as markers of power and authority. Other themes that emerge are those of hybridity, exoticism, androgyny, metamorphosis and the global market. These reworkings that cross cultures are complex sites that redouble the already bidirectional nature of reworkings *per se*.

This redoubling, this increasing complexity, is particularly evident in the refiguring of the dancing body. In these reworkings the body becomes a site of intersecting discourses as gender and sexuality are here coloured by ethnicity. The politics of cultural dialogue embodied here compel a further rethinking of 'the body'. The 'intercultural body', to use Halifu Osumare's concept, is a bodily text of appropriation which encompasses a combination of bodily practices and cultural multiplicity to challenge clear-cut paradigms of cultural theft of Orient by Occident. Pushing beyond the social construction and objectification of 'race', this 'intercultural body', she argues, is a *potentially* subversive means of transgressing/ transcending the controlling and racialising aspects of capitalism in a moment of increasingly complex economic and cultural exchange (Osumare 2002). Dancing solo, Shakti and Iwana use their own bodies as mobilising forces. What reverberates throughout is a sense of dialogic exchange and negotiation, as each engages with the processes of incorporation and inscription.

The discussion that follows considers the form and function of both *Swan Lake* and *The Legend of Giselle* in order to understand the internal operations and arising significance of these dances. I pay particular attention to the intersection between reworking and intercultural exchange. By bringing Iwana and Shakti's dances together I do not mean to efface their clearly distinct approaches and different cultural contexts. Rather, as I weave through this chapter, I allow themes to cross and morph between them such that similar agendas *and* significant contrasts become apparent. I hope that, by placing them together in this way, these dances will illuminate each other – each bringing the other into relief.

Shakti and *Swan Lake* (1998)

> Is it pole dancing or is it art?
> Think Playboy not Bolshoi.
>
> (Stewart 1999: 46)

Shakti's reworking, entitled *Swan Lake* (1998), is positioned as a site of conflicting discourses. A tracing of her representation of the swan woman reveals multifaceted arguments, as this Indo-Japanese woman appears on stage dressed like a G-string diva from a strip club and proceeds to dance perhaps the most prized roles from the classical ballet repertoire. As an intercultural performance artist, marked by the operations of orientalism, Shakti crosses boundaries between the Occident/ Orient and popular/high-art contexts. Within these already complex frames she presents a highly sexualised image which both reinforces and challenges the viewer's objectification of the performer. Her work is, perhaps, refreshingly free of political correctness and conservative feminist doctrine as she enjoys the power and pleasure of her sexuality. However, her image of woman may also be dangerously stereotypical and too easily consumable. I present a pendulous position which swings precariously between celebrating with Shakti her new image of a swan woman and questioning the extent to which this new swan woman is in any way 'new' at all – a different object of desire maybe, but

Plate 16   Swan Lake (1998) by Shakti

Photographer: Mino La Fanca

still an object, and one coded in camp and excess. This dance, and Shakti's particular dancing body, I argue, operates as a site of resistance, but only tenuously.

Her reworking of *Swan Lake* incorporates a series of exchanges of culture. Shakti transforms a nineteenth-century Russian dance text into a twentieth-century Indo-Japanese one, relocating the dance in terms of time and geography. The movement is also intercultural, in that the mix of dance forms evident cannot be placed into a single culture but embodies both Indian and American forms.

Furthermore, Shakti's work breaches boundaries between dance as erotic entertainment and dance as traditional 'high-art' form. The numerous signification systems, which are founded within myriad historical, geographical and artistic contexts, make this dance impossible to locate singularly. It requires the viewer to negotiate across normal boundaries and ignore established perimeters. Through the title, the music and the references to narrative, Shakti draws on our knowledge of the traditional *Swan Lake*, seemingly locating the viewer in a Western, 'high-art' context. However, the movement, costuming and setting shift our perceptions, engaging us in a process of reconceptualisation of *Swan Lake*, Indian classical dance, and Shakti as an Asian woman, bringing to the surface social, political and aesthetic issues. The location of the viewer in a Western, 'high-art' context is thereby estranged, and arguably Shakti instead asserts a post-colonial and (post)feminist experience.

Shakti trained in a range of classical Indian dance forms, yoga (including the tantra) and American modern dance. Her training was initially with her mother (Yae Chakravarty) who, states Shakti, 'was the first Japanese to bring the true form of Indian dance to Japan' (Shakti 1999a).[1] Her mother is the founder of the VasantaMala Indian Dance Institute in Tokyo and artistic director of the company. Shakti has also studied under various gurus of Indian dance: Guru Elappa (Bharata Natyam), Guru C. Archayalu (Kuchipudi), Guru Kelucharan Mahapatra (Odissi) and Swami Bua (yoga). She attempts in her dance to create a new form that is a blending of the techniques of classical Indian dance and the breathing (prana) and control of yoga (Shakti 1999a).

The company repertoire ranges from classical Indian dance pieces to Shakti's own brand of intercultural performance.[2] She has been performing her own work since the early 1980s. The subjects of her dances are often female figures from myth, which Shakti presents as strong and sexual beings. This subject matter is indicated by her performance titles, for example: *Salome*, *Eros of Love and Destruction*, *The Tibetan Book of the Dead*, *The Woman in the Dunes* and *The Pillow Book*. Speaking about *Eros of Love and Destruction*, Shakti states that it is 'about a woman's descent or ascent into herself and realizing all the potentials within. It's an exultation of being a woman and of being alive. It reveals her metamorphosis from self-love to self-destruction, from virgin to a vixen, from exotica to unrelenting erotica' (Shakti n.d.).

I viewed Shakti's reworking of *Swan Lake* when it was presented as part of the Edinburgh Fringe Festival (August 1999). The Garage Theatre venue, managed annually by Shakti, programmes a range of works under the title 'The Japan Experience'. In the press coverage of her *Swan Lake*, Shakti received controversial and mixed reviews, as demonstrated by the short quotation at the beginning of this section. Her dances are structured improvisations and are characterised by their free, energetic quality and unfettered erotic movement. Donald Hutera described her as 'the most audacious performer' at the 1999 Edinburgh Fringe and wrote that her *Swan Lake* is a 'wild ride' which 'risks vulgarity and camp' (Hutera 1999b: 63). In a similar vein Don Morris remarked (1999) that Shakti's swan is 'a shaker and a mover, and with the lusty-thighed Shakti personifying her, there is quite a lot to shake'.

While Shakti is not unused to mixed reviews, the controversy was, I suggest, further heightened because of the subject matter of her dance. For example Morris, in *The Scotsman*, wrote:

> She has ransacked reputable sources such as the *Tibetan Book of the Dead* and the *Kama Sutra* in pursuit of her own gyrating G-string spectacles, but never before has she defiled Tchaikovsky.
>
> (Morris 1999)

Reworkings *per se* do tend to attract mixed reviews – the traditional ballet critic, and even more so critics from the popular press, still seemingly find them, at best, curious though lacking – but what is it about Shakti's reworking of *Swan Lake* that leads a critic to state that Tchaikovsky has been 'defiled'? I suggest in this chapter that Shakti's dance is difficult to digest specifically because it is an intercultural and sexualised reworking of *Swan Lake* that blatantly contrasts the classically coded ballet.

Shakti's *Swan Lake* runs for 44 minutes and is in numerous sections which are defined by costume and music changes. The dance's structure runs parallel to the conventional ballet libretto and makes use of the most well-known sections of the music. The dance starts with Shakti costumed in a black halter-neck dress and sunglasses. The strains of Tchaikovsky's opening sequence play, but rather than Prince Siegfried drinking with his friends in the forest, Shakti walks confidently around the stage and performs a series of poses using gestures reminiscent of Indian dance traditions. She pays particular attention to the hands and arms, shaping them into *mudras*. Her arms circle overhead and then press down in front of her body, stopping at waist height; her fingers, which point towards each other, are stretched out with the middle three fingers pressing upwards and the thumb and little finger pressing downwards. Stylized gestural actions like these are contrasted by everyday gestures such as standing with her arms folded, and with her hands on her hips. Her body remains upright and she makes grounded and rhythmic steps. As the piece proceeds her leg actions become larger and more developed; for example, she flicks her leg out to the side from the knee and sharply swivels her pelvis around to the opposite side in order to step forward.

As the music continues, a full-length revolving mirror is uncovered upstage left. This mirror references both the lake and nightclubs and, as Hutera notes, is 'a fine metaphor for the self-reflective lake' (1999b: 63). It can also be seen as a metaphor for Shakti's self-conscious reworking of the ballet. Shakti gazes at herself and, dancing in front of the mirror, rocks her hips from side to side. Her persona has the strength and control of someone 'in the know'.

In the next section, which uses the 'vision scene' music, Shakti is dressed in a black fur coat that is opened to reveal a white bikini. The poses become more sexual in nature as she stands sideways on, pushes the side of her buttocks forward

Plate 17   Swan Lake (1998) by Shakti

Photographer: Mino La Fanca

and, with one hand touching her hip and holding the coat open and the other at her neck, arches her head back. She then begins to isolate her pelvis in forward pumping motions. The music changes to that which is usually used in act II by the *corps de ballet* leading into a *pas de deux* by Odette and Siegfried. As this music starts Shakti removes her coat and then executes her version of Odette's first appearance by the lake. Echoing the rippling chords of the harp, she performs deep arches of the back, rocks her hips and rotates her hands as her arm strokes up her torso. To the sound of a violin she gestures towards the audience, folding and circling from her elbows with her thumb and middle finger touching. These circling actions develop as she takes her right middle finger into her left hand and marks enlarged circles with her arms and torso. In a dramatic change of dynamic Shakti goes on to perform a wild 'dance of the cygnets'. As she crawls forward on her hands and knees her pelvis and rib cage pulsate. Her hands are held tense in a claw-like shape, with a contorted snarl her head flicks and twitches, and her very long hair flies in all directions. As she stands her whole body oscillates to the thumping rhythm of the music.

Next, dressed in a full-length black lace costume that hints at a medieval period, Shakti dances what appears to be her reworking of Odile in the ballroom scene. However, the music is not from the third act but from the swan scenes in act IV. Slowly she takes down her hair and, removing her choker, suggestively chews upon one end. She repeatedly walks around, and passes through, the revolving mirror. Her back leaning on the mirror, she slides down it to the floor, and then rolls through the mirror. As she leaves the stage she sets the mirror spinning. When she returns it is to the music which forms the dramatic climax in traditional versions, as Odette and Siegfried unite in love and death. Rather than appearing as a white swan finding freedom in death, however, Shakti is now dressed in a silver bikini with a glittery black velvet cape hanging over one shoulder. She swirls the cape and frenetically tosses her hair. Slowly she contorts her face into an orgasmic silent scream. Her body undulates and she touches her neck, face and torso.

For the final section of her *Swan Lake*, Shakti performs as a silver-clad swan to music played by Vanessa Mae, for the first time using music other than Tchaikovsky. Her movement is manic as isolated pulses pump through her hips, ribs, shoulders and head. Her whole body ripples and shakes. As she throws herself forwards and backwards, her hair flies dramatically. The work ends with Shakti in an intense state; on her knees she leans back, her face twisted and her hands held like claws at her throat.

Masaki Iwana and *The Legend of Giselle* (*Jizeru-den*) (1994)

> … having the courage to dance in opposition to a foregone conclusion, having the heart to dance a fruitless dance was recompense in itself.
>
> (Iwana 2002: 45)

In contrast to the brash excesses of Shakti, and stepping even further away from the ballet at its source, is Japanese butoh artist Masaki Iwana and his reworking *The Legend of Giselle* (*Jizeru-den*) (1994). This performance of a European canonical text in a butoh form radically alters and creates dissonance within the conventional Western understanding of the ballet (and dance *per se*). This appropriation brings the cultural specificity of *Giselle* to the fore and also refigures gender. Whereas *Giselle* conventionally reflects the reinforcement of the 'proper' order of class and gender (which, for example, Mats Ek's version reiterates; see chapter 1), Iwana attempts to strip the social body and tap into the subconscious. Extending the theme of cultural exchange and difference, he embraces 'the entire spectrum of life, the evil, ugly and dark' (Leask 1995: 69). His *Legend of Giselle* dislocates the ballet from its usual context and

Plate 18   The Legend of Giselle (1994) by Masaki Iwana

Photographer: Noriko Saitoh

form in a search for an ultimate freedom 'beyond oneself and beyond one's cultural, social and physical ego-bound identity' (ibid.: 64). Revealing the slippage between the lived body and its cultural representation, Iwana takes up the challenge of bodies and cultures, for, rather than presenting a fixed identity, the work implies an interactive and changing concept of cultural location.

Iwana's reworking of *Giselle* was performed in London at Chisenhale Dance Space as part of the 'East Winds Festival of New Butoh' (1995), and was also presented in Tokyo, Paris, Rome, Cologne and Chania, on Crete. At the 'East Winds' festival of workshops, performances and speakers, Iwana presented both his dance *Giselle* and a paper entitled 'Butoh has never existed anywhere' (reproduced in an adapted form in Iwana 2002). Iwana now lives and works in France, running a school and developing the butoh form through a focus upon change and dynamic (Leask 1995: 67). He began his dance career in 1975 outside the traditional butoh genealogy, coming to butoh following university studies and working as an actor. He trained in a range of forms including ballet, modern dance and gymnastics and then started to develop his own form of movement which he calls 'butoh blanc' (white butoh). This form, he says, stresses the philosophical advocacy of 'ankoku butoh' (black butoh, or the dance of darkness) – the form developed by Tatsumi Hijikata, the founder of butoh. Hijikata emphasised the ways in which a dancer must expose the darkness of his/her own existence in order to be open to that which lies dormant within us. Iwana develops this to emphasise 'that

Plate 19   The Legend of Giselle (1994) by Masaki Iwana

Photographer: Noriko Saitoh

such exposure should be so complete that it comes under the "white sun," meaning a perfectly clear and cloudless light' (Iwana 2002: 34).

Iwana has created at least one new solo work per year since 1977, and has toured these dances across Europe and in Japan. His first experiments in movement involved restricting his movements until, in the end, he stood still – beginning the process of inner awareness. Through his *Invisible* series (1980–81) (in which he stood still for one hour in natural light) and his *Decreasing* series (1982) (in which he crouched down and then rolled to the floor) he began to develop a methodology for dancing. It was not until 1985 that he called his dancing 'butoh'. His work ranges from improvisational dances to co-productions with musicians and video artists. The themes for works 'have been woman, masculinity in a woman, femininity in a man, man, holiness in baseness and other like subjects' (Iwana 2002: 15).

Butoh is not easily 'read' in Western terms, for the form has few features that are typical of Western concepts of dance. While butoh uses weight and gravity, and is theatrical and emotional, the form is not concerned with the development of choreographic ideas through a vocabulary of co-ordinated movement. Rather it focuses upon internal imaging to give rise to movement which energises a space to create an architecture that interacts with the viewers (Leask 1995: 67). Often evoking grotesque imagery and dark themes, dancers work to 'access the dance in the body' (ibid.: 69). Iwana states that 'the body is not a slave of society and order (*Shintai*) but should be an alive and changing sculpture fashioned by life itself (*Nikutai*) and the life is that which has encompassed individual history and experience' (cited in ibid.: 64). The embodiment of Japanese bodily concepts is an important feature of Iwana's reworking (see the section below entitled 'Fleshly metamorphosis and becomings in butoh').

In a similar manner to Fergus Early in *Sunrise*, an earlier reworking of *Giselle* created in 1979 (see chapter 1), Iwana uses almost no direct references to the ballet *Giselle* beyond the title and a few notes written for the performance – and these are key to a reading of this dance as a reworking of *Giselle*. In these notes he speaks of 'the Shinkokin poets of medieval times who, standing amidst ruins, were chilled and stimulated by the light of a frigid moon.' Inhabited by such thoughts, he goes on, 'Giselle herself approached me' (Iwana 2002: 46).

> The woman in me: memories which shoot straight up, cascading against the horizontal flow of time; and the unadulterated desires of 'mankind,' the desires that have existed since primeval times, the desires that exist in substances: these are the subjects of 'Giselle'. They are the pulses throbbing between the skin which is me, and space.
>
> Giselle Act two. Giselle stands motionless on top of a grave, struck by the beams of blue moonlight. She dances her past and her present. Then, charmed from the womb of Death by Giselle's dance, Albrecht (Giselle's sweetheart) appears before her. To no avail, 'Giselle' struggles to keep him from his fate.
>
> Just after daybreak: 'Where am I? Where am I to go?,' implores Giselle.
>
> (Ibid.)

Like Early's dance, this one occurs in the gaps of the ballet, creating another tale – responding to aspects of the 'tale' that go unseen or unsaid in the ballet. So while Iwana's expressive yet minimal dance suggests traces of Giselle's inner 'madness', death, rising and return to the grave, it also evokes other layers of her experience and Iwana's own creative interests.

Entering the stage dressed in a long black coat, Iwana stands in a central circle of warm yellow light. He begins to move painfully slowly, stepping forwards and rising onto the balls of his feet. He draws his arms in towards his body and his shoulders rise. Lowering himself onto his back foot, he leans backwards. A sudden pulse through the body leads to a drop of the pelvis downwards and causes the outwardly rotated knees to bend. As he shudders, he reaches an arm up over his head. The tension in the body is discernible, even palpable. As the dance progresses the movement continues to be internally focused – with Iwana glancing towards the audience only at a couple of points during the whole dance. The atmosphere is charged as his knees buckle and arms flare out, swinging from the shoulders in response to his collapsing knees and pelvis.

Iwana pulls his coat open from the chest down and his naked body, covered only by a thin pale coloured stocking, is revealed. He stands with heels raised and feet apart. The body is exposed and vulnerable. Following another period of erupting, fragmenting and stumbling movement, as Iwana shifts between precarious balances and loss of balance, he pulls at and eventually removes the white roll of paper that is attached to his pubic bone. Placing this false penis in his mouth, he slowly lowers himself to the floor. The body for the first time appears relaxed, its weight released into the floor. After lying in darkness and in silence for over two minutes, he slowly rolls towards the back of the stage and brings himself to a standing position. The false penis is still in his mouth as he crouches down to remove his coat fully. When he stands naked it becomes clear that his genitals are not visible – they are tucked away, leaving his body strangely de-sexed. The final images are of Iwana walking backwards towards the back wall, the stage bathed in blood-red light. Then he raises his heels and stands with his right foot on top of his left and allows his arms to drift overhead. The light changes to a deep green and he stands in this difficult pose with his body wavering. As Iwana maintains this unsteady position the lights fade and the piece ends.

While Iwana's particular butoh and this *Giselle* was developed in France, and I viewed it in a British context, the work still seems very Japanese and exotic. However, butoh is a particularly intercultural dance. It developed in its current form after World War II out of a Japanese postwar resistance to 'Americanisation', and was influenced by both German expressive modern dance and the traditional Japanese theatre arts: 'butoh artists negotiate the minefield of split cultural subjectivities, building their own worlds out of the cultural rubbish of Eastern and Western superpowers' (Dils and Albright 2001: 373). Recently it has mutated as the form has spread to other cultures. While this *Giselle* exemplifies features typical of butoh in the use and visual representation of the body, it also diverges from traditional forms. In this work Iwana evokes a fluid body that is liberated from both the cultural imperatives of butoh traditions and the colonialisation of the body embedded in conventional representations of *Giselle*.

Cultural (ex)change and hybridity

It is already clear that these two dances have embedded, and embodied, within them complex forms of cultural (ex)change. They are hybrid dances that newly fuse, and at times productively collide with, distinctive cultural forms. In the post-colonial writing of Homi Bhabha the hybrid resists the binary oppositions of racial and cultural difference. His model of hybridity is especially useful here, as he proposes a fluid and changing (rather than a hybrid but fixed) conceptualisation. Bhabha (1991: 211) characterises hybridity as a space 'in between' – a space in which 'new areas of negotiation of meaning and representation' evolve. Bhabha explains that the in-between space of hybridity is a 'cultural space for opening up new forms of identification that ... confuse the continuity of histori-cal temporalities, confound the ordering cultural symbols, traumatize tradition' (1994: 179). Further, he writes that a hybrid identity involves

> the regulation and negotiation of those spaces that are continually, contin-gently, 'opening out', remaking the boundaries, exposing the limits of any claim to a singular or autonomous sign of difference – be it class, gender or race ... difference is neither One nor the Other, but something else besides – in-between.
>
> (Ibid.: 219)

This concept of hybridity, articulating a postcolonial experience, mitigates notions of fixity and suggests an ambiguous place in between differing world views. It becomes possible, through this perspective, to locate Shakti and Iwana within 'the gaps' of cultural markers, forming places in which different cultures collide, trans-gressing each other's bounds rather than remaining separate. Such hybrid sites, writes Bhabha, are 'mutations' in which 'the trace of that which is disavowed is not repressed but repeated as something *different*' (1995: 34, emphasis in original). So, read through Bhabha, the dances of Shakti and Iwana might be seen to reveal the ambivalence of traditional discourses of authority. For, as a subversion of that which is authoritative (the ballet), these reworkings turn 'the discursive conditions of dominance into the grounds of intervention' (ibid.: 35). That is, in reversing colonialism, Shakti and Iwana place centre stage a denied form which estranges, therefore making explicit, the basis of dominant discourse.

While both these two dances reflect the fluid nature of hybridity, the modes of practice are quite different, embodying significantly distinctive forms of intercul-tural exchange, for, as Helen Gilbert and Jacqueline Lo note, hybridity 'is not a simple fusion of differences but rather a volatile interaction characterised by con-flict between and within the constitutive cultures' (1997: 7). It is the particular modes of volatile interaction and the distinctive aesthetics evident in the dances of Shakti and Iwana that I pursue for a while below.

Butoh and Iwana's butoh reworking of *Giselle* are particularly complex hybrid sites. 'The butoh aesthetic', write Sondra Fraleigh and Tamah Nakamura, 'loops historically from Japan to the West, and goes back to Japan' (2006: 13). Indeed the genealogy of butoh as form, and now as an international phenomenon, can be located interculturally. As Fraleigh comments: 'Butoh may be the most intercultural postmodern art we have' (Fraleigh 1999: 8). In its highly individualist and anti-establishment approach butoh acknowledges the history of modern Japan while 'honing new beginnings and freely plying global imagery. Beyond the Japanese box, Butoh finally spanned many culture and gender distinctions, bringing East and West together in its dance aesthetics and cross dressing' (Fraleigh 2004: 181).

Tracing butoh influences, Fraleigh and Nakamura note how butoh arises in the 'original expressionist "stew" of modern dance in the 1920s and 1930s' and discern the ways in which it embodies aspects of 'traditional Japanese aesthetics' (2006: 14). Butoh continues and breaches these traditional Japanese forms while also crossing other cultural borders and forms. Like the traditional Japanese forms of Noh and Kabuki, butoh reflects pre-modern Japanese aesthetics and values simplicity, incompleteness, emptiness, neutrality and abstraction (Barbe 2003). Like Noh, butoh often moves in an eternally slow time and, like Kabuki, uses white body paint – masking the performer's body. However, while embodying related aesthetics and echoing these forms superficially, butoh is anti-tradition and rejects these earlier forms as archaic and overly codified. Tatsumi Hijikata's first performances of butoh were wild and primal, returning to a more organic beauty – the beauty of an old woman carrying rice upon her back, or a child playing in the rain. Using parody, travesty, cross-dressing and burlesque, Hijikata's butoh was also bawdy and exaggerated. He looked behind the Japanese social mask to create performances that uncovered often ignored aspects of his society. Integrating elements of Japanese culture (classical dance, Japanese body postures, prewar popular entertainment and medieval grotesque paints) with European inspiration (from German expressionism, surrealism, dada and late pop art), Hijikata valued distortion, chance and improvisation (Fraleigh and Nakamura 2006).

Butoh is notoriously difficult to define. Indeed, Iwana suggests that, beyond Hijikata's dance, butoh has never existed – while existing everywhere (Iwana 2002: 40). He writes that dancers have 'merely given their private, personal dance the name "butoh"' (2002: 39). Resisting the attempts to locate or define butoh, he implies a notion of butoh that is far removed from the specifics of Japanese dance and culture, while still clearly embodying a traditionally non-Western philosophical position.

In his writings Iwana cites some characteristics of his to approach butoh:

1   When inner, hidden elements are fully actualized, the dancer's (or the human's) qualities as a material entity – e.g., the perfection of his or her ambiguity – will grow in *abstractness*. And when two hidden elements simultaneously awaken and become actualized, *duality* emerges. ...

2   The total opening of a living entity involves 'dark intentions' as perceived by the institutional society. ...

3   *Regression* and *limitations* are also recognitions characteristic to butoh. A living entity does not consist only of such aspects as *advance* and *expansion*. Rather, a living entity's substance is more apparent in contractions, perishing or withering. …

                                                    (Iwana 2002: 13, emphasis in original)

These characteristics he sets in contrast to the features of modern dance, such that, while the butoh dancer develops an 'inner landscape', the modern dancer pursues 'form and movement'; where the butoh dancer seeks 'transformation' the modern dancer emphasises 'expression'; and where the butoh dancer values 'presence' the modern dancer strives to attain 'techniques' (ibid.: 9–12). These dualisms are of course highly problematic and oversimplified (which Iwana himself acknowledges), yet they do provide useful insights into Iwana's approach to butoh and the reworking of *Giselle*.

Rather than telling a story, as in the narrative form of *Giselle*, Iwana evokes experiences and traces human consciousness through the body. While his reworking does have some parallels to the narrative of *Giselle* – for the work can be seen to suggest Giselle's metamorphosis from her physical body, through death, to what could be seen as her spiritual body as a Wili – this reading does not take into account the form and approach of butoh. This parallel reading of the conventional narrative is only very tentatively suggested in the dance and encompasses only a small part of Iwana's *Giselle*. Rather, prominence is given to hidden themes in the ballet and Iwana's own unfolding questions. What is it to embody the woman Giselle – her past and her present? What is it to die of a broken heart? To be betrayed? What is it to explore one's sexuality, perhaps for the first time? What is it to experience the desires of 'mankind'? To struggle against fate? These questions weave through the work, forming layers of images, evoking intersecting resonances at one time, for here meanings are not literal but ongoing and open to interpretation.

Instead of manifesting in outward display, as in ballet, Iwana's energy spirals inwards, tending towards awkwardness and dissipation. He emphasises ambiguity, imbalance and entropy, in contrast to ballet's clarity, harmony and flow of kinetic energy. As Fraleigh and Nakamura write: 'Contradicting the balanced essence of ballet, butoh plies the excitement of being off-balance, the psychic path of shaking and plodding. Its somatic subtly goes to hair-splitting extremes' (2006: 13).

This reworking is not, like ballet, choreographically structured in repeated patterns and motifs that occur in metered time, but is distinctly marked by its use of extended time and shows a distilled approach. Distillation in butoh is most often discussed in terms of the use of slow motion, stillness and the experience of time – for example, the moment of one intake of breath is extended into a ten-minute dance. Yet this concept, so important to butoh, is reflected in Iwana's dance not only in his use of time, but also in the uncovering and detailed expansion of single moments, of characters and emotions.[3] Iwana takes elements of the ballet and stretches these out, excavating images to expose the many layers and complexities within a single moment. This technique of distillation enables us to experience *Giselle* in a new way, as each distilled moment, each essence, is dilated and engorged.

Further the process of distillation and the experience of images over duration enables many readings and experiences to emerge that would not otherwise do so. During the opening sequences Iwana, dressed in a long black cloak, contrasting his white painted hands, hovers on his toes and reaches his arms above his head – as if hanging from a rope. Shifting his weight, he twists and turns, moving from the inside to the outside of his feet – falling from balance only to recover. Watching, I am not sure whether he is evoking the role of Giselle, the mother or, perhaps, Myrtha. Over time he is all of these women and none of them. The images created are ambiguous – suggesting inner tensions and conflicts, shifting histories and the merging of past and present – as his difficult balances on the balls of the feet evoke a sense of the body's fragility. Rather than explicitly representing the character of Giselle, he works from inside himself. As Kozel and Rotie note, Iwana has an ability 'to metamorphose, to blur the distinction between "being" and "other", and in the process to gain access to a mythic, archetypal realm mediated through images' (1996: 35).

Later in the work Iwana very slowly lowers from a standing position to lie on the floor. The action is suggestive of Giselle's death, leading to her rise as a spirit creature in act II. This structure also echoes the life–death cycle that is a common form in butoh. From the perspective embodied in butoh, there is no death as such in this cycle, only regeneration. Iwana's gradual and difficult lowering to the floor and eventual stillness, notes Leask, is a retreat into a 'death state' or into 'nothingness' (1995: 69). So while structurally Iwana appears to parallel Giselle's decent into madness and death, in butoh the 'death state' conveys the value of doing nothing and clearing thoughts so that a meditative silence is evoked. This is a place where the breaths in the body can become eloquent. In this present-centred aesthetic, 'consciousness has the opportunity to shift from its forward orientation to experience relief. Moments empty of thought and habit as we let go the compulsion to act or even think upon them' (Fraleigh 1999: 203).

Following this 'death state', Iwana slowly rises and, for the first time in the dance, his heels are grounded and his body is at ease. So while conventionally Giselle, as a Wili, becomes less substantial, less grounded, Iwana, for a moment at least, becomes more earthly, more centred. His gaze passes across the audience – acknowledging their presence. There is a sense of an intake of breath, a pause to reflect. His rising from the death state does not lead to a mythical world of spirits (as in a traditional *Giselle*) but to a moment of self-awareness and clarity. This moment is fleeting, however, as his weight shifts onto the edges of his feet and he is once more off-balance. His hands, arms and torso embody different rhythms, follow different 'stories', while remaining fully and essentially connected. Little by little Iwana peels away his coat as if shedding his skin. Unmasking the culturally mannered body, he reveals layers of self, through which we come to experience Giselle.

This *Giselle* is quietly intense, ambiguous, dark and in constant transformation. Pushing at boundaries of time and extreme states of being, and morphing from image to image, Iwana does not attempt to create an ethereal presence or narrative form as in ballet; his is a study of nature, time, death, sexuality. Transforming the ballet out of recognition, yet retaining references to it in the title and programme notes, Iwana holds *Giselle* in our sights, albeit in the corner of our peripheral vision as a shadowy intertext. In doing so this reworking embodies (ex)changes of culture in which East and West are brought together, allowing one culture to be seen through the lens of another.

While Iwana creates a hybrid reworking of *Giselle* through processes of distillation and dilation, Shakti's reworking is segmented and semi-narrative in structure. Her reworking encompasses overt intertextual references and multiple deconstructions. In particular she has developed her own individual and hybrid movement style, for her movement, which is clearly not from the ballet idiom, is neither exclusively from classical Indian nor from American modern dance forms – but a mix of these things and others (including Bollywood and erotic club dancing). Yet Shakti's classical Indian dance background is nonetheless the most evident. We see it through her use of features which are typical of classical Indian dance,[4] such as hand gestures (*mudras*), facial expressions (*abhinaya*), rhythmic and beating foot movements, and her generally earthbound movement quality. However, these features are performed in an unfettered manner which suggests a departure or development from classical Indian dance forms. For example, the foot rhythms and hand gestures are not developed as a defining element, as they are in 'traditional'[5] dances, but are only part of a full-bodied and sinuous movement form. For example, Shakti begins with a *mudra* around the face but then throws her hand backwards and arches her spine; her feet mark out a turn but her head swings rapidly in rotation. Her movements are unbound, even messy, in comparison with the codified geometry of classical forms. The exaggerated facial expressions that are a strong feature of her dance are not conventionally stylised. Rather than making a coquettish use of specific eye positions and the generally pleasant smile of classical Indian dance forms, Shakti grimaces and opens her mouth in orgasmic silent screams.

Shakti uses a mix of forms and crosses boundaries between forms to develop a dance style which has been described by critic Mary Brennan as 'classical Indian dance training allied to a kind of free-form Raks Sharki (*sic*)' (1999). The style could also be described as a postmodern or avant-garde Indian dance. Avant-garde classical Indian dance, Ananya Chatterjea writes,

> chooses to privilege what has been marginalized, often attends to the differentials enforced by class, caste, and gender inequities, and looks to define its own aesthetics and politics.
>
> (Chatterjea 1997: 294)[6]

Recent classical dancing in India has begun to break from tradition in terms of structure and content. In order to reflect feminist critiques and to embody a postcolonialist reassessment of power, contemporary female choreographers have reinterpreted traditions and myths by relating their dances to contemporary social realities (Bose 1998: 254). This view of change is also voiced by Chatterjea in her essay 'How can the brown, female, subaltern feminist speak?' (1997). In a parallel process to Shakti's reworking of *Swan Lake* (although with very different outcomes) Chatterjea describes how, in her work *Multitudinous Trio*, she attempted to choreograph reinterpretations of the legendary figures from a contemporary feminist perspective – 'reinterpreting myths so as to upset traditional conceptions' (Chatterjea 1997: 297).

Shakti's radical, sexualized *Swan Lake* can be seen as part of this shift in Indian dance. She uses choreographic variations or developments of Indian dance akin to those used by other choreographers.[7] Key to these variations is her use of a much less codified movement vocabulary, which is plural rather than 'purist' and suggests dialogues with different dance forms. Shakti also departs from tradition in terms of music, her form of improvisation and the use of a Western and secular subject matter as her source.

The accompaniment commonly used for bharata natyam (a particular form of Indian classical dance)[8] is South Indian classical (Carnatic) music. The form uses spoken syllables, song and instrumental sounds. The association between particular dances and their musical compositions are such that the dances are often identified on the basis of their musical content (Gaston 1999: 269). Discussing a traditional concert, for example, Gaston describes the Alarippu, which appears first in a traditional concert, as a dance which is performed to a fixed composition of mnemonic syllables. She goes on to describe a series of dances, noting the ways in which they alter rhythmically in accordance with the musical developments. Her account indicates that the dance relates to the music, with the spoken mnemonic rhythmic syllables suggesting the movement. 'Thus hard sounds such as "ta", "di", "gi", "na", "tom", direct percussive movements, while softer sounds, such as "longu", suggest other movements such as turns or jumps' (ibid.: 268). Dances that emphasise *abhinaya* are choreographed to poems set to music. These dances follow the narrative of the songs, expressing the moods and predicaments of the young woman at the centre of the tale.

Shakti's use of Tchiakovsky reflects both a radical departure and a maintenance of tradition. While in the style of music she uses – arguably the most canonical of Western classical music – there is an obvious rupture from the norms of Indian classical dance, her way of employing it is less radically different. Shakti maintains a clear rhythmic and dynamic relationship to the score. For example, in the music from act II, she performs a series of stepping turns around the stage as its rhythm changes, taking the precise length of the phrase. As a new phrase starts, she stops turning and performs a series of poses followed by soft padding foot patterns, again all in exact time to the musical patterns. This close relationship to the music reflects her traditional training.

The music also of course provides the viewer with the most direct connection to the ballet and thereby is a very important signifier. While the dance itself may have its own thrust, which could be said to be against the score, Shakti still uses the music to remind us of the ballet's narrative. Interestingly, while the costuming and movement suggest that Shakti follows the narrative of *Swan Lake*, evoking Odette and Odile respectively before evolving into the transcendent silver swan, close attention to the music leads to another possibility. It is all taken from acts I, II and IV, with none from Odile's dances. This could imply that Shakti's dance evokes not two women, but one – Odette. This reworking could be said to follow her story and her transformations through black, white, black and to silver rather than oppositions in women.

Although improvisation in classical Indian dance is not uncommon, it is normally allowed only within strict codes of prescribed movements. Shakti's whole dance is a structured improvisation. While her conceptual frame, costume changes and musical structure are set, the movement is not. Working through her practices in yoga, Shakti starts the dance 'cold'. She says that her body warms from the inside as she begins to perform (1999b). Therefore the dance starts with more recognisable movement, and as she warms up (in a mental and physical sense) the dance becomes less clearly defined. By the final section she has entered a trance-like state. Shakti remarks:

> I start more structured, and slowly the structure breaks and there is no structure any more – you become more free. But you have to have a structure to destroy, otherwise you don't get anywhere.
>
> (Shakti 1999b)

The overall structure she uses and ultimately destroys is a Western one – the libretto of *Swan Lake*. The use of a Westernised dance text as subject matter is outside the norm of subject matter for classical Indian dance. Traditional Indian dances, even as rendered on the concert stage, take religious forms and emphasise the dancer's dedication and love of the deity Krishna, with mythic narratives and personal transformations as common subjects. In traditional *Swan Lakes*, comparable themes of love and transformation exist, albeit in a Western and secular form; these subjects have here been translated across cultures. This translation or, perhaps more suitably, appropriation of a Western dance text is a potentially subversive postcolonialist twist, destabilising the neat binary categories of the Orient and the Occident.

This *Swan Lake* intervenes in the broad transnational, even globalising, sweep of the ballet genre, for the ballet genre has been adopted or imposed (as is often the case in colonialist situations) in many non-European countries. The implicit values inherent in the aesthetics and technique of ballet travel with it to these new locations. For example, Janet O'Shea notes that in postcolonial India 'ballet became the legitimizing standard' (1998: 54). O'Shea also describes the ballet instruction received by Rukmini Devi (one of 'two towering figures' who led the bharata natyam form in the early to mid-twentieth century (ibid.: 46). This ballet instruction, with the famous ballerina Anna Pavlova, was retained and incorporated into the 1930s reconstructed form of bharata natayam (ibid.: 54).

Shakti's ownership and ambivalence towards the ballet form marks this reworking as a political site of postcolonialist resistance. She freely makes this European export her own without embodying the inherent history or universalising aesthetics of the form. This resistance is also directed towards classical Indian dance, for Shakti rejects, or expands, 'traditional' Indian forms, which, as noted above, can already be seen as a postcolonial blend of Western and Indian forms. Shakti (literally) embodies, and her work represents, a complex hybrid site. As noted earlier, she is herself of mixed national and ethnic origin; the dance uses a blend of forms (Indian dance, modern dance and yoga, alongside influences from Japanese styles) and is based upon another form (ballet), while the work is performed in yet a different context (in this case Scotland). As the embodiment of hybridity, Shakti exists 'in between' positions.

What is evident is that both these intercultural reworkings bring to the fore the notion of ballet as a colonising form, so, whether or not these dances come from actual postcolonial situations, their interaction with ballet as a site of the coloniser means that they both intersect with postcolonial debates. Iwana's butoh reworking implicitly challenges notions of cultural stasis and monoculturalism in the discourses of ballet and Japan, while Shakti's Indo-Japanese – Western dance speaks back to the colonised history of India and the ballet.

These two dances by Shakti and Iwana represent a reverse appropriation of a Western classical ballet from a hybrid position. This hybrid position asserts the transactional nature of the postcolonial world, emphasising the mutuality of the colonising/colonised process. For, as Sara Suleri suggests, the facts 'frequently fail to cohere around the master-myth that proclaims static lines of demarcation between imperial power and disempowered culture, between colonizer and colonized.' She argues that, rather than there being a rigid demarcation between cultures, there is what she characterises as a 'ghostly mobility' between the colonised and the coloniser (Suleri 1995: 112).[9] In many ways these dances represent this shifting, 'ghostly mobility' – Shakti rendering it overt, and Iwana holding it as a lingering shadow. In their mobility these dances operate not on one single axis of power, but though a network of ghostly relationships, a network that suggests a much more discursive field through which Iwana and Shakti reiterate the narrative of neither the coloniser nor the colonised. Thereby they avoid binary categories and suggest instead an anti-monolithic model of exchange.

Through the hybrid position it becomes possible to view these reworkings of *Swan Lake* and *Giselle* as canonical counter-discourses, unveiling assumptions and ungrounding the perception of *Swan Lake* and *Giselle* as 'universal'. While all reworkings bring our attention, implicitly or explicitly, to concerns about purity, authenticity and ownership, these intercultural reworkings raise the stakes further. These two dances bring to the fore the impossibility of purity and the myth of originality, and, as Richard Schechner has pointed out, in 'hybrids and fusions' (that combine diverse cultural forms) there is the potential to subvert and overturn 'the colonial horror of "impurity" or "mixing"' (2002: 226).

It is important to note, however, that, while Iwana and Shakti's hybridity gives them the *potential* for taking a resistant stance, it not does not necessarily position their reworkings *as* resistant. For example, aspects of the imagery in *Swan Lake* by

Shakti in particular, such as the exotic and erotic modes of presentation, suggest a much less resistive stance, and both are strongly contained by the residual operations of orientialism.

Orientalism and the exotic

While these intercultural reworkings give rise to counter-canonical debates when viewed in a Western context, the bodies of Shakti and Iwana still unavoidably bear the impact of the continuing processes of colonisation by Western culture. Trinh T. Minh-ha makes the point that

> the third world representative the modern sophisticated public ideally seeks is the unspoiled African, Asian, or Native American, who remains more preoccupied with her/his image of the *real* native – the *truly different* – than with the issues of hegemony, racism, feminism, and social change.
>
> (Minh-ha 1995: 267)

Minh-ha's argument suggests that the 'first world' fantasy of the 'authentic' native envelops the 'third world' in a branding of 'difference'. This 'difference' is marked through 'orientalism', to use Edward Said's term. Said, in his influential postcolonialist work *Orientalism* (1995), makes clear that oriental culture and cultural forms, and, I would add, oriental bodies, have been exoticised due to the operation of orientalism. The categories of Orient and Occident are useful if problematic constructs. The terms are used by Said to denote a culturally constructed distinction: 'the "Orient" and the "Occident" are man-made' (1995: 5), and are more to do with imaginative geography than a fact of nature. Said's analysis of orientalism has been criticised for its construction of an inescapable dualism between the Orient and the Occident and the failure to locate a place from which the colonised can speak. However, he very usefully identifies long-lived and powerful forces of oppression. He argues that the images and stereotypes constructed by Western artists and scholars about the 'other' have produced unhelpful myths which repress and exoticise their subjects.

Exoticisation processes can be seen as a 'cultural cannibalism' (Root 1996: 30). The exotic 'other' (that which in the consuming culture is deemed to be 'different') is appropriated and constructed by the consuming culture – feeding curiosity and fantasy. It is important to note that this process is not an equal one but one in which cultural differences are abstracted and aestheticised, negating the people or the culture that is the source of the interest, thereby rendering it an exotic spectacle (ibid.). Viewing exoticism as a cannibalistic act makes overt the way in which the 'West' takes freely of the 'East' in order the satisfy Westerners' desires and fulfil romanticised images.

Such cannibalistic appropriations of the exotic 'other' have often been presented on the Western stage in ballet and modern dances.[10] As Pallabi Chakravorty notes, the popularity of the Eastern girl in Western ballets is one of the obvious examples of the unequal discourse of imperialism. This is evident, she writes, 'in the cultural appropriation of the "eternal" Orient as the repository of exotic customs and spiritual mysticism' (Chakravorty 2000–1: 110). While I shall not go into detail here, for it is not the focus of this work, the representation in dance of the exotic does influence readings of these reworkings. Exotic characters from far-off lands people many of Petipa's ballets. For example, *La Bayadère* (1877) is set in a lush and fantastical India and revolves around Nikiya, a sacred temple dancer, and *The Nutcracker* (1892) incorporates dances intended to represent Arabia, China and Spain.[11] The requirements of pointe work and *divertissement* in the classical style, however, meant that 'realistic' representations of Eastern dances were not possible, and not necessarily even desired. These imagined exotic worlds have little relationship to, or pretence of, realism; rather they are modes of colourful decoration and visual spectacle. However, as Deborah Jowitt notes, this did not restrain choreographers, as they 'doled out exoticism in judicious doses' (1988: 53). The image of the India reflected and created by these dances is that of 'a fantastic land of snake charmers, dancing girls, and spiritual mystique – a predominantly Hindu land with little heterogeneity' (Chakravorty 2000–1: 110).

International exhibitions and world fairs held in Europe and America at the turn of the nineteenth century promoted a fascination with all things from the East. Early modern dancers such as the American Ruth St Denis and the Canadian Maud Allan also embodied this curiosity. These dancers, like other contemporary artists, sought from the East 'a utopian vision of the past glories of classical civilizations' (Desmond 1993: 45). Further, the East was cast as 'an antidote to the chaotic urban conditions that threatened the middle and upper classes' (ibid.).

Following the fashion in the arts and in sciences for all things 'exotic', Allan and St Denis invoked a vision of the oriental in dances such as *Rhada* (St Denis, 1906) and *The Vision of Salome* (Allan, 1903). Their depiction of the 'oriental dance' had become so inscribed by the 1920s that Joan Erdman is able to characterise it thus:

> Certain features were perceived as essential: fluid boneless arm and shoulder motion, rhapsodic spirituality, costumes composed of swirling gossamer drapery and opaque veils, elaborate and wondrously vibrant jewelry, and hand movements intended to signal more than graceful positioning.
>
> (Erdman 1996: 288)[12]

Erdman emphatically states that '"Oriental dance" was an Occidental invention' (ibid.). This inventing of the Orient, as composed of exotic, mysterious, colourful figures, is a typical example of the process of orientalism in operation, a process described by Said as 'a Western style for dominating, restructuring, and having authority over the Orient' (1995: 3).

While Erdman focuses mainly upon orientalist visions of India, similar borrowings and re-presentations have been made of Japan. These '*Japonismes*' (a term commonly used in the visual arts to refer to artists – particularly French artists – and their works that have been heavily influenced by Japanese aesthetics) have received less attention in dance, yet such 'influences' can be seen in the work of Martha Graham and Mary Wigman. Indeed, Fraleigh notes how Japanese dancers studying New Dance abroad in the 1920s and 1930s 'encountered the East in several guises'. 'The early modern dance they witnessed and participated in', she writes, 'was often propelled by an "Oriental" craze' (2004: 179).

The popularity of butoh, its growing international following, can also been seen as part of an ongoing oriental fashion, as audiences, as well as Western post-modern theatre directors and choreographers, display a fascination for all things oriental. For example, oriental ideologies, forms and aesthetics are evident in the experimental theatres of Peter Brook, Robert Lepage and Robert Wilson. They reveal themselves too in the dance practices of Merce Cunningham and many of the early postmodern dancers at Judson Church.

Butoh and butoh-informed practices are now performed the world over. These practices are often described in ecstatic and spiritual terms. For example, as one reviewer eulogises; 'this naked dancer reaches inside of herself to draw out essential truths, those that we have suppressed, but long to reconnect with' (Liberatore 2005). Comments such as this reflect the ongoing Western tendency to look to the East for a spiritual truth, for the embodiment of universals, and for the recovery of a perceived innocence long since lost in the West. This mythologising of dance forms such as butoh is ingrained with undertones of exoticisation and is a form of new orientalism. Iwana too is troubled by responses to butoh in Europe: 'he is nagged by the suspicion that it might stem from the dance's seeming exoticism' (Misaki 1998: 70). Iwana also comments:

> I have no interest in those who see butoh as a kind of exotic spectacle of strange movements and bizarre gestures and who want to 'learn' it by some sort of rote process ... I find only marginal interest in butoh fanatics who covet butoh as an oddity and the dance 'experts' whose pride hangs on the thread of conventional technique.
>
> (Iwana 2002)

Kazuo Ohno's dance *Suiren* (Water Lilies, 1987), while not immune to the mystifications of Western audiences, provides an interesting reversal of the processes of orientialism and exoticization. Ohno, who with Hijikata was one of the leading founders of butoh, dances this duet with his son Yoshito Ohno. With Claude Monet's impressionist paintings *Water Lilies* as his inspiration, Kazuo Ohno draws on themes outside of Japan. Using Monet as his foil, he incorporates *Japonisme*, for Monet borrowed liberally from the aesthetics and culture of Japan, creating paintings of an orientalist landscape – as constructed at his home in Giverny. 'Behind *Surien*', Fraleigh and Nakamura poetically write, 'ones senses the transparency and spiritual luminosity of Monet's work, the surface of the water, motionless or gently rippling, emerging through the flat leaves of the Water Liles, and floating flowers in repose like the lotus lilies of Buddhist tranquillity' (2006: 94).

Yet this dance is in no way a simple homage or imitation of Monet. Rather *Surien* estranges and displaces Monet and the traditions of self-portraiture in Western art. Mark Franko suggests that Ohno 'appears to practice a form of reverse "japonisme" from within one of the Occident's own sublimating representations of Japan: the water-lily series. That is, a Japanese artist frames himself in a Western image of Japan to express his desublimated vision of Western emotionalism' (1995: 102).

Ohno's dance, its revisiting and transformation of Western art, provides a useful lens through which to consider *The Legend of Giselle*. Taking *Giselle* as his starting point, Iwana transforms the Western concepts of Romanticism theatricalised therein. As the embodiment of Western Enlightenment thought and French bourgeois ideology, the Romantic ballet *Giselle* rejects authoritarianism and celebrates passion, emotion, melancholy and the sense of mystery in life. On the surface Iwana's butoh dance shares parallel concerns. Yet, while ballet expresses these ideas through outward display, Iwana internalises them. He turns to his own sensation of passions and emotions, such that we perceive his shifting experiences rather than see the demonstration of them. Through this turning inside of Western Enlightenment he reveals by way of contrast the idealised surfaces of the Romantic ballet.

While Iwana risks orientalist objectification, Shaki's female body is doubly colonised as orientalist, and patriarchal ideologies work in tandem. The non-Western female body is mapped and controlled from within its own culture, and from without by Western orientalists. Chatterjea states that the subaltern female body

> has been subject to relentless tabooing and reconstruction through the process of colonization, national cultural revivalism and the creation of new national identity through the woman's body.
>
> (Chatterjea 1997: 297)

This process has been particularly evident in its effects upon the subaltern performing female body (ibid.). In the discourse of orientalism, and as a result of patriarchal constructs, it becomes clear that the stereotypical oriental female performer is perceived to be at once an excessively sexualised being and a sexually repressed, controlled woman.[13]

The double colonisation of the female body has been 'redoubled' by many Western feminisms.[14] Western feminisms have naturalised differentiated experiences of patriarchal oppression under a European model. This form of feminist colonisation is implicitly confronted in Shakti's work. Shakti's hybrid performance/body evades and elides the search by the 'first world' for a real or authentic 'third world' representation. She stands in opposition to (re)produced authenticity, which, as a product of hegemony (as a counterpart of universalism), constitutes a silencing of radical oppression. Shakti is anti-authentic and her work militates against universalist readings. She uses what is hers and what is not hers, refusing to be reduced to a single 'real' identity. Hence she echoes (post)feminist agendas in her assertion of a fluid identity which cannot be generalised or essentialised.

One of the ways Shakti challenges assumptions about the Orient (views which are mirrored by Western feminisms) is to refuse to sit safely within the bounds of tradition. By 'opening up' the codified language of classical Indian dance, and overtly 'breaking the rules' of what has been constructed as a symbol of 'Indianness', she calls into question images of India as a tradition-centred culture.

As an intercultural performance, Shakti's *Swan Lake* interrupts the notion of an authentic performance tradition, emphasising instead multiplicity and plurality. So although her Edinburgh fringe venue promotes 'The Japan Experience', the experiences on offer reflect multiple and complex visions of 'otherness'. While working against a white hegemony, she simultaneously flaunts and uses her 'difference'. However, her 'difference' is founded upon a concept of 'other' which is a not singular or 'pure' 'otherness', but a 'difference' which is of a number of locations. As Erdman asks: 'what is "the other" when one belongs to more than one place?' (1996: 291).

Shakti's *Swan Lake*, as seen by the predominantly Western audience at the Edinburgh Fringe Festival, is both familiar and foreign, in a place between the Orient and the Occident. So while the extent to which any Asian woman, whose body has already been exoticised, can create a more mutable identity is questionable, this *Swan Lake*, as an intercultural experience, which operates through a plurality of cultural and artistic signifiers, functions so to as destabilise neat power. Challenging the constricting bounds of exoticism, Shakti constructs a mutable identity that reflects the urban societies (in the 'East' and the 'West') in which she locates herself. For although the Orient, argues Said, cannot be discussed as a 'free subject of thought or action' (1995: 88), in this work Shakti deconstructs typical 'Eastern' and 'Western' forms. Through the stripping of context, alteration of subject matter and transformation of form, the performance requires an audience to examine how it recognises cultural forms and what stereotypes are associated with them.

Shakti's work is as much, if not more, 'about' a reconfiguration of Indian dance forms as it is 'about' a reworking of ballet. In its reconfiguration of Indian dance and ballet, her *Swan Lake* presents a current sensibility. However, is it, asks Erdman, like other new Indian choreographies, a form of 'new orientalism'? For Erdman, 'new orientalism' is founded upon the ways in which dances combine 'Western sensibilities, technological sophistication, and international audience appeal with indigenous Indian themes and/or movement' (Erdman 1996: 298).

Following Erdman's characterisation of the 'new orientalism', Shakti's *Swan Lake* might well been seen to be deeply mired in the orientalism it seeks to deconstruct. As a reworking of a Western dance form that uses a contemporary form of Indian dance and is performed at an international arts festival, the dance is clearly marketed to an international audience. The publicity images Shakti uses to promote her dance also play on the orientalist expectations of a Western consumer. For example, her use of sheer fabrics and heavy make-up are reminiscent of fantasy representations of women from a harem.[15] Through such images she engages in a form of self-exoticisation, reinforcing the reading of her work as exotic and continuing the over-inscription of the colonial body which limits the subversive potential of her work.

It becomes obvious through this discussion that dances cannot be imagined autonomously. These dance texts, like all texts, can only be read in the light of cultures, contexts and other texts. The non-Western images used may seem to be dominant (or at least resonate most strongly to 'Western' eyes through their 'difference'), but there are reminders that these works would not have been possible without the prior incarnations of *Giselle* and *Swan Lake*, the classic ballets. These ballets, with all their cultural imperatives, continue to rumble in the background within the new, culturally hybrid works – even if the ballet is not literally embodied in movement.

While a reworking may seek to exceed the colonising source text, that source remains as an inevitable trace (or, more strongly, essence). This aspect of the reworking is echoed in Gayatri Chakravorty Spivak's (1995) accounts of postcolonialism. Spivak makes clear that the only things that one really deconstructs are things in which one is deeply mired.[16] For, she argues, deconstructive practices can speak only in the language of the things they criticise. Because of this predicament it becomes necessary to ask the question: To what extent is it possible to rework a privileged discourse, that of the ballet canon, without reinscribing Western privilege?

The difficulties of a deconstructive process may limit, but do not negate, the possibilities of a reworking process. Shakti's *Swan Lake*, as discussed above, speaks across a number of languages, and Iwana avoids an overtly deconstructive process, while using an inherently deconstructive form. Although the ballets upon which these dances are based are reflected in these works, fundamental features of the ballet canon have been removed – most importantly the language of ballet itself. The replacing of the codified form of ballet with a butoh-based movement language and a deconstructed version of classical Indian dance forces an audience to relocate its perspective.

The complex relationships between colonial/postcolonial and regulated/subversive bodies are noted by Susan Bennett in *Performing Nostalgia*:

> The post-colonial body is constantly susceptible in its gestures, in its languages, of cultural expropriation. It is the body that colludes with postmodernism in a global economy that appropriates and markets exotic practices in a showcase called multiculturalism. Yet it is also the body which holds out the hope of exceeding the regulated performances of the past.
>
> (Bennett 1996: 148)

It is to the body, its representation and materiality, that I now turn. Firstly, in the following section, I investigate the ways in which Shakti radically challenges the ballet image of woman – re-presenting Odette and Odile in a highly sexualised manner. I then turn to consider the potential of Iwana's body as a deregulatory and unruly force, noting the ways in which his deterritorialised body provides an active site of subversion.

Enter the silver swan: excess and the erotic

Brennan writes that she 'will never see *The dance of the little swans* in quite the same light thanks to those pelvic shunts' (1999). Indeed, Shakti's representation of the Swan is less about a mystical creature full of grace, as evident in traditional versions, and more to do with creatures from a natural world who fight and mate. She says of her 'dance of the cygnets':

> Do little swans really flitter and flutter around on their toes? No, they are kind of wild. I would think of the 'dance of the little swans' as more of a mating dance ... a savage one ... with their webbed feet and strong beaks. The swan is a creature of the wild – it is not tame – they're proud creatures but free.
>
> (Shakti 1999b)

The Petipa/Ivanov *Swan Lake* is often criticised within feminist dance literature for its representation of women as dualistic and disempowered. For example, Christy Adair writes that in Odette we have '"the woman on a pedestal" of male fantasy' while, on the other hand, 'Odile provides the other extreme of fantasy as "a woman to be used"'(1992: 107). Both of these roles, Adair argues, disempower women by placing control in the hands of men. Sally Banes, in her more recent text *Dancing Women*, essentially follows this argument, stating:

> So in *Swan Lake* there is a binary division that sorts women into the categories of wicked and good, expressed in oppositions between active and passive, assertive and yielding, strong and gentle.
>
> (Banes 1998: 61)

And she continues:

> Yet the monster and the angel are wrapped up in a single woman, for one ballerina dances both roles, suggesting an underlying female dualism.
>
> (Ibid.: 61–2)

Shakti considers that her version of the swan woman surpasses the traditional duality of the good Odette and the evil Odile. Shakti's swan is not only performed by one dancer, but is also a single character who transforms as the dance progresses. In this version the white swan evolves through the work into a transcendent, powerful silver swan. This transformation process is marked by a series of costumes that are variously removed and layered throughout the dance. Shakti starts the dance in a black fur coat and then reveals the white G-string bikini beneath it; the white bikini is later covered by a black lace dress, as she transforms into the Black Swan. The white bikini can still be seen through the black lace. The costuming reinforces the interrelationship between the black swan and the white swan, who are presented as containing elements of each other – neither is entirely black or white. Indeed, as Shakti would have it, the black and the white swan are not separate, dualistically opposing women but different aspects of one woman. The final costume change is into a silver bikini. This costume references back to the white bikini but in its glittering fabric and slicker design is clearly a move away from that prior image.

Following the philosophies of tantric yoga, which Shakti practises, the black and white swans are projections of the inner and opposing forces inside all of us, for yoga is based on a philosophy in which everything is viewed as having two aspects. Following the one living divinity (Brahma), who separates Itself into Him (Shiva) and Her (Shakti), opposites are evident in all aspects of life. Everything has two elements: male and female, now and then, here and there, self and other-than-self, and good and evil. These opposites are in a continuous relationship and are considered essential parts of the divine process.

In the practice of yoga there is an attempt to reach a union and transcendence of these opposites. Shakti's vision of *Swan Lake* therefore can be usefully illuminated by this philosophy. The opposites of good and evil in the forms of Odette and Odile are brought together and embodied by the Silver Swan – who transcends them both. This transcendent silver swan woman is neither all purity nor all evil, but is a woman who embodies both good and evil. She is free in her desires and enjoys both aspects of her self in a shimmering illusion of silver. Shakti suggests that her Silver Swan has the freedom to be whatever she wants to be and that:

> You could be a virgin *and* a whore. You could be creative *and* destructive. There is no need to deny one side of you, but I think people have the tendency to deny the black or the white … one is bad or one is good.
>
> (Shakti 1999b)

Further, she maintains that:

> In a Western context it is a struggle between good and evil. But then in an Eastern context good and evil are one. So what is good and what is evil – you don't have one without the other – which is also true in the Western *Swan Lake* – we just don't have the princes and the romance there because it's all within you.
>
> (Ibid.)

Shakti's Silver Swan is a very desirous and sexualised swan/woman. Her movements are powerful and dynamic, sexual and demonic. Her body writhes and pulsates as she crawls across the floor and rhythmically thrusts her pelvis and flings her hair. She performs with an abandonment unusual in Western dance and is overt in the sexual nature of her movement images. This overt display of sexuality is at times uncomfortable for the audience and is certainly a shift from the carefully hidden and restricted sexuality of the ballet swan woman.[17]

The ballet swan woman may display her crotch and legs, she may arch backwards in a sensuous pose, but we are not supposed to notice. The narrative of *Swan Lake* may well suggest sexual consummation, but we are encouraged politely to ignore it. Instead we are to celebrate Odette's pure, non-sexual love, as if sexuality and eroticism would somehow sully the otherwise perfect image. It is Odile who is a sexual temptress and, as Banes has pointed out, her overt and assertive qualities assign her as evil, as dangerous (1998: 61). While never actually overtly sexual, Odile, on account of her ability to seduce the Prince, is branded wicked.

The hiding, or suppression, of sexuality evident within classical ballet is also echoed in the history of classical Indian dance. As a religious form, classical Indian dance expressed an erotic love (*sringara rasa*) for the divine. Before British colonial rule in India these dances were performed by female temple dancers, or *devadasis* (literally meaning 'servant of god'). These women, commonly from a family line of such women, were dedicated to god and became his brides in particular temples. *Devadasis*, in comparison to other Hindu women, were better educated, were permitted more freedom and were not required to be chaste, making them somewhat marginal figures (O'Shea 1998: 49). Mandakranta Bose writes that *devadasis* 'lived wholly under the will of temple priests and royal patrons, a situation that fostered abuse and turned many of these women into courtesans' (Bose 1998: 252). By the nineteenth century British-influenced reformers 'came to view the *devadasis* not as auspicious wives of god but rather as "common prostitutes"' (O'Shea 1998: 50). The associations of the dance with prostitution led to a stigmatisation and suppression of the dancers and their dance forms.

In the 1930s, following the attempted eradication of temple dancing by imperial Britain, interest in dance was revived as part of the celebration of Indian nationalism. The dance in this postcolonial nationalist incarnation was taught to non-*devadasi* girls and 'purified' in an attempt to remove the sexual associations of the dance. It was performed by upper- and middle-class girls, and the erotic content of the form was hidden. This view is exemplified by Rukmini Devi (a leading teacher of bharata naytam), who

> held the element of *sringara*, or erotic sentiment, as a symbol of the form's degradation which needed to be replaced with *bhakti* – devotionalism – devoid of sexual referent.
>
> (Cited in O'Shea 1998: 47)

As a postcolonial form, a form carrying within it the impact of British colonial rule, sexuality has been replaced by the representation of a non-sexual devotional love. These Indian reformist changes are intermingled with Victorian notions of gender and sexuality and reveal a 'British colonial disdain for all cultural practices not within the realm of Western Protestantism' (O'Shea 1998: 50). It is possible to argue thereby that the attitudes towards sexuality evident within both ballet and Indian dance (following colonial rule) are deeply rooted in Western culture, which 'generally considers sex to be a dangerous, destructive, negative force. Most Christian tradition, following Paul, holds that sex is inherently sinful' (Rubin 2000: 321).

Feminists have always been vitally interested in sex, but there has been a strand in second-wave feminism that considers sexual liberalisation as an extension of male privilege (Rubin 2000: 338). Shakti is well aware of these views, and her gleeful disregard for the politically correct and her obvious pleasure in her own body sits uncomfortably with these feminist perspectives. In its representation of female eroticism and desire, her *Swan Lake* work brings to the fore the universalising and, in terms of erotica, repressive tendencies of much feminist theory. She argues that it is the portrayal of

> sexuality and eroticism that people are always trying to suppress, but it is the basis of life and there is no way to deny that, and there is nothing wrong with it. And a woman, or even a swan, is a very sexual creature, we give birth. ... To portray desire, to be desirous is totally natural.
>
> (Shakti 1999b)

Further, she states:

> Everybody is interested in sex. Everybody has a body, and everybody is interested in pleasing the body. Sexual pleasures and sexual desire are not to be suppressed.
>
> (Ibid.)

It might well be that Shakti's representation of sexuality and her pleasure in the erotic come not as a corrective to the feminist doctrines of the West, but rather from the Hindu concept of the goddess Shakti. Within Hinduism Shakti is an active and powerful female energy. The goddess is the focus of tantric practices and is considered the force of liberation and the life energy of the universe (Klostermaier 1998: 80). Interestingly, in tantricism, it is the body, rather than the spirit, that is central to divinity, for the goddess Shakti is identified with *prakrti* (nature/matter). This focus on and within the material body as a place of female power is clearly evident in *Swan Lake* and Shakti's conceptualisation of her own performance practices. In using the positive qualities associated with her namesake as a symbol of women's power, Shakti draws an interesting link between the esoteric traditions of Shaktism and feminisms.

The work could also be positioned within the frame of pre-colonial, and prenationalist, Indian dance. These earlier dance forms were, as discussed above, more erotic in style. While Shakti's dance is a modern incarnation and is in a secular context, her readmission of explicitly erotic and sexual content sets her work in opposition to the colonial 'cleansing' of Indian dance. Shakti revels in the *sringara* (erotic) and sees no dichotomy between sexuality and spirituality.

Tanjore Balasarawati, who was a leading bharata natyam teacher from a *devadasi* family, echoes this view. Balasarawati maintains:

> Bharatanatyam is a form of yoga ('yoking') grounded in *bhakti* ... and expressed in the erotic idiom of *sringara*. *Sringara* is *bhakti*-in-dance; there is, and can be, no dichotomy between *bhakti* and *sringara*.
>
> (Cited in O'Shea 1998: 48)

Shakti's perception of the relationship between spirituality and sexuality is evident in a discussion regarding attitudes towards sexual expression within different cultures, where she states:

> Christianity and Eastern religion is very different: Christianity has more sin and guilt, whereas Hindu religions don't have that sin or guilt. You've seen those temple sculptures – the joy of the Karma Sutra and everything. It's all over the sculptures, it's on the walls of the temple, it's under the sunshine, it's something to be praised as a gift from the gods.
>
> (Shakti 1999b)

Whatever the conceptual basis of the erotic in this *Swan Lake*, Shakti's swan woman, in her G-string and with her sexualised display in movement, in many ways resembles a Western nightclub stripper. The bikini, lace, shiny silver fabric and fur coat reflect the attire that is traditionally associated with strippers, as is the continual emphasis upon dress, for stripper's routines usually focus upon clothing and its removal. So, while Shakti both removes and layers clothing, the way the costume becomes part of the work links her dance with stripping routines. For example, she first enters the stage in a black fur coat and in sunglasses, then dances with the coat hanging draped from her elbows and eventually, after these teasing images, reveals herself dressed in the white G-string bikini. While she does not strip to a fully nude body (and this is not an insignificant difference) she does proffer her almost fully exposed body using sexualised and sexually mimetic movement.

The sexualised movement performed by strippers brings the audience's attention to the female body and, in particular, to the genitals. They arch their backs, spread their legs and protrude their buttocks (Dodds 1997: 222). This collection of movements for sexual display is also clearly evident in Shakti's work. She repeatedly arches backwards, causing her breasts to protrude directly towards the audience and to strain at the seams of her bikini top. Her 'Dance of the cygnets' starts with Shakti on all fours, crawling across the floor and repeatedly thrusting with her rib cage and pelvis. In another recurring movement she sits on the floor with her legs spread wide apart and pushes her pelvis forward and between her legs so her crotch is presented to the viewer.

The use of an erotic presentational style and movement language is further complicated when the position of eroticism as a trope of the exotic is taken into account. As Root writes:

> One of the most persistent tropes of exoticism is the fascination with the erotic possibilities of the colony, which in effect becomes the eroticization of racial power. Exoticism always seems to pertain to sex in some way. ... Exotic images of women have to do with colonial fantasies of power, and the sexual availability of women classified as exotic is for the most part dependent on the ability of the colonist to coerce.
>
> (Root 1996: 40)

Swan Lake heightens the already sexualised image of the oriental woman, reinforcing the concept of her as sexually available to the Western male desire. Conversely, however, I can also conceive that Shakti reappropriates her own sexuality not only from the male gaze but also from the colonising and eroticising gaze by the very 'overtness' of the display and her powerful stance. Shakti takes control of her sexuality in a manner which mitigates the 'colonial fantasies of power'.

One of the final images in the dance of the Silver Swan is the performance of a ritual behind a bowl of flames.[18] As Shakti sets the flame alight, her focus is intense and her face pulls into exaggerated contortions of pained ecstasy. The light cast onto her face and body flickers, creating dark shadows, suggesting some inner demon is present and further subverting the audience's perceptions. This silver swan woman is dangerous and may just bite back!

Shakti's body/body usage is excessive. Her overtly curvaceous body folds, her breasts undulate, her thighs brush against each other and her buttocks are puckered. Her movement is untamed, wild and contorted. Her expressions are exaggerated – stretching her face into extreme configurations. In her-mid forties, Shakti exceeds the bounds of established boundaries – she is excessive and her behaviour is considered 'inappropriate'. She is anathema to the body aesthetics embedded in the classical canon, for the classical canon promotes an idealised, contained and controlled body. This body has become in modern times associated with the young, slim, perfect body of films and advertisements. In contrast, the excessive body (or, in Mary Russo's terms, the 'grotesque' body, 1994), is materialistic, debased, and has orifices, genitalia and other protuberances (belly, breasts, buttocks, etc.). Shakti attacks the image of the classical body through a celebration of her sexuality and her self-evident confidence and pleasure in her own body.

However, the way Shakti presents her work to the Western spectator is problematic and hastens the recommodification of her work and her body into a colonial system. This sublimation of her work into the colonizer's agenda is magnified by her entry into the global economy of sex.

Fleshly metamorphosis and becomings in butoh

While Shakti presents an overtly sexualised body, Iwana integrates gender through metamorphosis and androgyny. His slim body is hairless and often almost naked. His genitals are concealed. He performs shifting, contorting and transforming movements – at one moment twitching irregularly and at the next moment still – hardly breathing. Blurring between states and genders, he revises the ethereal, feminine body of the Wilis, for he is neither masculine nor feminine. Throughout the dance the markings of his sex are hidden or removed. Firstly he uses a phallus (a white paper roll forms a false penis), then removes this phallus, and finally reveals his body and pubic hair with his genitals tucked out of sight. Becoming feminised (through lack) he evokes neither a fully male nor a fully female presence – he suggests instead an androgynous, yielding and transformative gender-bending.

The blurring and crossing of genders is evident in Japanese cultural histories and traditions. For example, Fraleigh tells of the great goddess Amaterasus, who dressed up in male clothes. She also notes that the national dress of Japan, the kimono, is worn by both sexes (1999: 58). Iwana's gender-bending is located in this cultural context and in particular draws on previous butoh practices and also conventions within the Japanese theatre forms – Kabuki and Noh – in which in men commonly perform female roles. Only male actors play the Kabubi form, and these actors learn to perform the movement patterns, postures and speech typical of both female and male roles, later specialising in one or the other. The art of the *onnagata* – the playing of female roles – requires the actors to take up as little space as possible and generally be modest and self-effacing. To achieve this physically they bend their knees to reduce their height, walk with their knees together and slightly pigeon-toed, keep their hands, elbows and arms close to the body, and speak in a falsetto.

In butoh itself there is also a tradition of cross-dressing. Butoh founders Tatsumi Hijikata and Kazuo Ohno often performed in women's costumes. Appearing in extravagant attire such as in *Admiring La Argentina* (1977), Ohno, a 79-year-old man, wears an old-fashioned black velvet dress, a crumpled pink hat, and high-heeled shoes. His face and hands are painted white and his lips are bright red. As he dances he adjusts his hat, lowers his eyes and flutters his eyelids. With curving arms and mincing steps, he becomes like a grotesque spectre of a young girl. Similarly, in *Suiren* (White Liles, 1987), Ohno wears a beaded lace dress, long gloves and a hat from the 1900s. Appearing worn and slightly tattered, Ohno traces uncertain paths across the stage. His portrayal of this fragile feminine figure avoids the effects of neo-conservative drag, in which the enacted presentation of the opposite sex reinforces gender binaries, creating instead a performance of gender that 'is foreign to us because it speaks of disparate sexes in one body without invoking paradox or inviting us to delude ourselves about the 'truth' (Franko 1995: 105).

Using the insights of Barthes and the Bunraku puppet theatre, Mark Franko (1995) suggests that Ohno's crossed-dressed performance does not refer to the fixing and subverting of identities that is often part of Western theatrical cross-dressing. Instead he abandons both illusion and delusion, holding polarities at bay. As with Bunraku puppets, which mock the opposites of animate/inanimate, gender signs are obscured and dissolved (Franko 1995: 105).

Iwana similarly blurs gender such that plural gender signs are evoked, without giving rise to a paradox. Iwana does not signal this blurring of gender through cross-dressing, however – rather he is neither male nor female, but both, as his body, costume and movement all blur – creating a productive gender ambiguity. Also, taking a step further, he attempts to empty his body of notions of gender – such that at the same time as we encounter gender pluralism we also experience gender through lack. His concealed genitals mark this lack most explicitly.

Iwana lists five methods by which he changes his genitalia for performance (2002: 18):

1   existence/absence of my own pubic hair when dancing totally naked
2   extremely small genital covers
3   artificial female genitalia with artificial pubic hair
4   artificial penises
5   asexual genitalia.

Describing how he creates 'asexual genitalia' as used in his reworking of *Giselle*, he writes:

> I tie my scrotum and penis with a rubber band, leaving my testicles unbound. I then tuck the penis and scrotum under towards my anus and fix them there with a very small genital cover, with the testicles slightly raised. I then put on a slightly larger genital cover, whose colour is the same as that of my genital area, to further stabilize these appendages. On top of all this I wear women's seamless stockings of a uniform denier 0.3mm or thinner, which I call my skin costume.
>
> (Iwana 2002: 18)

Through this tucking away of his genitals, alongside the addition of the paper roll as an artificial penis and the physical form of his own body (which appears pre-pubescent, despite the evidence of his pubic hair), Iwana creates a highly androgynous figure.

Emilyn Claid (1998, 2006) has interestingly discussed androgyny and its performative potential in dance. Rejecting both classical transcendent notions of androgyny and androgyny as a negation of gender, she intriguingly positions androgyny as an illusion, an imaginary construct, as a 'movement between masculine and feminine qualities, between identities, rather than a union of male and female' (1998: 50). Further, she writes:

> As a verb, to androgynize, the body in action temporally spans between identities that emerge in the gaps between things. As androgynizing bodies, we no longer have fixed identities – we become performing hybrids, and hybrid bodies span the divide between things.
>
> (Claid 2006: 182)

Via his use of 'genital covers', combined with the exposed pre-pubescent appearance of his body, Iwana is androgynised in just such a way. Further his danced movement, which shifts between states and dynamics, creates neither fully masculine nor fully feminine qualities, while evoking imaginary glimpses of both. And these imaginary glimpses of female presences are amplified, for Giselle the young woman from legend reverberates throughout this reworking, while remaining at the same time absent. Her ghostly presence becomes confused with Iwana's own ambiguously gendered body, such that the performance opens space and time for the play of multiple possibilities of gender, not constrained by static binary codes, to become present in the dance.

Iwana's reworking of *Giselle*, then, challenges the gendered aesthetic of the ballet body in a fundamental manner. Going beyond the restylisation of gender or a parody of gender, he blurs boundaries such that polarity of male/female binaries are no longer meaningful. Iwana's butoh also blurs the dualisms of body/mind and flesh/spirit, for the butoh body – 'butoh-tai' in Japanese – relates to both the physical and the mental. The concept of 'butoh-tai' reflects the fundamentally non-Cartesian assumptions of Japanese thinkers, who, emerging from an intellectual environment permeated by Buddhism, discuss the body as spirit and speak of the unified body-mind.

Chikako Ozawa-de Silva (2002), introducing Western readers to the influential writings of Yuasa Yasuo and Ichikawa Hiroshi, provides useful insights into theories of the body in contemporary Japanese philosophy in the hope that her writing will 'benefit and change Western sociologies of the body' (2002: 23). Yuasa Yasuo's book *The Body: Toward an Eastern Mind-Body* was first published in 1977 and was translated into English in 1987. Ichikawa Hiroshi's most influential texts, *Seishin toshite no Shintai* (The Body as Spirit), first published 1975, and *Mi no Kôzô: Sintairon wo koete* (Structure of the Body: Overcoming the Theory of the Body, 1993), have not as yet been translated into English.

Ichikawa's main thesis of 'the body as spirit' employs the phenomenological insights of Husserl, Marcel, Sartre and Merleau-Ponty, shifting and developing this work through Eastern perspectives. In Ichikawa's writings it is clear that the mind is unified with the body and that 'human beings *are* physical existence, and cannot live apart from the "lived body"' (Ozawa-de Silva 2002: 24, emphasis in original). This body is so familiar to us that it is difficult to grasp, yet he writes: 'if we can grasp the body in the situation we live in everyday, we will realize that the body is much closer to what we understand by the word "spirit"' (cited ibid.).

Elaborating this idea, Ichikawa develops a concept of the body as unfinished 'potential' in which the lived body is understood to have many layers. Using the Japanese word *mi* (body as potential whole) he discusses shifting meanings of the body, from fruit, flesh, the way of the body, the garments on the body, life, self, socialized self and social status, gradually moving outwards to encompass '*Mi* as whole existence' (Ozawa-de Silva 2002: 28). The *mi* includes the body, mind and heart and is related to the concept of *ki* (spiritual energy), which provides a connection between nature and the body – an organising force field and dynamic unity.

These ideas lead Ichikawa to that of 'meta-bodies', which extend the body beyond the limitations of the skin. 'Meta-bodiness' includes various modes of deepening awareness of both the internal individual self and the social external self. Through the meta-body the dichotomy of nature and culture dissolves, for once we grasp the embodied nature of human beings' existence nature can no longer be seen as outside culture (Ozawa-de Silva 2002: 29).

Interestingly, and uncommonly from a Western perspective, Ichikawa and Yuasa both discuss their ideas in relation to actual bodily practices – in particular yoga and meditation. Indeed, Yuasa developed his theories with a deep knowledge of Ki-meridian systems of Chinese acupuncture, alongside Western neurology and medicine (Ozawa-de Silva 2002: 30). Yuasa sees these bodily practices as essential processes of self-cultivation through which it is possible for individuals to attain deeper awareness. His critical review of concepts of 'normality' and 'health' lead him to write that 'cultivation means pursuing a way of life that is more than the average way of life' (cited ibid.: 32).

Iwana's form of butoh practice can be understood as a form of self-cultivation that challenges the crude materiality of the body through non-dualistic routes. Seeking the 'body as a living entity' (or a 'human body') (Iwana 2002: 8), he embraces both inner and external nature to reveal forms and movements previously unseen, for in this work movement, time and space emerge from the body, rather than being imposed upon it. This type of body practice – which has 'as its end not power, but the recognition of body–mind integration' (Ozawa-de Silva 2002: 36) – is common within Japanese traditions, yet these forms of 'discipline' contrast with Western tendencies to treat the body as an object to be controlled and dissected.

Iwana makes a parallel point when he writes that, in ballet,

> the body has been finely segmented and reintegrated geometrically like in differential and integral calculus, thereby eventually overcoming the limits of the dancing entity with inner strength strong enough to confront external time and space. While this inner strength is different from inner nature, to me it is the desperate beauty and radiance of a dancing entity that has given up on becoming a human as a material entity.
>
> (2002: 19, n.5)

Ballet bodies, he argues, are only partial bodies, subjected to constant refinement or crystallisation; they are regulated in such a way that accessing the 'body as living entity' becomes difficult. And Romantic ballet goes further. Not only is the body regulated and controlled, but the narrative reinforces Western tendencies to make clear distinctions between the physical world and the spirit world – portraying the material body as clearly distinct from spirit. Yet Iwana makes no such distinction: his is a transformative dance that does not separate the physical and the spiritual.

Butoh requires finding a personal dance through one's emotional, physical and intellectual self and then removing the 'I' from the dance, for butoh values a quality of 'emptiness' – a quality akin to the setting aside of the ego. The butoh-tai then seeks an individually 'authentic' dance, and this dance rejects completion and stability, making finished form an impossibility. It is this approach that gives rise to Iwana's constant state of flux, as he lets go of all shapes that can be identified, following instead pathways of indeterminacy. As Fraleigh notes: 'In Butoh bodily control goes the way of imagistic morphology, the metaphysics of *becoming* through metamorphosis, not arriving, but always in processing of integration and dissolution' (Fraleigh 2004: 29, emphasis in original).

Echoing the philosophical writings of Gilles Deleuze and Félix Guattari (1988), the butoh body is in a constant state of 'becoming'. The becoming body is never complete, never finished. Going beyond any view of the body as a unitary structure in which organs are interrelated and hierarchically organised, the body as Deleuze and Guattari perceive it is not singularly bound or even hybrid, but is deterritorialised and in process. By avoiding order stratification, they enable flow along escape lines or lines of transgression that can open up heterogeneous meanings. Further, they write: 'Becoming is certainly not imitating, or identifying with something. Becoming is a verb with a consistency all of its own: it does not reduce, or lead back to, "appearing", "being", "equalling" or "producing"' (Deleuze and Guattari 1988: 239). These becomings are not simply a matter of choice, however, and they 'always involve a substantial remaking of the subject' (Grosz 1994: 174). Through these conceptualisations of the body Deleuze and Guattari 'problematize our most common assumptions regarding identity, relations between subject and object, substance, matter, corporeality' (ibid.: 164).

Iwana's butoh body, as a becoming body, is a body without boundaries. Reverberating with a sense of deterritorialisation, his dancing emphasises processes of deconstruction. This body creates 'escape lines' through metamorphosis. By transforming himself into various forms of human and non-human being – animal, spirit – or, when human, teasing out the underside of social history – disreputable women, the diseased, the mad – he uses his body to drag the body from its pedestal.

Iwana deterritorialises not only his own body but also, through the process of reworking, many interrelated bodies. Here the relationships between bodies – Iwana's own 'real' body, his butoh 'performing' body, all those past bodies in both butoh and ballet – begin to intersect and morph, doubling and tripling in any moment of watching, as the bidirectional focus of reworkings redoubles in complexity.

However, while complex and becoming, Iwana's body is still culturally marked (even if that cultural location is a hybrid). This is important to remember. As discussed in the previous chapter with reference to the plurality of embodiments in *O (a set of footnotes to Swan Lake)*, while celebrating and asserting the potential of the mutable body it is crucial that we retain an awareness of, and an intimate connection to, the material specificity of the flesh, for the body is sexed and cultured. Not to pay attention to this would result in the theorising of a universal performing body, and it is such universals that the intercultural reworkings discussed here contest. It is also critical that these bodies are grounded in the reality of the intercultural markets and commercial worlds which surround them, and it is to these specific contexts I now, albeit briefly, turn.

Commodification, appropriation and the global market

Both Shakti and Iwana perform internationally, touring the globe to present their dance in small- to mid-scale venues, as part of performance festivals and theatre seasons. Unavoidably they both enter into economic contexts that apply to any commodity – artistic or otherwise. These economic contexts in relation to inter-cultural performance are particularly invasive, impacting upon audience percep-tion and reception. In addition, the artists' desire to appeal to these international markets may affect publicity design, aesthetic directions and production choices. As such the effects of the global market are insidious and significant.

Shakti, in particular, bears the imprints of these markets. Indeed, as I watch Shakti, shadows of the sex industry and the illegal trafficking of women across global markets loom at the edges of my awareness. These shadows darken my experience. While I have considered her work in the light of Indian philosophies and suggested ways in which she promotes a challenge to conservative, anti-sexual discourse, bringing to the fore the subversive potential of this dance, I have to question the extent to which she is able to achieve these subversions when so heav-ily laden with sex. As a female performer who incorporates orientialist fantasies of sexual availability, displaying her body and performing clearly sexualised movements, she may also be too easily assimilated into a commercial economy and do too little to avert this commodification.

The reviews of Shakti's work in the tabloid press, which describe her as 'Love Shak' and 'Sexy Shakti' and her dances as 'steamy' and 'sizzling' (Anon 1999), suggest that this is, at least in part, the case. This assimilation has been hastened by her own publicity, which emphasises the titillating aspects of her show via images of her in provocative poses and dressed in revealing clothing such as biki-nis and sheer fabrics. In her press releases and interviews she has also repeatedly pointed towards the erotic nature of the work, and she often highlights the places in which it has been banned as a result of its erotic content/imagery. The viewer cannot help but be influenced by the context enacted in the publicity surround-ing the performance – indeed the sexual references and images may well be a key factor in an audience's attendance – and Shakti's work is thereby received, unavoidably, in the context of the commercially sexualised body.

The way sex is used as a selling tool places this dance on the borders of dance as art and erotic dancing. However the female appropriation of sexual display in live performance, even within patriarchal norms, acts as a threat to hegemony. Female sexual pleasure, especially self-pleasure, while bordering on the structures of pornographic viewing, can be empowering to women. So although this perfor-mance could be dismissed as simply an erotic display, it is creatively erotic, and operates in such a manner as to challenge the status quo of hegemonic eroticism as it celebrates a woman's sexuality, and in doing so challenges audiences to examine their preconceptions.

Moreover, sexual images formerly regarded as unacceptable are now boldly displayed and accepted as art, and society shifts the once proscribed into the mainstream. Shakti's ownership of sexuality is an interesting shift, as many artists have disassociated their work from pornography through claims of 'artistic merit' (Campbell 1996: 272). In this formulation, sexual representation, contained within an aestheticised form, is admissible. For it is claimed that, if the sexual display has a 'serious purpose', then it is acceptable: purposes of gratification are not. In Shakti's work such distinctions are hard to qualify as barriers between high and low culture; 'trashy' and 'arty' are traversed and disregarded.

Conclusion

I started this chapter with a quotation that includes the words: 'it is the strangeness of the unknown (how it can re-arrange our perceptual field) that calls us to travel across the bridge of difference', and goes on, 'when familiar territory is given up, the traveler can stand in a new familiar, in the place where worlds (and they are whole worlds) meet' (Fraleigh 1999: 17). Crossing cultures, these reworkings, then, give up and challenge fixed territories, calling us to revisit the 'known' through the perspective of what is perhaps rather 'less known'. Whether the known is the ballet, butoh or classical Indian dance, these works invite an audience to 'travel across the bridge' forming in between spaces such that that which appears customary comes to be considered anew. For when experiencing these intercultural reworkings the viewer oscillates between the familiar and the unfamiliar, the native and the foreign, developing and transferring meanings in anti-hegemonic, imaginative ways.

Shakti's *Swan Lake* addresses the here and now and reflects the multicultural, postmodern societies in which she lives. While using two historically rooted forms (ballet and Indian dance), the dance deconstructs these sources to focus on today – on the 'stories' of modern life. Challenging the bounds of exoticism and constructing a mutable identity, Shakti controls her own image to take pleasure in her own sexuality, and draws interesting links between pre-colonial forms of Indian dance, Shaktism and feminisms.

However, Shakti's representation of the swan women as unproblematically sexual leaves her open to consumerist tendencies and deeply tainted within orientalist structures. While her Silver Swan has a very different identity to that presented in classical ballet versions, it is still problematic. Her erotic performance falls into the traps of essentialism – in which woman's sexuality is unquestioningly celebrated as liberation. This does not discount, however, the ways in which this new *Swan Lake* brings into focus established notions of *Swan Lake*, Indian dance and eroticism, shifting traditional angles and fields of vision.

Iwana's *The Legend of Giselle* also significantly shifts perspectives, as he enters deep inside Giselle, allowing her to enter him, becoming a catalyst for his own exploration. All that explicitly remains of the ballet is its shadowy ghost, which we can sense only in imaginative ways – as if seen in our peripheral vision. Using processes of distillation and dilation, Iwana expands sensations of love and death to breathe new life into the work. He evokes particularly Japanese concepts of embodiment and works against dualisms of body and mind, morphing between states. Full of ambiguities, and thoroughly unfixing and deconstructing identities, his is an androgynised Giselle that slips in between in a continuous process of becoming.

Inserting cultural differences, these dances implicitly reveal the unspoken assumption of 'whiteness' in conventional ballet, increasing the repertoire of identity spaces available to audiences through depth and diversity. These reworkings thereby enable Western audiences to reorient their perceptions of ballet and the East. In doing so, what becomes evident is the notion of ballet as a colonising form, as Shakti's Indo-Western dance speaks back to the colonised history of India and the ballet while Iwana implicitly challenges monocultural readings and notions of cultural stasis. His inherently intercultural dance addresses both the monocultural history of Japan and the closed imperatives in readings of *Giselle* – speaking back to the colonising impulse of ballet.

Chapter 6

Conclusion

Transgressive desires

As a form of intertextual palimpsestuous practice, reworkings are hybrid texts that evoke, at the very least, a bidirectional gaze. These dances have the potential to demythologise the dances of the ballet canon, for as canonical counter-discourse (which may be intentional or otherwise) reworkings engage in cultural debates that have sought to deconstruct and rewrite the ideologies embedded within canonical practices. Emphasising two recurring aspects of reworkings, on the one hand I brought to the fore the ways in which these dances have reconceptualised gender, sexuality and race, creating a proliferation of identities, bringing viewers' attention to previously unseen and unnoticed perspectives. On the other hand I suggested that, however radical or subversive any particular reworking may be, the canon continues to reverberate within them as they simultaneously reveal and reiterate their sources.

In this conclusion I assemble some of the key thrusts and, albeit briefly, bring together some of the many *Swan Lakes* discussed throughout the book, enabling comparison and a consideration of their collective force as reworkings of one of the most iconic of ballets. In the first section, 'Reworkings as canonical counter-discourse', I consider reworkings as they teeter at the edges of successful difference and fatal reappropriation. In 'The double gesture: moving beyond binaries', reworkings are positioned as productively 'in between'. It is possible that these dances, as hybrid palimpsests that shift between histories, geographies and perspectives, are able to go beyond binaries, embodying mutability and interconnectedness instead. The following section, 'Diversity and difference: (re)inscribing the body', brings to the fore the ways in which these dances have refigured the body. Through difference and diversity they deregulate gender, race and sexuality, as the markers of identity are realised as only partial and provisional, belonging to particular times and contexts. I then turn, in 'Pleasure and power: the (re)-eroticised body', to a consideration of the erotic within reworkings, for the ways in which the male and female dancer have been eroticised within particular reworkings have served to reframe sexuality such that men and women have the potential to enjoy the pleasure and power of their own sexuality, without recourse to dominant orthodoxies.

Reworkings as canonical counter-discourse

The dances discussed throughout this book have reworked the most canonical of ballets and have been shown to unveil and dismantle the basic assumptions of specific canonical texts. The multiple versions of *Swan Lake* variously divest this canonical text of its (specious) authority and authenticity, reinvesting it anew with a more local relevance. These reworkings can be usefully understood as a form of canonical counter-discourse. Yet these dances do not simply offer an unrelenting critique or an uncritical celebration; rather they reconfigure their source texts for other readings. They make us aware of the continuum of images and experiences, releasing canonical ballets from their status as seemingly frozen events of the past, while also reflecting images of the present. Instead of denying the past these dances make explicit the ways in which the past resonates in the present. Reverberating with processes of *becoming* rather than being caught in the illusion of *being*, they bring to our attention the provisionality of knowledge and the illusory nature of truth. For an essential feature of these dances is that they emphasise departure and process. The source text is significantly altered in order to give rise to a new dance that has significantly different resonances and meanings, mapping out alternative aesthetic terrains. Thereby, as they challenge previously hermeneutic bodies of knowledge, reworkings help us recognise our assumptions and shift our perceptions.

As a particular kind of intertextual practice, reworkings evoke particular obligatory intertexts from within their very substance such that these dances rely on, or at least use, the viewer's awareness of intertextual references. Importantly, however, they also challenge these intertextual references via a rewriting project as they work to destabilise power. Provoking, at the very least, a bidirectional gaze, these dances are never (even in their most 'whole' forms) fully 'closed'. They always remain 'open', inviting viewers to read and re-read the reworking and the ballet at the source.

Using the strategies of intertextuality, reworkings shift from the sign of authenticity to that of performativity to manifest a resistive stance, for these dances encourage the viewer to read the discourse between texts and to become a co-creator of meaning. Rather than relying on the mind of the resisting audience member to read canonical ballets 'against the grain', the potential of reworkings is that they embody and play out resistance in the act of performance itself. Thereby reworkings demythologise their sources such that the viewer becomes unable to consume myth innocently and is able to recognise the mythic transcendence of the source and its simultaneous deconstruction.

It is evident, however, that, while reworkings reveal myth, they do not vanquish it, for this is a very difficult thing to do. Barthes writes, 'the very effort one makes in order to escape its [myth's] stranglehold becomes in its turn the prey of myth' (1993: 135). These dances are held in a tense relationship between the canon and counter-canon. For while reworkings express a desire to transgress the bounds of their sources, they simultaneously reinvoke the source within their very substance.

This desire to transgress, while also desiring to have, has been shown to place these dances in a paradoxical position, for the status quo of the ballet canon, which frames reworkings, resonates continuously.

For example, the reworkings of *Swan Lake* by Bourne and Ek are limited in their radicalising potential because of the way in which they reinscribe the theatrical values of conventional ballet and reiterate (at least partially) the heterosexual matrix, such that they are commodified within the frame of the canon. As these examples demonstrate, the citing of the dominant norm does not necessarily displace that norm. Rather the dominant norm may well be reiterated as a desired object. There is a tension therefore in reworkings between transgression and desire. Reflecting what Foster describes as a 'magnetic contradictoriness' (1995a: 110), reworkings express both a distaste and a fascination for the ballet.

This dual stance is embodied in reworkings through their bidirectional nature, and this is both the strength and the weakness of these dances. Tiffin's (1995) discussion, cited in chapter 1, of the risk of contamination and neo-assimilation within postcolonial counter-discursive texts, applies equally to reworkings. A parallel argument is found in chapter 5 when, paraphrasing Spivak (1995), it is noted that one is deeply mired in the things one deconstructs. Similarly in chapter 3, regarding Foster's use of parodic strategies, I cited Hutcheon, who writes that 'you are always implicated in the value you choose to challenge' (Hutcheon 1988: 223). The ambiguous status of parody means that while parody trans-contextualises it also incorporates, for parody operates as a form of 'authorised transgression' (Hutcheon 1985: 75). Reworkings as particularly bidirectional texts that refer to an obligatory intertext (whether overtly operating via parody or not) are similarly bound, and it may well be that their transgression takes place only within limited contexts.

Reworkings, like a Bakhtinian carnival, might be seen to mark only a fleeting emancipation. In his discussion of carnival Bakhtin writes that 'one might say that carnival celebrated temporary liberation from the prevailing truth and from the established order; it marked the suspension of all hierarchical rank, privileges, norms, and prohibitions' (Bakhtin 1984: 10). From this perspective reworkings are presented in a context in which transgressions take place in the safe knowledge that, as the curtain lowers, the status quo will be reasserted. However, while this model suggests the containment of subversion and a neat closure, with no noticeable political transformative effect, these dances, which variously challenge the canon and the representations within it, demonstrate strategies through which some leakage is bound to occur.

The reworkings discussed through this book demonstrate the potential to resist the nostalgic and authoritative frame of the canon, revealing gaps and omissions, elucidating assumptions and privileges, exposing gender and ethnic specificities. They exist therefore as sites of struggle and may act as catalysts for change. If this is the case, the hybrid and bidirectional nature of reworkings does not undermine their resistive value; rather it acts as the very basis of resistance. For while in reworkings the source ballets may retain their mythic status, we do come to understand them differently.

Consider the multiple reworkings of *Swan Lake* – they shift between a kind of unfaithful faithfulness, in the manner of Bourne and Ek, to wilful deconstructions, such as those by Foster and Hoghe. These dances are overtly double-coded and dialogic texts that present a purposeful re-reading of their sources – rejecting the false illusion of absolute or unequivocal meaning. Hence they serve to demythologise their source texts in a self-conscious manner. The multiplicity of perspectives evident avoids the entrenchment of any one approach, authority or reading, and displays a deregulation of the past. Reworkings thereby reflect a counter-tradition in which the past is embodied in multiple ways and becomes complex rather then singular and linear. The historical canon is thereby recognised as a collection of texts that can be opened up, and may fly apart and be reconstructed at the whim of those who would perform them.

Reworkings can enter into and change canonical ballets, radically reinscribing them rather than endorsing the values of the source text. Thereby a politically motivated reworking can reconstitute the canon and become a vehicle for values other than those of the Western, white heterosexual male. Importantly, particular reworkings have also contributed to a decentring of the European norms and have given voice to different cultural perspectives. Reworkings such as those by Iwana and Shakti, and also by Tankard, have been shown to question imperial and colonial, as well as the accompanying orientalist, power structures. These forces try to maintain neat order and have excluded non-white, non-Western voices from the canon. By forming intercultural texts, these artists have demonstrated the way in which reworkings can operate effectively to contradict the geographical, historical and cultural assumptions of the canon. As Tiffin has written: the 'processes of artistic and literary decolonisation have involved a radical dis/mantling of European codes and a post-colonial subversion and appropriation of the dominant European discourses' (Tiffin 1995: 95). Interestingly, Iwana and Shakti do not rework only European discourses as represented in ballet but also the dance forms of bharata natyam and butoh respectively. These dances highlight the false perception of India and Japan as tradition-bound cultures, and it becomes clear that cultural contexts and cultural forms are not stable or knowable containers. In addition, these intercultural reworkings make explicit the complex axis of race, gender and sexuality, undercutting the assumptions of whiteness in gender and sexuality studies.

The double gesture: moving beyond binaries

Placing a rift in the tropes of same/other reworkings does not just refer to other texts in a neutral or innocent fashion. Rather the intertextual practice of reworkings is specific and purposeful in its use of prior texts, for, as discussed above, reworkings, like other counter-discourses, are involved in destabilising power. Recognising that the canonical can never be erased, these dances are hybrid in form and reinforce the fact that hegemonic processes require continual deconstruction. This process is also evident in all reworkings because of the operations of the bidirectional gaze. Reworkings implicitly and at times explicitly resist binary categories. Existing as hybrid texts, they blend or fluctuate in such a manner as to challenge the fixity of referents to shift 'in between'.

The hybrid asserts the transactional nature of power, texts and bodies. The site of the hybrid is a site of fluctuation and mutation that can estrange the basis of dominant discourse. Through a blend of the familiar and the unfamiliar, reworkings create a disorientation which can be unsettling, for as they are not totally new they show us the otherness within the same, for it is the invisible which animates the visible. While it should be noted that hybridity presents the *potential* for resistance but does not assume a resistive stance, these dances create a dialogic signifier which is unstable and oscillating rather than single and discrete, remaking boundaries and exposing the premise of their sources.

Drawing on the epistemology established by Deleuze and Guattari, Braidotti (1994) suggests that the hybrid subject is a nomadic and becoming subject that can flow between connections, which may, but does not necessarily, connect by appropriation. The process of becoming, as discussed in relation to *O (a set of footnotes to Swan Lake)* and also *The Legend of Giselle* (chapters 3 and 5 respectively), is never complete. As it does not lead back, or reduce, to a subject or a source, it can never fix into binary oppositions. A reworking that operates in this way emphasises process and change; from this perspective reworkings can be seen to be about constant transformation, not arrival. In particular the reworkings discussed in part II reflect a commitment to process and resistance to closure. While, as pointed out in chapter 1, all reworkings by their very nature suggest a sense of process, a sense of continual renewal, these reworkings are especially 'incomplete' and defiant of single definitions. They represent an ongoing dialectic between hegemonic centrist systems and the peripheral subversion of them. They are dynamic, not static. As Tiffin (1995: 96) notes in relation to postcolonial counter-discourse, reworkings do not seek to subvert the dominant with a view to taking its place; rather, they operate to continually consume their own biases, while at the same time they expose and erode those of the dominant discourse.

All the reworkings discussed operate in at least two directions at once, but some reveal an especially 'both/and' approach rather than the stance of the 'not/but'. The promise of these reworkings is that they may, in Braidotti's (1994: 5) terms, bring 'interconnectedness' to the fore via the shifts between unlikely encounters and unexpected sources. Beyond binaries between texts and between bodies, these reworkings can be seen to embody a 'double gesture'. This double gesture indicates a way out of dualisms and offers instead the possibility of a discursive mobility. I am suggesting here that the double gesture operates in reworkings to form a palimpsestuous effect (either literally within the dance and/or through the viewer's active engagement with the dance through memory and imagination). In this way the source text is experienced as an intense presence through its absence, for if we have memories of that prior text, we always feel its presence shadowing the one we are directly experiencing. In reworkings prior texts do not vanish but are present through the bodies and lines traversing the stage, through our memories and associations. Indeed in this way reworkings might well be helpfully understood as palimpsests. Layering emergent and residual narratives, forms and choreographies, reworkings remind us that clean breaks do not occur; rather the past is constantly reconfigured and reconstructed, and we attain new perspectives while retaining previous histories.

Thereby double gesture undoes conventional binaries of same/other, canon/counter-canon, old/new, past/present, and mythologised/demythologised. Without simply discounting the ballet, these dance-makers lay claim to what is theirs and what is not theirs to give glimpses of possible alternatives while still allowing us to know the ballet, but to know it differently.

Diversity and difference: (re)inscribing the body

Choreographers, through the processes of reworking, have encompassed changing attitudes towards gender, sexuality and cultural difference, unsettling the bodies of their predecessors. They have reworked the ballet and re-represented the ballerina and the male dancer by appropriating, trans-contextualising, and transforming their identities. This appropriation and transformation is such that the categories of identity become open to the convergence of multiple discourses at the site of identity – rendering categorisations problematic.

The reinscription and self-representation of the body is a key issue within reworkings. The insidious and persuasive construction of the body within the ballet canon, which tends to inscribe the body as object, makes the reworking of the body a particularly critical task. Here the body is located as a potential site of resistance, a site that can critique and challenge hegemony, for the body is never simply a passive object but a site that maintains the possibility of strategic reinscription.

The reworking of the body has been shown to usefully alter the source text and embody strategies of resistance. Indeed the reconfiguration of the body via diversity and difference is an important concept within reworkings, for it is the nature of reworkings to create difference, and as a collective group of dances they render diversification. While it is clear that the reconfiguration of the body is more thorough in some reworkings than in others, if we look, for example, to reworkings of *Swan Lake*, by sheer number and as a collective force they speak to the impossibility of coherence, illuminating provisionality and constructedness. In line with Butler, who states that her 'recommendation is not to solve this crisis of identity, but to proliferate and intensify this crisis' (Butler 1990: 121), the bodily reinscriptions evident in reworkings refigure the body by creating multiple and heterogeneous representations. The promise of these dances is that they may offer such a proliferation of bodily inscriptions that identities can no longer be perceived as natural and indeed may no longer be categorisable at all.

In reworkings identity is signed as particularly fictive – the deliberate reinscription of the body marks identity as a construct. Because reworkings self-consciously 'repeat' the dances of the past they bring the performativity of gender and race into the open – failing to (re)iterate, and thereby failing to (re)produce, the bodily acts of their sources. Whether they repeat in such a way as to displace norms or become reincorporated varies across dances. However, whatever the degree of displacement, or not, of norms within specific dances, the body's ability to frac-ture has been shown to provide a significant site for feminist, queer and cultural decolonisation. Rather than reinstating the highly coded bodies of the ballet canon, reworkings have rechoreographed the body such that a wider variety of bodily incarnations are encompassed, allowing for divergence and multiplicity, as opposed to uniformity and sameness.

Significantly these dances bring otherwise marginal bodies to the centre. For reworkings can present unpredictable and disruptive self-representations and cre-ate idiosyncratic vocabularies that challenge the codification of their sources. This approach inscribes subjectivity and suggests ways in which the canon can be per-ceived more flexibly. Each of these dances literally embodies the experiences and interests of its maker/dancers – as each is made and performed through its maker's own, very specific, body. These independent makers perform themselves in solo/duet and small chamber groups to mark out their own identities, identi-ties that are not easy to categorise. They contrast the seemingly universal canon and operate in variance to the hierarchical structures of ballet companies.

Pleasure and power: the (re)-eroticised body

A number of the reworkings discussed throughout this book reclaim the pleasures of eroticism and sexuality in contrast to the ballet's repressed and hidden repre-sentations. Ek's swan women are assertive, sexual women and his Prince holds the promise of a more contingent masculinity. Bourne, by inserting a homosexual reading in *Swan Lake*, emphasises desire in alternative ways, while he simultane-ously suppresses the potential power of eroticism. In the versions of *Swan Lake* by de Frutos, Foster, Shakti and myself, eroticism becomes explicit. While the modes of eroticism in each of the works differ, in reclaiming the erotic it is possible to present bodies and sexualities positively in a form of erotic agency – this has been of particular importance for women and is central to queerness. The erotic agency evoked operates within the frames of power and pleasure, and it is useful to consider what the nature and form of this agency is and to ask how successful it is in opening up genders and sexualities.

Shakti (see chapter 5) asserts her own pleasure and sexuality, reclaiming the erotic, while exposing her body. The erotic pleasure reflects the esoteric traditions of Shaktism rather than being driven by a corrective of Western feminist doc-trines. This powerful female force is celebrated in this dance as Shakti practises a tantric yoga that releases sexual energies. However, the power of the global econ-omy of sex impacts upon her dance, and her body, as she risks being viewed in the same frame as a stripper. This frame could consume her, but the nature of her dance as a reworking, which clearly has an agenda other than titillation, her inter-action with the audience, and her all too fleshy body work against the fetishistic properties of stripping. Equally problematic, however, is the trope of the erotic within the exotic, and this holds her erotic agency within orientialist structures. Nevertheless, while problematic, Shakti does challenge conventional representations of Odette and successfully asserts an eroticism that calls into question previous categorisations.

My own reworking, *footnotes* (chapter 3), explores erotic agency and the haptic. The dance performed naked in the video and the almost translucent costume I wear throughout the live performance, alongside the sinuous sensuality of the movement style, do not graphically present sex but are erotic. The erotic body in *footnotes* is a site of tactile, fluid pleasure – this is a female pleasure that is multiple and diffuse as I write my own body, an erotic body that resists and invites the viewer's objectification. The installation format, the video projections, and the improvised movement form work together to hinder sexual gratification, creating instead a haptic presence. This haptic presence, which focuses on kinaesthetic and proprioceptive awareness and emphasises tactile impressions rather than a visual sense, evokes a seductive relationship between the viewer and the performer. The live body is presented in an ever-changing fluid form that resists the viewer's objectification while also laying itself open to be viewed. These haptically erotic bodies engulf the viewer in a flow of tactile impressions, arousing while evading sexual gratification.

Rather than presenting the erotic as a reclaimed positive force, Foster (chapter 3), as an erotic agent, dismantles the appearance of the sexual offering. Using a range of techniques such as overdisplay and parody, she overtly explores looking-at-to-be-looked-at-ness and refuses the erotic by dismantling the structures of viewing – shifting and challenging the gaze to deautomatise the way she is viewed. Framing herself between a pair of curtains attached to a headdress, she demonstrates the objectivication of the ballerina while giving her a powerful, 'knowing' voice. In this dance Foster creates a new language of desire based upon an interaction with her audience in which they and she enjoy the pleasure of resistance.

Another key aspect of erotic agency in *The Ballerina's Phallic Pointe* is Foster's concept of the ballerina-as-phallus. As phallus the ballerina makes overt her status within the symbolic system. The imagery used by Foster also suggests the more subversive possibilities of the penis and the dildo. By reading the ballerina-as-penis, with all the specificity and materiality that the penis embodies, the ballerina is significantly reinscribed. The reference to dildos also inserts a lesbian erotic agency. This lesbian eroticism threatens the normative bipolarized sexuality of the ballet and asserts that bodies do not always line up into expected categories as sexual practices proliferate. Thereby the conception of the ballerina is shifted as a subjective and fluid identity is inserted into her conventional appearance of fixity.

Sexual desire is the driving force of queerness, and de Frutos (chapter 4) claims and refigures erotic territories for homosexual men to evoke queer rifts. Revealing the inherent sexual queerness of *Swan Lake*, while exploiting its romantic associations, his (homo)sexually overt dance reveals a gap between kinaesthesia and morphology in a disruption of naturalised and white heteronormativity. Disrupting the conventional aesthetics of the male dancing body, he foregrounds his penetrability, in contrast to the impenetrability of masculine heterosexuality. This penetrable portrayal of desiring males deflates masculinist norms, asserting a corporeality that is specifically located in his own experiences as a gay man.

These radical reworkings embody feminist and queer recuperations of the sexual body as an erotic politics of the body is fashioned as part of a flux of identities, in a plurality of styles. They open up categories of gender, sexuality and the erotic, intervening in the representation systems that objectify the body. Reclaiming the erotic, these dances use erotic agency as a strategy to intervene in the cultural construction of women as fantasy objects and to disrupt the impenetrability of masculinist desire, articulating instead the 'subject-performer' – presenting the subjective pleasure of their maker's/dancers' own bodies. This marks a significant response and reaction to the perceived limitations of sexuality in the ballet *Swan Lake*.

Because of the operation of the 'double gesture' in reworkings, the reframing of the body becomes explicit, as viewers see the body in new, reappropriated and erotic ways. Destabilising normative modes of viewing, these dances disrupt conventional heterogeneous paradigms of desire, encouraging a model of spectatorship in which audiences look beyond the immediate and to the simultaneous habitation of multiple and overlapping formations. Beyond binary oppositions to the ballet, they play across absence and presence, opening the imagination to see differently and not simply 'other than'. While engaging in simultaneous processes of dematerialising and materialising, these dances enter, extend, shift and mutate that which already exists in a celebration of diversity. This story continues, and the diversity of voices that articulate yet to be imagined futures and terrains leave me dreaming of a plethora of *Swan Lakes*, anticipating new perspectives and possible directions.

Notes

Introduction

1 For example, see the plethora of reviews of Bourne's *Swan Lake*. A good collection of reviews of this work can be found in *Theatre Record* (Sept 1996).

2 These dances in chronological order are:
Swan Lake (1976) by Jacky Lansley; *Lac de Signes* (1983) by Susan Foster; *Swan Lake* (1987) by Mats Ek; *Swan Lake* (1995) by Matthew Bourne; *Schwanengesänge* (1997) by Philippe Talard and José Luis Sultan, *Swan Lake* (1998) by Birgit Scherzer; *The Hypochondriac Bird* (1998) by Javier de Frutos; *Swan Lake* (1998) by Shakti; '*... and then the lake engulfed them*' (1999) by Örjan Andersson; *BirdBrain* (2001) by Garry Stewart; *O (a set of footnotes to Swan Lake)* (2002) by Vida Midgelow; *Swan Lake* (2003) by Peeter Jalakas and Sasha Pepelyayev of Van Krahl Theatre; and *Swan Lake, 4 Acts* (2005) by Raimund Hoghe.

3 Detailed historical, choreographic and musical analysis of the ballet can be found in Roland Wiley (1985) and Cyril Beaumont (1952). But, to give a very brief synopsis, the ballet tells the story of Prince Siegfried, who while out on a hunting trip encounters Odette, an enchanted swan-woman, and falls in love with her. The only way that the spell that holds Odette can be broken is if Siegfried remains faithful to her. Later, at a ball, Siegfried meets Odile. Odile – the daughter of the evil sorcerer Von Rothbart – is disguised as Odette, and seduces Siegfried. Deceived by appearances, he pledges to marry her and in so doing breaks his vow of fidelity to Odette. Endings of the ballet differ. In some versions Odette and Siegfried plunge into the lake and in others Siegfried battles with the sorcerer to emerge victorious. 'In either case, love triumphs over deception' (Anderson 1992: 110).

1 Reworking the ballet

1 Here I am referring to the reworkings by Mark Morris, Mats Ek and Matthew Bourne respectively.

2 For a discussion of the renowned reconstructions by Millicent Hodson and Kenneth Archer, see their essay in Adshead-Lansdale and Layson (1994).

3 Adshead (1988) provides a model for this type of analysis.

4 See my discussion later in this chapter on mythification. I point out here that reworkings rely on a mythic version as a source rather than any particular staging.

5 Barthes first published his reflections upon the processes of myth in 'Myth today' in 1957 as part of collection of essays entitled *Mythologies* (1993). This was followed by

'Change the object itself – mythology today', in *Image, Music, Text* (1977), in which he revisits his earlier work in the light of new developments. Barthes's account of the processes of myth are vivid and his writings animate contemporary culture. His work is overtly politicised and runs in parallel with the erasure of differences that the canon embodies. Pollock writes that using Barthes analysis of mythic structures

> avoids distracting arguments over who and what is or is not, should or should not be[,] in which canon. Beyond the cultural wars over its contents … we need to pierce the naturalising carapace of myth to delineate the social and political investments in canonicity which make it so powerful an element in the hegemony of dominant social groups.
>
> (Pollock 1999: 9)

6 For example, Fredric Jameson argues that the past in postmodernism has been reduced to a commodity in which we can 'only "represent" our ideas and stereotypes about that past' (Jameson 1993: 79). The revisiting of the past in postmodern art, he argues, is an indictment of consumer capitalism and is a symptom of a society that has become incapable of dealing with time and history. Jameson laments the loss of 'real' history to nostalgia. He maintains that postmodernism's fascination with the past keeps us 'imprisoned in the past' and that through the replication of a mythic past we are prevented from confronting the present. The postmodern remake presents a retro-past in which the history is presented in a nostalgic non-critical mode. Further, Jameson has stated that 'we are condemned to seek History by way of our own pop images and simulacra of that history, which itself remains forever out of reach' (ibid.). Widdowson supports this view, stating:

> In this scenario, postmodernism is the last great gambit of capitalism to defeat opposition, contestation and change. … We are left in a world of radically 'empty' signifiers'. No meaning. No classes. No history. Just a ceaseless procession of simulacra, the past is played and replayed as an amusing range of styles, genres, signifying practices to be combined and re-combined at will. … The only history that exists here is the history of the signifier and that is no history at all.
>
> (Cited in Jenkins 1991: 67)

7 While for clarity I stress the bidirectional nature of these works, it is important to note that reworkings, like other texts, may also suggest to the viewer not just two, but many directions. I use bidirectionality, however, to highlight the necessary feature of simultaneity in these dances. In addition, my use of bidirectionality relates to Hutcheon (1985), who also uses this term to describe the operation of parody.
8 Derrida's term *différance* usefully expresses the constantly deferred and differential nature of meanings. See Norris (1987).
9 The language used here both attempts to 'speak back' to Bloom's (1997) father–son model and also evokes Wittgenstein's (1953) model of 'family resemblances'.

2 Canonical crossings

1 Similar arguments have also been expressed by Noël Carroll (1984) and Deborah Jowitt (1984).

2 For example, in Pierre Lacotte's 1972 historical reconstruction a silk scarf is used by James to capture the sylph. The scarf operates as a dual signifier of embracing and smothering, love and death. In contrast Bourne's more direct gardening shears are overtly dangerous, and James's action becomes less ambiguous in intent.

3 By cross-casting I am referring to the placing of men into normally female roles (or vice versa). In cross-casting the performer retains their own gender identity and does not attempt to take on the characteristics (in costume or overt gestures) of the opposite sex. In cross-dressing the performance is costumed across normative gender lines. For example, a male dancer wears a tutu. This type of cross-dressing is evident in *Swan Lake* by Mats Ek, *Coppélia* by Maguy Marin and *The Hard Nut* by Mark Morris – the work that is used to exemplify this strategy here.

4 It is somewhat slippery but useful to attempt to distinguish between cross-dressing and drag. Drag I posit, following Butler (1990), involves performing the signs of gender such that there is a dissonance between sex, gender and gender performance, whereas in cross-dressing the visual signs of the opposite gender may be presented (for example, via costume) but the performative signs of that gender are not necessarily embodied. *Crossing the Stage: Controversies on Cross-Dressing* (1993), edited by Lesley Ferris, provides a collection of illuminating examples of cross-dress/drag and a range of perspectives on these debates. Interestingly in this book she suggests that contemporary drag (as opposed to the simpler cross-dressing) 'answers to a viable gay aesthetic' (1993: 9).

5 Jann Parry was one of the few critics who did mention the homosexual aspects of the work. She writes that, 'with William Kemp as the swan to Ben Wright's prince, the love affair is homoerotic ... they are complementary halves of a whole, finally united in the ballet's apotheosis as the curtain closes' (1996: 1163).

6 Banes quotes Roger Abrahams, who suggests that, similarly, folklorists are in a postmodern or poststructuralist period, and that this is evident 'insofar as we seek to add both historical and ethnographic specificity to the way in which we present out collections' (Banes 1994: 381).

7 In August of 1992 the tabloid press widely published photographs of the Duchess of York, commonly referred to as 'Fergie', topless and having her feet kissed by her formal financial advisor John Bryan.

3 Female bodies and the erotic

1 Carter notes that 'the artistic endeavour of thousands of women performers has been relegated to the dustbin by discourse' in the writings of feminist dance scholars (1999: 227). She discusses how they critiqued the ballet in a manner as to cast all women within it as passive and objectified, such that the ballet seemed to embody 'the oppressive hegemonies of patriarchy' (ibid.).

2 The eroticisation of the ballerina was particularly explicit during the Romantic era in the writings of critics such as Théophile Gautier (1811–72). The image of the ballerina as erotic object has continued through to the present day and is evident in publicity imagery and reviews.

3 Foster is editor of *Choreographing History* (1995b) and *Corporealities: Dancing Knowledge, Culture and Power* (1996a), as well as the author of *Reading Dancing: Bodies and Subjects in Contemporary American Dance* (1986) and *Choreography and Narrative: Ballet's Staging of Story*

and Desire (1996b). Foster has also published numerous essays and papers, including 'Textual evidences' (1995c); 'Harder, faster, longer, higher – a postmortem inquiry into the ballerina's making' (1995a); 'Dancing bodies' (1997) and 'Closets full of dances: modern dance's performance of masculinity and sexuality' (2001), which contains an analysis of Matthew Bourne's reworking of *Swan Lake.*

4 The elements of *Swan Lake* and *Giselle* most overtly used on stage are: sections of libretto; movement sequences and positions (such as Odette's distinctive arm gestures and Giselle and Albrecht's *pas de deux*); costume (in the first section Foster wears a traditional short classical tutu); and fragments of music ('The dance of the cygnets' and Odette and Siegfried's *grande pas de deux* from the end of act 1 are both played whole).

5 While I use the notion of a 'postmodern dance style' here, there is not of course a single or easily defined movement style that characterises postmodern dance. Rather I use this term to indicate the attitude towards the body that is evident in 'softer' techniques, such as release-based practices, as well as more individual, idiosyncratic ways of moving that have become associated with postmodern choreography.

6 See, for example, the work of Yvonne Rainer (USA) and current British choreographer–dancers such as Emilyn Claid, Liz Aggiss, Wendy Houston and Carol Brown (UK/NZ), who have explored different strategies for establishing alternative performer–audience relationships.

7 Mulvey (2001) argues that scopophilia, the drive towards visual pleasure, as explored in Freud's work, is one of the central features of the cinematic experience.

8 This image makes reference to Odette but also suggests other iconic roles, such as *The Dying Swan* (1907, ch. Fokine).

9 The phrase 'anxiety of influence' used by Hutcheon refers to the book *The Anxiety of Influence* by Harold Bloom (1997). In this book, as well as in more recent texts such as *The Western Canon* (1995), Bloom suggests that all literary texts are a misreading of those that precede them (see chapter 1 for a discussion of reworkings and the 'anxiety of influence').

10 In her endnotes to 'The ballerina's phallic pointe' Foster states that her definition of the ballerina-as-phallus follows the ideas established by Lacan, de Lauretis, Bernheimer and Taussig (1996a: 23, n.33).

11 Foster notes that the gazes of men are also brought to our attention, problematising men's identification with the male dancer on stage. She writes:

> his point of identification on-stage is an effeminate man, a man in tights, through whom he must pass on his way to the object of his fascination, or on whom he can focus within a homosexual counter-reading of the performance.
>
> (Foster 1996a: 3)

12 I would like to express my gratitude to these collaborators in the making of footnotes. Thanks are also due to Kate, Eve, Lei, Brian, Chris, David, Valerie and Alysn who gave their time and support to this project. The performance was made possible through financial support received from Arts Council England, the National Lottery and the University of Northampton. The work was premiered at the University of Northampton on 3 February 2002.

13 *O (a set of footnotes to Swan Lake)* (2002) developed out of *O* (2001). However, *O*, unlike the subsquent *footnotes*, was presented in a conventional 'end on' performance mode and incorporated fixed choreography.

14 Performance credits:

Awaking Aurora: Performed by Fiona Warne, Cathy Spalton, and Dominic Phillips. Music edited and part composed by Sally Hall.

The Original Sylph: Choreographed and performed by Vida Midgelow. Music by Adolphe Adam.

The Collection: Co-directed by Vida Midgelow and Jane Mulchrone. Performed by Vida Midgelow, Darren Adams, Ceroc Central, and Haraam. Music by Mickey Skeedal. Edited by Tim Coley.

15 Feminist writers such as Adair (1992) and Novack (1993) have noted this dual stance towards ballet.

16 Recent examples of feminist dance scholarship have critiqued the previously used binary models that often left dance, particularly ballet, in an impossible situation. See Carter (1999, 2001), Banes (1998) and Albright (1997).

17 Skinner Releasing Technique is a way of moving developed by American movement practitioner Joan Skinner. The technique uses poetic and anatomical imagery to encourage an experiential and efficient body usage.

18 The perception of sameness is brought about as a result of the processes of mythification (see chapter 1).

19 An extended discussion of these ideas is found in Dolan (1988) and a review of different perspectives can be found in Brooks (1997).

4 Princely revisions

1 See Burt (1995) and Kopelson (2001) for detailed discussions of Nijinsky and homosexuality.

2 Expo '98 opened in Lisbon on 22 May and ran until 30 September 1998. The event was an officially sanctioned world exposition, as recognised by the BIE, the Bureau International des Expositions. It was a 'specialised exposition', with a specific theme, 'The oceans: a heritage for the future'.

3 This lecture performance is entitled 'Throwing the body into the fight' (2000).

4 Jameson's view leaves little room for a critical role for postmodernism. He argues that in postmodernism pastiche has eclipsed parody:

> Parody finds itself without vocation; it has lived, and that strange new thing pastiche comes to take its place. Pastiche is, like parody, the imitation of a peculiar mask, speech in dead language: but it is a neutral practice of such mimicry, without any of parody's ulterior motive, amputated of the satiric impulse, devoid of laughter and of any conviction. ... Pastiche is thus blank parody, a statue with blind eyeballs.
>
> (Jameson 1993: 74)

5 In this essay Burt discusses the work of Mark Morris, Michael Clark and Bill T. Jones. He describes these choreographers as 'artistic radicals and gay men who are open about their homosexuality', but also usefully points to the fact that, while these artists may make unequivocally queer dances, there is no direct correlation between 'artistic and sexual radicalism' (2001: 236).

6 This view of the erotic can interestingly be seen to resonate with Georges Bataille's concepts. For Bataille, eroticism and love are associated with death, pain and anguish. Linking

eroticism and sacrifice, he argues that the erotic impulse tears us from ourselves, for 'if love exists at all it is, like death, a swift movement of loss within us, quickly slipping into tragedy and stopping only with death' (Bataille 1986: 239). While Bataille is problematic from a feminist perspective, he offers an interesting way of viewing the erotics of *Bird*, for in this work the two men's risk of pain and death bring passion in life.

7 Albright discusses the difficulties of the word disability. Usefully pointing to the negative '*dis in disability*', she notes ways in which the 'politics of naming are, needless to say, fraught through and through with the politics of identity' (1997: 59).

5 Intercultural encounters

1 Shakti uses the term 'true' Indian dance. This is highly problematic, as shall be discussed later in this chapter. However, for my purpose this comment points to Shakti's pride in her heritage (family and dance). Her comments also suggest that she has a need to locate herself within an established 'respected' form(s) even while working in opposition to it (them).

2 While not the focus of this study, this repertoire – from classical dance pieces to experimental works – demonstrates two attitudes towards classical Indian dance. Many artists strive to locate the most 'authentic' form possible of the 'reinvented' tradition, while others are trying to free themselves from the perceived ties of tradition an create dances that express a more current sensibility.

3 I would like to thank Fran Barbe (a London-based butoh practitioner) for pointing this out and for being so kind as to discuss Iwana's work with me.

4 See Iyer (1997) for a discussion of different styles of classical Indian dance.

5 Indian nationalists revived classical Indian dance, following its suppression under British imperial rule, in the 1930s. In this new context the dance forms and purpose were significantly altered; see O'Shea (1998) Gaston (1999) and Bose (1998).

6 Chatterjea suggests that a differentiation needs to be drawn between 'modern' dance and avant-garde dance in India: 'The avant-garde is often marked by ambiguity: traditional forms and modes are critiqued in their contemporary incarnation. It looks beyond the neo-classical dance celebrated by "modern" or modernizing India and beyond the models of modernity created by the West' (1997: 294).

7 Coorlawala notes several postcolonial choreographers that have divorced their dances from the Hindu religion and questioned the classical norms. She lists Mrinalini Sarabhai, Kumudini Lakhia, Narendra Sharma, Bharat Sharma and Malika Sarabhai (2001: 401).

8 Bharata Natyam is one of a number of styles of classical Indian dance. Other styles are Kathakali, Kathak, Manipuri, Odissi, Kuchipudi and Chaau (See Iyer, 1997).

9 The notion of cultural exchange as 'ghostly mobility' is developed by Suleri (1995) in a discussion of the historical documentation of English India in the eighteenth century.

10 For case studies of the representation of 'the exotic' in ballet and modern dance, see for example, Jowitt (1988), Garafola (1998), Erdman (1996), Koritz (1997) and Desmond (1993).

11 Fisher (2003–4) interestingly discusses the portrayals of the Middle East and the hybridisation of Russian ballet's orientalism evident in the many Christmas versions of *The Nutcracker* that are performed in America every year.

12 Erdman very interestingly points to the interaction between these Western 'oriental dances' and the regeneration of Indian dance in India. She writes: 'But it was mainly

the interest of Westerners in indigenous Indian dance which encouraged India's Westernized elites to search for their own traditions and reconstruct them for staged public performances' (1996: 290).

13 As Elaine Showalter comments, 'the Oriental woman behind the veil of purdah stood as a figure of sexual secrecy and inaccessibility for Victorian men in the 1880s and 1890s.' She goes on to link the veil to female sexuality and to the veil of the hymen in order to argue that 'the veil thus represented feminine chastity and modesty; in rituals of the nunnery, marriage, or mourning; it concealed sexuality' (1992: 145).

14 The 1970s phase of feminist activity was particularly problematic in its blindness concerning race. During this period the emphasis of the women's liberation movement was on the union of women in a single sisterhood (Aston 1995: 78). This approach disenfranchised 'difference', sweeping over the historical and cultural conditions of gender, race and class. Chandra Talpade Mohanty, in her foundational critique of Western feminisms – 'Under Western eyes' (1995) – suggests that Western feminisms naturalise differentiated experiences of patriarchal oppression under a European model. In this model, the monolithic 'average third world woman' of Western feminist imagination

> leads an essentially truncated life based on her feminine gender (read: sexually constrained) and being 'third world' (read: ignorant, poor, uneducated, tradition bound, domestic, family-oriented, victimized, etc.).
>
> (Mohanty 1995: 261)

This image is contrasted with the implicit self-construction of the 'Western woman' as an educated and modern woman who has freedom over her own body. Western feminism's construction of the 'third world woman' appropriates and colonialises her as fully as imperial colonialisers did. The 'third world woman' has become the object of Western feminist speculation, a gaze that has already been coloured by the gaze of orientalism. Through such critiques of Western feminisms it is clear that the complexities that characterise women's lives have been problematically constituted as a homogeneous group 'on the basis of secondary socio-logical and anthropological universals' (ibid.: 262).

15 For example, in her publicity images for *Swan Lake* Shakti is dressed in a translucent white jacket, which is open at the front to reveal a white strapless bikini top. She has a gold choker around her neck and is posed with her back arched. In the publicity for *The Pillow Book* she is draped in a silky red fabric and is lying across a set of steps.

16 This is a parallel argument to that presented by Linda Hutcheon (1988, 1989) in her discussion of postmodern deconstructive strategies.

17 See Hanna (1993), O'Shea (1998), Gaston (1999) and Bose (1998) for more detailed and interesting discussions of the *devadasis* and the changing status of women in classical Indian dance.

18 This ritual sequence was part of the Edinburgh Festival performance I attended in August 1999 but does not appear in the earlier 1998 video recording of this dance.

References and bibliography

Acocella, Joan (1993) *Mark Morris*, New York: Noonday Press.

Adair, Christy (1992) *Women and Dance: Sylphs and Sirens*, Basingstoke: Macmillan.

Adshead, Janet (ed.) (1988) *Dance Analysis: Theory and Practice*, London: Dance Books.

Adshead-Lansdale, Janet (1999) 'Creative ambiguity: dancing intertexts', in J. Adshead-Lansdale (ed.) *Dancing Texts: Intertextuality in Interpretation*, London: Dance Books.

Adshead-Lansdale, Janet and Layson, June (eds) (1994) *Dance History: An Introduction*, London and New York: Dance Books.

Albright, Ann Cooper (1997) *Choreographing Difference: The Body and Identity in Contemporary Dance*, Middletown, CT: Wesleyan University Press.

Anderson, Jack (1992) *Ballet and Modern Dance: A Concise History*, Hightstown, NJ: Princeton Book Company/Dance Horizons.

Anon (1999) 'Love Shak', *Daily Star*, 18 June.

Aschengreen, Erick (1974) 'The beautiful danger: facets of the Romantic ballet', trans. P. McAndrew, *Dance Perspectives*, 58, Summer: 1–52.

Ashcroft, Bill G. Griffiths and H. Tiffin (eds) (1995) *The Post-Colonial Studies Reader*, London: Routledge.

Aston, Elaine (1995) *An Introduction to Feminism and Theatre*, London and New York: Routledge.

Bachelard, Gaston (1994) (first published 1958) *The Poetics of Space*, Boston: Beacon Press.

Bakhtin, Mikhail (1981) *The Dialogic Imagination: Four Essays by M. M. Bakhtin*, trans. C. Emerson and M. Holquist, Austin and London: University of Texas Press.

——(1984) (first published 1965) *Rabelais and his World*, trans. H. Iswolsky, Cambridge, MA: MIT Press.

Balanchine, George and Mason, Francis (1984) *Balanchine's Festival of Ballets*, Vol. 2, London: Comet.

Banes, Sally (1987) *Terpsichore in Sneakers*, Middletown, CT: Wesleyan University Press.

——(1994) *Writing Dancing in the Age of Postmodernism*, Hanover: Wesleyan University Press.

——(1995) 'Choreographic methods of the Judson Dance Theatre', in *Border Tensions: Dance and Discourse*, Proceedings of the Fifth Study of Dance Conference, Guildford: University of Surrey, Department of Dance Studies.

——(1998) *Dancing Women: Female Bodies on Stage*, London and New York: Routledge.

Banes, Sally and Carroll, Noël (1997) 'Marriage and the inhuman: La Sylphide's narratives of domesticity and community', in L. Garafola (ed.) *Rethinking the Sylph: New Perspectives on the Romantic Ballet*, Hanover, NH, and London: University Press of New England for Wesleyan University Press.

Bannerman, Henrietta (2000) 'Matthew Bourne interviewed by David Leonard', in S. Jordan (ed.) *Preservation Politics: Dance Revived, Reconstructed, Remade*, Conference Proceedings, University of Surrey, Roehampton, November, London: Dance Books.

Barbe, Frances (2003) 'Instances of Wabi Sabi: looking at butoh dance through a new lens', unpublished booklet, Canterbury: University of Kent.

Barrett, Michèle (1992) 'Words and things: materialism and method in contemporary feminist analysis', in M. Barrett and A. Phillips (eds) *Destabilizing Theory: Contemporary Feminist Debates*, Cambridge: Polity.

Barrett, Michèle and Phillips, Anne (eds) (1992) *Destabilizing Theory: Contemporary Feminist Debates*, Cambridge: Polity.

Barthes, Roland (1975) (first published 1970) *S/Z*, trans. R. Miller, New York: Hill & Wang.
——(1977) *Image, Music, Text*, trans. S. Heath, London: Fontana.
——(1993) (first published 1957) *Mythologies*, trans. A. Lavers, London: Vintage.

Bataille, George (1986) (first published 1957) *Eroticism*, trans. Mary Dalwood, London: Marion Boyars.

Baudrillard, Jean (1993) 'The evil demon of images and the precession of simulacra', in T. Docherty (ed.) *Postmodernism: A Reader*, New York and London: Harvester Wheatsheaf.

Bauer, Una (2006) 'Melting Away', *Performance Research*, 11/2: 145–7.

Beaumont, Cyril W. (1952) *The Ballet Called Swan Lake*, London: Cyril W. Beaumont.

Benjamin, Andrew (1994) *Object Painting*, London: Academy Editions.

Bennett, Susan (1996) *Performing Nostalgia: Shifting Shakespeare and the Contemporary Past*, London: Routledge.

Berger, John (1972) *Ways of Seeing*, London: Penguin.

Bernheimer, Charles (1992) 'Penile references in phallic theory', *Differences*, 4/1: 116–32.

Bhabha, Homi (1991) 'The third space', in J. Rutherford (ed.) *Identity, Community, Culture, Difference*, London: Lawrence & Wishart.
——(1994) *The Location of Culture*, London: Routledge.
——(1995) (first published 1985) 'Signs taken for wonders', in B. Ashcroft G. Griffiths and H. Tiffin (eds) *The Post-Colonial Studies Reader*, London: Routledge.

Bharucha, Rustom (1993) *Theatre and the World: Performance and the Politics of Culture*, London: Routledge.
——(2000) *The Politics of Cultural Practice: Thinking through Theatre in an Age of Globalization*, Hanover, NH: Wesleyan University Press.

Bloom, Harold (1995) *The Western Canon*, London: Macmillan.
——(1997) (first published 1973) *The Anxiety of Influence*, Oxford: Oxford University Press.

Bohlin, Peter (1988) 'Shaking off tradition', *Ballett International*, 11/4: 32.

Bollen, Jonathan (2001) 'Queer kinesthesia: performativity on the dance floor', in Jane Desmond (ed.) *Dancing Desires: Choreographing Sexualities on and off the Stage*, Madison: University of Wisconsin Press.

Bordo, Susan (1994) 'Feminism, postmodernism, and gender skepticism', in Anne C. Herrmann and Abigail J. Stewart (eds) *Theorizing Feminism: Parallel Trends in the Humanities and Social Sciences*, Boulder, CO, and Oxford: Westview Press.
——(1999) (first published 1993) 'Feminism, Foucault and the politics of the body', in J. Price and M. Shildrick (eds) *Feminist Theory and the Body: A Reader*, Edinburgh: Edinburgh University Press.

Bose, Mandakranta (1998) 'Gender and performance: classical Indian dancing', in L. Goodman with J. de Gay (eds) *The Routledge Reader in Gender and Performance*, London: Routledge.

Bourdieu, Pierre (1993) *The Field of Cultural Production*, Cambridge: Polity.

Braidotti, Rosi (1991) *Patterns of Dissonance: A Study of Women in Contemporary Philosophy*, Cambridge: Polity.

——(1994) *Nomadic Subjects*, New York: Columbia University Press.

Brennan, Mary (1999) 'A whole new take on a classic', *The Herald*, 23 August.

Brennan, Patrick (2003) 'Beauty and the beast' *Irish Examiner*, 6 October.

Briginshaw, Valerie (1988) 'Analysis of variation in choreography and performance: Swan Lake act II pas de deux', in J. Adshead (ed.) *Dance Analysis: Theory and Practice*, London: Dance Books.

——(1991) 'Postmodern theory and its relation to dance', in *Postmodernism and Dance*, Chichester: West Sussex Institute of Higher Education.

——(2001) *Dance, Space and Subjectivity*, Basingstoke: Palgrave.

Brook, Barbara (1999) *Feminist Perspectives on the Body*, London: Longman.

Brooks, Ann (1997) *Postfeminisms: Feminism, Cultural Theory and Cultural Forms*, London: Routledge.

Burnside, Fiona (1994) 'Matthew Bourne and Kim Brandstrup', *Dance Theatre Journal*, 11/2: 38–41.

——(1996) 'Review: Cannes dance festival', *Dance Theatre Journal*, 9/3: 25–6.

Burt, Ramsay (1995) *The Male Dancer: Bodies, Spectacle, Sexualities*, London: Routledge.

——(2001) 'Dissolving into pleasure: the threat of the queer male dancing body', in Jane Desmond (ed.) *Dancing Desires: Choreographing Sexualities on and off the Stage*, Madison: University of Wisconsin Press.

——(2005) 'Raimund Hoghe – "Sacre. Rite of Spring"', *Ballet–Dance Magazine*, March; http://ballet-dance.com/200503/articles/Hoghe20050223.html [accessed 20 April 2007].

Butler, Judith (1988) 'Performative acts and gender constitution', *Theatre Journal*, 40/4: 519–31.

——(1990) *Gender Trouble: Feminism and the Subversion of Identity*, London and New York: Routledge.

——(1993) *Bodies that Matter: On the Discursive Limits of Sex*, London and New York: Routledge.

Campbell, Patrick (1996) 'Bodies politic, proscribed, perverse', in P. Campbell (ed.) *Analysing Performance: A Critical Reader*, Manchester: Manchester University Press.

Carlson, Marvin (1990) *Theatre Semiotics: Signs of Life*, Bloomington: Indiana University Press.

Carroll, Noël (1984) 'The return of the repressed: the re-emergence of expression in contemporary American dance,' *Dance Theatre Journal*, 2/1: 16–19, 27.

Carson, Fiona (2001) 'Feminism and the body', in S. Gamble (ed.) *The Routledge Companion to Feminism and Postfeminism*, London and New York: Routledge.

Carter, Alexandra (1999) 'Staring back, mindfully: reinstating the dancer – and the dance – in feminist ballet historiography', *Proceedings of the Society of Dance History Scholars*, Riverside, CA: SDHS.

——(2001) 'Changing views: a critical history of second wave feminist and post-feminist debate and its manifestation in writings on ballet', *Proceedings of the Society of Dance History Scholars*, Riverside, CA: SDHS.

Case, Sue-Ellen (1991) 'Tracking the vampire', *differences: A Journal of Feminist Cultural Studies*, 3/2: 1–20.

Chakravorty, Pallabi (2000–1) 'From interculturalism to historicism: reflections on classical Indian dance', *Dance Research Journal*, 32/2: 108–19.

Chatterjea, Ananya (1997) 'How can the brown, female, subaltern feminist speak?', in S. E. Friedler and S. B. Glazer (eds) *Dancing Female: Lives and Issues of Women in Contemporary Dance*, Amsterdam: Harwood Academic.

——(2001) 'Chandralekha: negotiating the female body and movement in cultural/political signification', in A. Dils and A. C. Albright (eds) *Moving History/Dancing Cultures: A Dance History Reader*, Middletown, CT: Wesleyan University Press.

Chin, Daryl (1991) 'Interculturalism, postmodernism, pluralism', in Bonnie Marranca and Gautam Dasgupta (eds) *Interculturalism and Performance*, New York: Performing Arts Journal Publications: 83–95.

Christiansen, Rupert (1996) 'Lakeside adventures', *Dance Theatre Journal*, 12/4: 29–31.

Citron, Marcia, J. (1993) *Gender and the Musical Canon*, Cambridge: Cambridge University Press.

Claid, Emilyn (1998) 'Yes! No! Maybe … The practice of illusion in dance theatre performance', Unpublished doctoral thesis, University of Surrey.

——(2001) 'Seduced by Odette', *Dance Theatre Journal*, 17/3: 39–43.

——(2002) 'Playing seduction in dance theatre performance', *Discourses in Dance*, 1/1: 29–46.

——(2006) *Yes? No! Maybe … Seductive Ambiguity in Dance*, New York and London: Routledge.

Colebrook, Claire (2002) *Gilles Deleuze*, London: Routledge.

Connell, R.W. (2004) 'The social organization of masculinity', in Stephen Whitehead and Frank Barrett (eds) *The Masculinities Reader*, Cambridge: Polity.

Coorlawala, Uttara (2001) 'Ananya and Chandralekha – a response to "Chandralekha: negotiating the female body and movement in cultural/political signification"', in A. Dils and A. C. Albright (eds) *Moving History/Dancing Cultures: A Dance History Reader*, Middletown, CT: Wesleyan University Press.

Copeland, Roger (1990) 'Founding mothers: Duncan, Graham, Rainer and sexual politics', *Dance Theatre Journal*, 8/3: 3–9, 27–9.

——(1993) 'Dance, feminism and the critique of the visual', in H. Thomas (ed.) *Dance, Gender and Culture*, London: Macmillan.

——(1994) 'Reflections on revival and reconstruction', *Dance Theatre Journal*, 11/3: 18–20.

——(1997) 'Mark Morris, postmodernism, and history recycled', *Dance Theatre Journal*, 13/4: 18–23.

Crane, Debra (1996) Review, *The Times*, 13 September; *Theatre Record*, 9–22 September: 1161.

Crisp, Clement (1996) Review, *Financial Times*, 13 September; *Theatre Record*, 9–22 September: 1162.

Daly, Ann (1992) 'Dance history and feminist scholarship: reconsidering Isadora Duncan and the male gaze', in L. Senelick (ed.) *Gender in Performance: The Presentation of Difference in the Performing Arts*, Hanover, NH: University Press of New England.

Deleuze, Gilles (1994) *Difference and Repetition*, New York: Columbia University Press.

——(1996) *Cinema 1: The Movement-Image*, trans. H. Tomlinson and B. Habberjan, Minneapolis: University of Minnesota Press.

Deleuze, Gilles and Guattari, Félix (1988) *A Thousand Plateaus: Capitalism and Schizophrenia*, trans. B. Massumi, London: Athlone Press.

Dempster, Elizabeth (1993) 'Revisioning the body: feminism, ideokinesis and the New Dance', *Writings on Dance*, 9, Autumn: 10–21.

——(1995) 'Women writing the body: let's watch a little how she dances', in E. Goellner and J. Murphy (eds) *Bodies of the Text: Dance as Theory, Literature as Dance*, New Brunswick, NJ: Rutgers University Press.

——(1995–6) 'Releasing with Joan Skinner', *Writings on Dance*, 14, Summer: 17–25.

Derrida, Jacques (1976) *Of Grammatology*, trans. Gayatri Chakravorty Spivak, Baltimore: Johns Hopkins University Press.

——(1978) *Writing and Difference*, Chicago: University of Chicago Press.

Desmond, Jane (1993) 'Dancing out the difference: cultural imperialism and Ruth St Denis's "Radha" of 1906', *Writings on Dance*, 9, Autumn: 40–54.

——(1999) 'Engendering dance: feminist inquiry and dance research', in S. H. Fraleigh and P. Hanstein (eds) *Researching Dance: Evolving Modes of Inquiry*, London: Dance Books.

——(ed.) (2001) *Dancing Desires: Choreographing Sexualities on and off the Stage*, Madison: University of Wisconsin Press.

Despoja, Shirley Stott (1994) 'Aurora', in Australian Dance Theatre, Aurora Theatre Programme.

Diamond, Elin (2001) 'Brechtian theory/feminist theory: towards a gestic feminist criticism', in C. Counsell and L. Wolf (eds) *Performance Analysis: An Introductory Coursebook*, London and New York: Routledge.

Dils, Ann and Albright, Ann Cooper (eds) (2001) *Moving History/Dancing Cultures: A Dance History Reader*, Middletown, CT: Wesleyan University Press.

Diprose, Rosalyn (1994) 'Performing body-identity', *Writings on Dance*, 11–12.

Dodds, Sherril (1997) 'Dance and erotica: the construction of the female stripper', in H. Thomas (ed.) *Dance in the City*, Basingstoke: Macmillan.

Dolan, Jill (1985) 'Gender impersonation on stage: destroying or maintaining the mirror of gender roles', *Women and Performance*, 2/2: 4–11.

——(1988) *The Feminist Spectator as Critic*, Ann Arbor: University of Michigan Press.

Donald, Ralph, R. (2004) 'Masculinity and machismo in Hollywood's war films', in Stephen Whitehead and Frank Barrett (eds) *The Masculinities Reader*, Cambridge: Polity.

Douglas, Mary (1966) *Purity and Danger: An Analysis of Concepts of Pollution and Taboo*, London: Routledge & Kegan Paul.

Dyer, Richard (1992) *Only Entertainment*, London: Routledge.

Eco, Umberto (1984) *Postscript to the Name of the Rose*, trans. W. Weaver, New York: Harcourt, Brace, Jovanovich.

Erdman, Joan (1996) 'Dance discourses: rethinking the history of the "oriental dance"', in G. Morris (ed.) *Moving Words: Re-writing Dance*, London: Routledge.

Faludi, Susan (1992) *Backlash: The Undeclared War against Women*, London: Vintage.

Featherstone, Mike (1999) *Love and Eroticism*, London: Sage.

Ferris, Lesley (1993) *Crossing the Stage: Controversies on Cross-Dressing*, London and New York: Routledge.

Feuer, Jane (2001) 'A mistress never a master?', in Jane Desmond (ed.) *Dancing Desires: Choreographing Sexualities on and off the Stage*, Madison: University of Wisconsin Press.

Findlay, Heather (1999) (first published 1992) '"Freud's fetishism" and the lesbian dildo debates', in J. Price and M. Shildrick (eds) *Feminist Theory and the Body: A Reader*, Edinburgh: Edinburgh University Press.

Fisher, Jennifer (1997) 'Relational sense, towards a haptic aesthetic', *Parachute*, 87, July–September: 4–11.

Fisher, Jennifer (2003–4) '"Arabian coffee" in the land of sweets', *Dance Research Journal*, 35/2–36/1: 146–63.

Forte, Jeanie (1990) 'Women's performance art: feminism and postmodernism', in S. E. Case (ed.) *Performing Feminisms: Feminist Critical Theory and Theatre*, Baltimore and London: Johns Hopkins University Press.

——(1992) 'Focus on the body: pain, praxis and pleasure in feminist performance', in J. Reinelt and J. Roach (eds) *Critical Theory and Performance*, Ann Arbor: University of Michigan Press.

Fortier, Mark (1997) *Theory/Theatre: An Introduction*, London and New York: Routledge.

Foster, Hal (ed.) (1985) *Postmodern Culture*, London: Pluto Press.

——(1999) *The Return of the Real*, Cambridge, MA: MIT Press.

Foster, Susan Leigh (1986) *Reading Dancing: Bodies and Subjects in Contemporary American Dance*, Berkeley and London: University of California Press.

——(1995a) 'Harder, faster, longer, higher – a postmortem inquiry into the ballerina's making', *Border Tensions: Dance and Discourse*, Proceedings of the Fifth Study of Dance Conference, Guildford: University of Surrey, Department of Dance Studies.

——(ed.) (1995b) *Choreographing History*, Bloomington: Indiana University Press.

——(1995c) 'Textual evidences', in E. Goellner and J. S. Murphy (eds) *Bodies of the Text*, New Brunswick, NJ: Rutgers University Press.

——(1996a) 'The ballerina's phallic pointe', in S. Foster (ed.) *Corporealities: Dancing Knowledge, Culture and Power*, London and New York: Routledge.

——(1996b) *Choreography and Narrative: Ballet's Staging of Story and Desire*, Bloomington and Indianapolis: Indiana University Press.

——(1997) 'Dancing bodies', in J. Desmond (ed.) *Meaning in Motion*, Durham, NC, and London: Duke University Press.

——(2001) 'Closets full of dances: modern dance's performance of masculinity and sexuality,' in Jane Desmond (ed.) *Dancing Desires: Choreographing Sexualities on and off the Stage*, Madison: University of Wisconsin Press.

Foucault, Michel (1977a) (first published 1975) *Discipline and Punish: The Birth of the Prison*, trans. A. Sheridan, Hamondsworth: Penguin.

——(1977b) *Language, Counter-Memory, Practice: Selected Essays and Interviews*, ed. Donald F. Bouchard, Ithaca, NY: Cornell University Press.

——(1980) *Power/Knowledge: Selected Interviews and other Writings 1972–1977*, New York: Pantheon.

Fraleigh, Sondra Horton (1999) *Dancing into Darkness: Butoh, Zen, and Japan*, Pittsburgh: University of Pittsburgh Press; London: Dance Books.

Fraleigh, Sondra (2004) *Dancing Identity: Metaphysics in Motion*, Pittsburgh: University of Pittsburgh Press.

Fraleigh, Sondra and Nakamura, Tamah (2006) *Hijikata Tatsumi and Ohno Kazuo*, New York and London: Routledge.

Franko, Mark (1993) *Dance as Text: Ideologies of the Baroque Body*, Cambridge: Cambridge University Press.

——(1995) *Dancing Modernism/Performing Politics*, Bloomington and Indianapolis: Indiana University Press.

Freedman, Barbara (1990) 'Frame up: feminism, psychoanalysis, theatre', in S. E. Case (ed.) *Performing Feminisms: Feminist Critical Theory and Theatre*, Baltimore and London: Johns Hopkins University Press.

Frow, John (1990) 'Intertextuality and ontology', in M. Worton and J. Still (eds) *Intertextuality: Theories and Practices*, Manchester and New York: Manchester University Press.

Gamble, Sarah (ed.) (2001) *The Routledge Companion to Feminism and Postfeminism*, London: Routledge.

Garafola, Lynn (ed.) (1998) *Rethinking the Sylph: New Perspectives on the Romantic Ballet*, Hanover, NH, and London, Wesleyan University Press.

Garraghan, Deveril (1999) 'Too many cooks mix the metaphors: Marin and Spink and the Sandman link', in J. Adshead-Landsdale (ed.) *Dancing Texts: Intertextuality in Interpretation*, London: Dance Books.

Gaston, Anne-Marie (1999) 'The reconstruction of Bharata Natyam', *Proceedings of the Society of Dance History Scholars*, Riverside, CA: SDHS.

Gatens, Moira (1999) (first published 1992) 'Bodies, power and difference', in J. Price and M. Shildrick (eds) *Feminist Theory and the Body: A Reader*, Edinburgh: Edinburgh University Press.

Gere, David (2001) 'Effeminate gestures: choreographer Joe Goode and the heroism of effeminacy', in Jane Desmond (ed.) *Dancing Desires: Choreographing Sexualities on and off the Stage*, Madison: University of Wisconsin Press.

Gerschick, Thomas (2000) 'Toward a theory of disability and gender', *Signs: Journal of Women in Culture and Society*, 25/4: 1263–8.

Gibson, James (1966) *The Senses Considered as Perceptual Systems*, Boston: Houghton Mifflin.

Gilbert, Helen and Lo, Jacqueline (1997) 'Performing hybridity in post-colonial monodrama', *Journal of Commonwealth Literature*, 32/1: 5–19.

Gilbert, Helen and Tompkins, Joanne (1996) *Post-Colonial Drama: Theory, Practice, Politics*, London and New York: Routledge.

Gilbert, Jenny (1996) Review, *Independent on Sunday*, 15 September; *Theatre Record*, 9–22 September: 1162.

Goldberg, Marianne (1987–8) 'Ballerinas and ball passing', *Women and Performance: A Journal of Feminist Theory*, 2/6: 7–31.

——(1997) 'Homogenized ballerinas', in J. Desmond (ed.) *Meaning in Motion*, Durham, NC, and London: Duke University Press.

Grant, Jennifer (1988) 'AMP and the Featherstonehaughs at the ICA', *Dance Theatre Journal*, 6/3: 31, 38.

Green, Amy S. (1994) *The Revisionist Stage: American Directors Reinvent the Classics*, Cambridge: Cambridge University Press.

Griggers, Cathy (1994) 'Lesbian bodies in the age of (post)mechanical reproduction', in L. Doan (ed.) *The Lesbian Postmodern*, New York: Columbia University Press.

Grosz, Elizabeth (1990) 'Inscriptions and body maps: representations of the corporeal', in T. Threadgold and A. Cranny-Francis (eds) *Feminine/Masculine and Representation*, Sydney: Allen & Unwin.

——(1994) *Volatile Bodies: Towards a Corporeal Feminism*, Bloomington and Indianapolis: Indiana University Press.

——(1999) (first published 1992) 'Psychoanalysis and the body', in J. Price and M. Shildrick (eds) *Feminist Theory and the Body: A Reader*, Edinburgh: Edinburgh University Press.

——(2001) 'Transgressive bodies', in C. Counsell and L. Wolf (eds) *Performance Analysis: An Introductory Coursebook*, London and New York: Routledge.

Guest, Ivor (1955) 'Parodies of Giselle on the English stage (1841–1871)', *Theatre Notebook*, 9/2: 38–46.

Hall, Donald E. (2003) *Queer Theories*, Basingstoke: Palgrave Macmillan.

Hallet, Bryce (1994) 'Beauty taps into present', *The Australian*, 3 September.

Halperin, David (1995) *Saint Foucault: Towards a Gay Hagiography*, New York and Oxford: Oxford University Press.

Hammonds, Evelynn M. (1999) (first published 1997) 'Toward a genealogy of black female sexuality: the problematic of silence', in J. Price and M. Shildrick (eds) *Feminist Theory and The Body: A Reader*, Edinburgh: Edinburgh University Press.

Hanna, Judith Lynne (1993) 'Classical Indian dance and women's status', in H. Thomas (ed.) *Dance, Gender and Culture*, Basingstoke: Macmillan.

Haraway, Donna (1992) 'The promises of monsters: a regenerative politics for inappropriate/d others', in L. Grossberg, C. Nelson and P. A. Treichler (eds) *Cultural Studies*, London: Routledge.

Hardwick, Viv (2005) 'Swan strong', *Northern Echo*, 10 February; http://archive.thenorthern echo.co.uk/2005/2/10/23326.html [accessed 20 July 2007]

Hargreaves, Martin (2000) 'Haunted by failure, doomed by success: melancholic masculinity in AMP's *Swan Lake*', *Proceedings of the Society of Dance History Scholars*, Riverside, CA: SDHS.

Holledge, Julie and Tompkins, Joanne (2000) *Women's Intercultural Performance*, London and New York: Routledge.

hooks, bell (1981) *Ain't a Woman: Black Women and Feminism*, Boston: Southland Press.

Howes, David (1991) *The Varieties of Sensory Experience*, Toronto: University of Toronto Press.

Hutcheon, Linda (1985) *A Theory of Parody: The Teachings of Twentieth-Century Art Forms*, London and New York: Methuen.

——(1988) *A Poetics of Postmodernism: History, Theory, Fiction*, London and New York: Routledge.

——(1989) *The Politics of Postmodernism*, London and New York: Routledge.

——(2006) *A Theory of Adaptation*, London and New York: Routledge.

Hutchinson Guest, Ann (2000) 'Is authenticity to be had?', in S. Jordan (ed.) *Preservation Politics: Dance Revived, Reconstructed, Remade*, Conference Proceedings, University of Surrey, Roehampton, November, London: Dance Books.

Hutera, Donald (1999a) 'Giselle', *The List*, 19–26 August: 44.

——(1999b) 'Feast for the eyes', *Dance Now*, 8/3: 56–63.

Huxley, Michael (1988) 'Are you right there Michael, are you right?: Fergus Early', in J. Adshead (ed.) *Dance Analysis: Theory and Practice*, London: Dance Books.

Irigaray, Luce (1985a) (first published 1974) *Speculum of the Other Woman*, trans. G. C. Gill, Ithaca, NY: Cornell University Press.

——(1985b) (first published 1977) *This Sex which is Not One*, trans. C. Porter, Ithaca, NY: Cornell University Press.

——(1999) (first published 1980) 'When our lips speak together', trans. C. Burke, in J. Price and M. Shildrick (eds) *Feminist Theory and the Body: A Reader*, Edinburgh: Edinburgh University Press.

Iwana, Masaki (2002) *The Intensity of Nothingness: The Dance and Thoughts of Masaki Iwana*, trans. Teiko Seki, Reveillon, Normandy: La Maison du Butoh Blanc.

Iyer, Alessandra (1997) 'South Asian dance: the traditional/classical idioms', *Choreography and Dance*, 4/2: 5–17.

Jacobs, Laura (1993) 'Jawbreaker', *New Dance Review*, 5/3: 3–5.

Jameson, Frederic (1993) 'Postmodernism, or the cultural logic of late capitalism', in T. Docherty (ed.) *Postmodernism: A Reader*, New York and London: Harvester Wheatsheaf.

Jencks, Charles (1993) 'The emergent rules', in T. Docherty (ed.) *Postmodernism: A Reader*, New York and London: Harvester Wheatsheaf.

Jenkins, Keith (1991) *Re-thinking History*, London and New York: Routledge.

Johnson, Barbara (1980) *The Critical Difference*, Baltimore: Johns Hopkins University Press.

Johnson, Dominic (2005) 'The poised disturbances of Raimund Hoghe', *Dance Theatre Journal*, 2: 36–40.

Jones, Amelia (1998) *Body Art/Performing the Subject*, Minneapolis: University of Minnesota Press.

Jordan, Stephanie (1992) *Striding Out: Aspects of Contemporary and New Dance in Britain*, London: Dance Books.

Jowitt, Deborah (1984) 'The return of drama: new developments in American dance', *Dance Theatre Journal*, 2/2: 28–31.

——(1988) *Time and the Dancing Image*, Berkeley: University of California Press.

——(2006) 'Swan's Way', *Village Voice*, 15 May; www.vilagevoice.com/dance/0620,jowitt, 73215,14.html [accessed 19 July 2007].

Kealiinohomoku, Joann (1993) 'An anthropologist looks at ballet as a form of ethnic dance', in R. Copeland and M. Cohen (eds) *What is Dance?*, Oxford and New York: Oxford University Press.

Kiernander, Adrian (1995) 'Meryl Tankard's Australian Dance Theatre', *Theatre Forum*: 4–9.

Kimmel, Michael, S. (2004) 'Masculinity as homophobia: fear, shame and silence in the construction of gender identity', in Stephen Whitehead and Frank Barrett (eds) *The Masculinities Reader*, Cambridge: Polity.

Klostermaier, Klaus K. (1998) *A Short Introduction to Hinduism*, Oxford: One World.

Kopelson, Kevin (2001) 'Nijinsky's golden slave', in Jane Desmond (ed.) *Dancing Desires: Choreographing Sexualities on and off the Stage*, Madison: University of Wisconsin Press.

Koritz, Amy (1997) 'Dancing the Orient for England: Maud Allan's *The Vision of Salome*', in J. Desmond (ed.) *Meaning in Motion*, Durham, NC, and London: Duke University Press.

Kozel, Susan and Rotie, Marie-Gabrielle (1996) 'The reorientation of butoh', *Dance Theatre Journal*, 13/1: 34–5.

Kristeva, Julia (1982) *Powers of Horror: An Essay in Abjection*, trans. L. S. Roudiez, New York: Columbia University Press.

Kuppers, Petra (2001) 'Deconstructing images: performing disability', *Contemporary Theatre Review*, 11/3–4: 25–40.

Lansley, Jacky (1979–80) 'Fergus Early in "Sunrise"', *New Dance*: 13.

Latrell, Craig (2000) 'After appropriation', *Drama Review*, 44/4: 44–55.

Lavender, Andy (2001) *Hamlet in Pieces: Shakespeare Reworked: Peter Brook, Robert Lepage, Robert Wilson*, London: Nick Hern.

Leask, Josephine (1995) 'East winds blowing west', *Dance Now*, 4/1: 64–9.

LeBihan, Jill (2001) 'Feminism and literature', in S. Gamble (ed.) *The Routledge Companion to Feminism and Postfeminism*, London and New York: Routledge.

Lehman, Peter (ed.) (2001) *Masculinity: Bodies, Movies, Culture*, New York and London: Routledge.

Lepecki, André (2004) 'Concept and presence: the contemporary European dance scene', in Alexandra Carter (ed.) *Rethinking Dance History: A Reader*, New York and London: Routledge.

——(2006) *Exhausting Dance: Performance and the Politics of Movement*, New York and London: Routledge.

Liberatore, Wendy (2005) '"Decay of the Angel" is eloquent, transcendent', *Daily Gazette*, 10 October; www.maureenfleming.com/pages/reviews_pages/20051010_gazette.html [accessed 19 July 2007]

Lloyd-Jones, David (1995) 'The music of Swan Lake', Sadler's Wells Theatre programme.

Lorde, Audre (1984) *Sister Outsider: Essay sand Speeches*, Trumansburg, NY: Crossing Press.

Lorraine, Tamsin (1999) *Irigaray and Deleuze: Experiments in Visceral Philosophy*, Ithaca, NY, and London: Cornell University Press.

Lyotard, J.-F. (1984) (first published 1979) *The Postmodern Condition: A Report on Knowledge*, trans. G. Bennington and B. Massumi, Manchester: Manchester University Press.

Mackrell, Judith (1992) *Out of Line: The Story of British New Dance*, London: Dance Books.

——(1996) Review, *The Guardian*, 14 September; *Theatre Record*, 9–22 September: 1164.

Manning, Susan (1997) 'The female dancer and the male gaze: critiques of early modern dance', in J. Desmond (ed.) *Meaning in Motion*, Durham, NC, and London: Duke University Press.

——(2001) 'Looking from a different place: gay spectatorship of American modern dance', in Jane Desmond (ed.) *Dancing Desires: Choreographing Sexualities on and off the Stage*, Madison: University of Wisconsin Press.

Marinis, M. de (1993) *The Semiotics of Performance*, Bloomington: Indiana University Press.

Marks, Laura, U. (1998) 'Video haptics and erotics', *Screen*, 39/4: 331–48.

Marshall, Barbara (1992) *Teaching the Postmodern*, London: Routledge.

Meyer, Moe (1994) 'Introduction: reclaiming the discourse of camp', in M. Meyer (ed.) *The Politics and Poetics of Camp*, New York and London: Routledge.

Midgelow, Vida (2003) 'Reworking the ballet: refiguring the body and Swan Lake", Unpublished PhD thesis, University of Surrey.

Minh-ha, Trinh T. (1995) (first published 1989) 'Writing postcoloniality and feminism', in B. Ashcroft, G. Griffiths and H. Tiffin (eds) *The Post-Colonial Studies Reader*, London and New York: Routledge.

——(1999) (first published 1992) 'Write your body and the body in theory', in J. Price and M. Shildrick (eds) *Feminist Theory and the Body: A Reader*, Edinburgh: Edinburgh University Press.

Misaki, Eri (2002) (first published 1998) 'New York dance fax', in M. Iwana, *The Intensity of Nothingness: The Dance and Thoughts of Masaki Iwana*, trans. Teiko Seki, Reveillon, Normandy: La Maison du Butoh Blanc.

Mohanty, Chandra Talpade (1995) (originally published 1984) 'Under Western eyes', in B. Ashcroft, G. Griffiths and H. Tiffin (eds) *The Post-Colonial Studies Reader*, London and New York: Routledge.

Morris, Don (1999) 'Swan Lake', *The Scotsman*, 16th August.

Morris, Gay (1996) '"Styles of the flesh": gender in the dances of Mark Morris', in G. Morris (ed.) *Moving Words: Re-writing Dance*, London and New York: Routledge.

Morris, Mark (1995) 'Synopsis', Hard Nut Theatre programme, Mark Morris Dance Group.

Mulvey, Laura (1981) 'Duel in the sun', *Framework*, 15–17: 12–15.

——(2001) (first published 1975) 'Visual pleasure and narrative cinema', in C. Counsell and L. Wolf (eds) *Performance Analysis: An Introductory Coursebook*, London and New York, Routledge.

Nead, Lynda (1992) *The Female Nude: Art, Obscenity and Sexuality*, London and New York: Routledge.

Norris, Christopher (1982) *Deconstruction: Theory and Practice*, London: Methuen.

——(1987) *Derrida*, London: Fontana.

Novack, Cynthia (1990) *Sharing the Dance: Contact Improvisation and American Culture*, Madison: University of Wisconsin Press.

——(1993) 'Ballet, gender and cultural power', in H. Thomas (ed.) *Dance, Gender and Culture*, Basingstoke: Macmillan.

Nugent, Ann (1995) 'Altered states', *Dance Theatre Journal*, 12/2: 6–20.

O'Shea, Janet (1998) '"Traditional" Indian dance and the making of interpretative communities', *Asian Theatre Journal*, 15/1: 45–63.

Osumare, Halifu (2002) 'Global break dancing and the intercultural body', *Dance Research Journal*, 34/2: 30–45.

Owens, Craig (1985) 'The discourse of others: feminists and postmodernism', in Hal Foster (ed.) *Postmodern Culture*, London: Pluto Press.

Ozawa-de Silva, Chikako (2002) 'Beyond the bind/body? Japanese contemporary thinkers on alternative sociologies of the body', *Body and Society*, 8/2: 21–38.

Parry, Jann (1996) Review, *The Observer*, 15 September; *Theatre Record*, 9–22 September: 1163.

Pavis, Patrice (1992) *Theatre at the Crossroads of Culture*, London: Routledge.

——(ed.) (1996) *The Intercultural Reader*, London: Routledge.

Percival, John (2003) 'BirdBrain, Queen Elizabeth Hall, London', The Independent, 12 May; http://arts.independent.co.uk/theatre/reviews/article104408.ece [accessed 20 June 2007].

——(2005) 'Double visitation', *danceviewtimes*, 7 March; www.danceviewtimes.com/2005/winter/10/bird.htm [accessed 2 August 2005].

Phillips, Katie (2005) 'Absurdism, Anarchy and Mime', *Dance Theatre Journal*, 20/1: 21–25.

Poesio, Giannandrea (1994) 'Giselle, part III', *Dancing Times*, April: 688–97.

——(1998) 'Review', *The Spectator*, 31 January.

Pollock, Griselda (1999) *Differencing the Canon: Feminist Desire and the Writings of Art's Histories*, London and New York: Routledge.

Price, Janet and Shildrick, Margrit (eds) (1999) *Feminist Theory and the Body: A Reader*, Edinburgh: Edinburgh University Press.

Rich, Adrienne (1980) (first published 1972) 'When we dead awaken: writing as re-vision', in A. Rich, *On lies, Secrets and Silence*, London: Virago.

Riffaterre, Michael (1990) 'Compulsory reader response: the intertextual drive', in M. Worton and J. Still (eds) *Intertextuality: Theories and Practice*, Manchester: Manchester University Press.

Riley, Denise (1999) (first published 1988) 'Bodies, identities, feminisms', in J. Price and M. Shildrick (eds) *Feminist Theory and the Body: A Reader*, Edinburgh: Edinburgh University Press.

Rimmer, Valerie (1993) 'The anxiety of dance performance', in H. Thomas (ed.) *Dance, Gender and Culture*, Basingstoke: Macmillan.

Robertson, Allen (1995) 'High voltage', *Dance Now*, 4/3: 2–11.

Roebuck, Chris (2004) '"Queering" the king: a remedial approach to reading masculinity in dance', in Alexandra Carter (ed.) *Rethinking Dance History*, New York and London: Routledge.

Root, Deborah (1996) *Cannibal Culture: Art, Appropriation, and the Commodification of Difference*, Boulder, CO: Westview Press.

Rose, Margaret (1993) *Parody: Ancient, Modern and Post-modern*, Cambridge: Cambridge University Press.

Rowe, Karen E. (1993) 'Feminism and fairy tales', in J. Zipes (ed.) *Don't Bet on the Prince: Contemporary Feminist Fairytales in North America and England*, Aldershot: Scolar Press.

Roy, Sanjoy (2007) 'Sacre – The Rite of Spring', *The Guardian*, 10 April; http://arts.guardian.co.uk/theatre/dance/reviews/story/0,,2053226,00.html [accessed 20 April 2007].

Rubidge, Sarah (1996) 'Does authenticity matter?', in P. Campbell (ed.) *Analysing Performance: A Critical Reader*, Manchester: Manchester University Press.

——(2000) 'Identity and the open work', in S. Jordan (ed.) *Preservation Politics*, London: Dance Books.

Rubin, Gayle (2000) (originally published 1993) 'Thinking sex', in M. Cooper and D. Simmons (eds) *Multicultural Dimensions of Film: A Reader*, New York: McGraw-Hill.

Russo, Mary (1995) *The Female Grotesque: Risk, Excess, and Modernity*, London: Routledge.

Sacks, Anne (1996) Review, *Evening Standard*, 12 September; *Theatre Record*, 9–22 September: 1161.

Said, Edward, W. (1995) (first published 1978) *Orientalism*, Harmondsworth: Penguin.

Salas, Roger (2000) 'Review', *El Pais*, 1 June.

Sanders, Julie (2006) *Adaptation and Appropriation*, London and New York: Routledge.

Schechner, Richard (2002) *Performance Studies – An Introduction*, London and New York: Routledge.

Schneider, Rebecca (1997) *The Explicit Body in Performance*, London and New York: Routledge.

Sedgwick, Eve (1990) *Epistemology of the Closet*, Berkeley: University of California Press.

——(1993) *Tendencies*, Durham, NC, and London: Duke University Press.

Selden, Raman, Widdowson, Peter and Brooker, Peter (1997) *A Reader's Guide to Contemporary Literary Theory*, London and New York: Harvester Wheatsheaf.

Shakti (1999a) 'Swan Lake', company programme.

——(1999b) Personal interview with author, tape recording, August.

——(n.d.) 'Profile', www.shakti.jp/text/English/profile-new1.htm [accessed 20 July 2007].

Shildrick, Margrit and Price, Janet (1996) 'Breaking the boundaries of the broken body', *Body and Society*, 2/4: 93–113.

Showalter, Elaine (1992) *Sexual Anarchy: Gender and Culture at the Fin de Siècle*, London: Virago.

Siegmund, Gerald (2006) 'Raimund Hoghe', http://kulturserver-nrw.de/home/rhoghe/ [accessed 27 July 2006].

Slemon, Stephen (1990) 'Modernism's last post', in I. Adam and H. Tiffin (eds) *Past the Last Post*, Calgary: University of Calgary Press.

Smith, A. William (1992) 'Flickers: a fifty-year-old flicker of the Wiedman tradition', in *Dance Reconstructed: Conference Proceedings: A Conference on Modern Dance Art*, Past, Present, Future, New Brunswick, NJ: Rutgers University Press.

Smith, Hazel and Dean, Roger (1997) *Improvisation, Hypermedia, and the Arts Since 1945*, Amsterdam: Harwood Academic.

Solomon, Alisa (1993) 'It's never too late to switch – crossing toward power', in Lesley Ferris (ed.) *Crossing the Stage: Controversies on Cross-Dressing*, London: Routledge.

——(1997) *Re-Dressing the Canon: Essays on Theatre and Gender*, London and New York: Routledge.

Spackman, Helen (2000) 'Minding the matter of representation: staging the body (politic)', *Contemporary Theatre Review*, 10/3: 5–22.

Spivak, Gayatri Chakravorty (1995) (first published 1988) 'Can the subaltern speak?', in B. Ashcroft, G. Griffiths and H. Tiffin (eds) *The Post-Colonial Studies Reader*, London: Routledge.

Stallybrass, Peter and White, Allon (1986) *A Politics and Poetics of Transgression*, London: Methuen.

Stewart, Gabe (1999) 'Dance review, Swan Lake', *The List*, 26 August–9 September.

Suleiman, Susan Rubin (1985) '(Re)writing the body: the politics and poetics of female eroticism', in S. Suleiman (ed.) *The Female Body: Western Culture – Contemporary Perspectives*, Cambridge, MA: Harvard University Press.

Suleri, Sara (1995) (first published 1992) 'Woman skin deep: feminism and the postcolonial condition', in B. Ashcroft, G. Griffiths and H. Tiffin (eds) *The Post-Colonial Studies Reader*, London: Routledge.

Suvin, Darko (1988) 'Weiss's Marat/Sade and its three main performance versions', *Modern Drama*, 30/3: 395–419.

Taylor, Christie (2006) 'Dance: joy is in the air', The Times, 7 May; http://entertainment.timesonline.co.uk/tol/arts_and_entertainment/article712973.ece [accessed: 27 July 2006]

Tegeder, Ulrich (1983) 'Create characters, special people', *Ballett International*, May: 16–19.

Thomas, Helen (2003) *The Body, Dance and Cultural Theory*, Basingstoke: Palgrave Macmillan.

——(2004) 'Reconstruction and dance as embodied textual practice', in Alexandra Carter (ed.) *Rethinking Dance History: A Reader*, New York and London: Routledge.

Thornham, Sue (2001) 'Feminism and film', in S. Gamble (ed.) *Routledge Companion to Feminism and Postfeminism*, London and New York: Routledge.

Tiffin, Helen (1995) (first published 1987) 'Post-colonial literatures and counter-discourse', in B. Ashcroft, G. Griffiths and H. Tiffin (eds) *The Post-Colonial Studies Reader*, London: Routledge.

Tobias, Tobi (1984) 'Manchild in the promised land: Mark Morris', *Dance Magazine*, 68/12: 28–30.

Ulzen, Karen van (1990–1) 'Not quite modern ballet', *Dance Australia*, 51: 45.

Wagner, Geoffrey (1975) 'Three modes of adaptation', in G. Wagner, *The Novel and the Cinema*: Rutherford, NJ: Farleigh Dickinson University Press; London: Tantivy Press.

Warner, Marina (1995) *From the Beast to the Blonde*, London: Vintage.

Warner, Michael (ed.) (1993) *Fear of a Queer Planet: Queer Politics and Social Theory*, Minneapolis: University of Minnesota Press.

Weeks, Jeffrey (1985) *Sexuality and its Discontents: Meanings, Myths and Modern Sexualities*, London: Routledge & Kegan Paul.

Werner, Katja (2003) 'Tanzgeschichten', *Dance Europe*, December; http://kulturserver-nrw.de/home/rhoghe/en/en_tanzgeschichten.htlm [accessed 27 July 2006].

Wesemann, Arnd (1997) 'Fun with a swan', *Ballett International*, 6, June: 62.

Wiley, Roland John (1985) *Tchaikovsky's Ballets: Swan Lake, Sleeping Beauty, Nutcracker*, Oxford: Clarendon Press.

Wittgenstein, L. (1953) *Philosophical Investigations*, trans. G. E. M. Anscombe, Oxford: Blackwell.

Wolff, Janet (1990) *Feminine Sentences: Essays on Women and Culture*, Cambridge: Polity.

——(1997) 'Reinstating corporeality: feminism and body', in J. Desmond (ed.) *Meaning in Motion*, Durham, ND, and London: Duke University Press.

Worton, Michael and Still, Judith (eds) (1990) *Intertextuality: Theories and Practice*, Manchester: Manchester University Press.

Wright, Elizabeth (1996) 'Psychoanalysis and the theatrical: analysing performance', in P. Campbell (ed.) *Analysing Performance*, Manchester and New York: Manchester University Press.

Zarrilli, Philip (1992) 'For whom is the king a king? Issues of intercultural production, perception and reception in Kathakali King Lear', in J. Reinelt and J. Roach (eds) *Critical Theory and Performance*, Ann Arbor: University of Michigan Press.

Zile, Judy van (1995) 'New trends in Korea', in R. Solomon and J. Solomon (eds) *East Meets West in Dance: Voices in the Cross-Cultural Dialogue*, Amsterdam: Harwood Academic.

Zipes, Jack (ed.) (1993) *Don't Bet on the Prince: Contemporary Feminist Fairytales in North America and England*, Aldershot: Scolar Press.

——(1994) *Fairy Tale as Myth, Myth as Fairy Tale*, Lexington: University Press of Kentucky.

Videography of the key works cited

Andersson, Örjan (1999) '… and then the lake engulfed them', Helsinki City Theatre Dance, personal copy of the choreographer.

Bourne Matthew (1992) *The Nutcracker*, Adventures in Motion Pictures, The Place Videoworks Collection.

——(1996, stage premiere 1995) *Swan Lake*, Adventures in Motion Pictures, BBC2, 26 December.

——(1997, stage premiere 1994) *Highland Fling – A Romantic Wee Ballet*, Adventures in Motion Pictures, Spring Loaded, The Place Videoworks Collection, recorded at The Place Theatre, 27 February.

Coralli, Jean and Perrot, Jules, revised by Petipa, Marius (1983, stage premiere by J. Coralli and J. Perrot, 1841) *Giselle*, Kirov Ballet, producer O. Vinogradov, NVC Arts.

De Frutos, Javier (1998) *The Hypochondriac Bird*, The Place Videoworks Collection, recorded at Queen Elizabeth Hall, 22 October.

Ek, Mats (1990, stage premiere 1987) *Swan Lake*, Cullberg Ballet, producer M. Reutersweard, RM Associates.

——(1993, stage premiere 1982) *Giselle*, Cullberg Ballet, producer M. Reutersweard, Summer Dance, BBC2, August.

Foster, Susan (1983) *Polylogue (Lac de Signes)*, personal copy of the choreographer.

——(1996, premiere 1994) *The Ballerina's Phallic Pointe*, recorded at Highways, California, 21 June, personal copy of the choreographer.

Hoghe, Raimund (2005) *Swan Lake, 4 Acts*, personal copy of the choreographer.

Ivanov, Lev, Redman, Vincent and Wright Peter (1994, stage premiere by L. Ivanov, 1892) *The Nutcracker*, Birmingham Royal Ballet, producer J. Pleydell-Bouverie, BBC1, 27 December.

Iwana, Masaki (1995, premiere 1994) *The Legend of Giselle*, Chisenhale Dance Space Archive, recorded at Chisenhale Dance Space, 17 February.

Marin, Maguy (1994) *Coppélia*, Lyon Opera Ballet, producer T. Grimm, RM Arts and Danmarks Radio.

Midgelow, Vida (1995–6) *Awaking Aurora*, personal copy of the author.

——(1997–8) *The Original Sylph*, personal copy of the author.

——(2002) *O (a set of footnotes to Swan Lake)*, personal copy of the author.

Midgelow, Vida and Mulchrone, Jane (1999) *The Collection*, personal copy of the author.

Morris, Mark (1992, stage premiere 1991) *The Hard Nut*, Mark Morris Dance Company, producer J. Kingberg, BBC2, 28 December.

Petipa, Marius, staged by Konstantin Segeyev (1983, stage premiere by M. Petipa, 1890) *The Sleeping Beauty*, Kirov Ballet, producer S. Kononchuk, USSR Gosteleradio and NVC Arts.

Petipa, Marius and Ashton, Frederick, staged and choreographed by Natalia Markarova (1988, stage premiere by M. Petipa and L. Ivanov, 1895) *Swan Lake*, London Festival Ballet, producer T. Grimm, Danmark Arts with RM Arts and Channel 4.

Petipa, Marius, Cecchetti, Enrico and Wright, Peter (1995, stage premiere by M. Petipa, 1884) *Coppélia*, Birmingham Royal Ballet, producer S. Marks, BBC2, 23 December.

Scherzer, Birgit (1998) *Swan Lake*, personal copy of the choreographer.

Shakti (1998) *Swan Lake*, Vasanta Mala, personal copy of the choreographer.

Shaw, Susan (producer) (1999) Javier de Frutos, *The South Bank Show*, ITV, January.

Stewart, Garry (2001) *BirdBrain*, personal copy of the choreographer.

Taglinoni, Filippo, reconstructed by Pierre Lacotte (1972, stage premiere by F. Taglinoni, 1832) *La Sylphide*, Paris Opera Ballet, producer Y. A. Hubert, Le Service de la Musique, Kultur (NTSC Formate).

Tallard, Philippe and Sultan, José Luis (1997) *Schwanengesänge*, Mannheimer Ballet, personal copy of the choreographer.

Tankard, Meryl (1994) *Aurora*, Australian Dance Theatre, personal copy of the choreographer.

Index

eBooks – at www.eBookstore.tandf.co.uk

A library at your fingertips!

eBooks are electronic versions of printed books. You can store them on your PC/laptop or browse them online.

They have advantages for anyone needing rapid access to a wide variety of published, copyright information.

eBooks can help your research by enabling you to bookmark chapters, annotate text and use instant searches to find specific words or phrases. Several eBook files would fit on even a small laptop or PDA.

NEW: Save money by eSubscribing: cheap, online access to any eBook for as long as you need it.

Annual subscription packages

We now offer special low-cost bulk subscriptions to packages of eBooks in certain subject areas. These are available to libraries or to individuals.

For more information please contact webmaster.ebooks@tandf.co.uk

We're continually developing the eBook concept, so keep up to date by visiting the website.

www.eBookstore.tandf.co.uk